The Venezuelan Conspiracy

Another clear and present danger for the USA

ISBN: 978-1-4251-1832-7

*We at Trafford believe that it is the responsibility of us all, as both individuals
and corporations, to make choices that are environmentally and socially sound.
You, in turn, are supporting this responsible conduct each time you purchase a
Trafford book, or make use of our publishing services. To find out how you are
helping, please visit www.trafford.com/responsiblepublishing.html*

*Our mission is to efficiently provide the world's finest, most comprehensive
book publishing service, enabling every author to experience success.
To find out how to publish your book, your way, and have it available
worldwide, visit us online at www.trafford.com/10510*

www.trafford.com

North America & international
toll-free: 1 888 232 4444 (USA & Canada)
phone: 250 383 6864 ♦ fax: 250 383 6804
email: info@trafford.com

The United Kingdom & Europe
phone: +44 (0)1865 722 113 ♦ local rate: 0845 230 9601
facsimile: +44 (0)1865 722 868 ♦ email: info.uk@trafford.com

10 9 8 7 6 5

This book is dedicated to those individuals whose involvement and support gave inspiration for this story.

- With sincere gratitude to the Admirals, Officers and the men and women of the ARMADA DE VENEZUELA, COMANDO DE GUARDACOSTAS and Captain Nicholas Goschenko for the friendship, support and protection provided during a dangerous period.

- To Jason Paul Geary, my son and best friend who personally experienced the spite, evil and wrath of the CIA and the U. S. Coast Guard as a result of his fathers refusal to participate in the Conspiracy against Venezuela.

- To the Deep Throat somewhere within the US Government who secretly provided the critical information that thwarted the stonewalling efforts of the government's lawyers.

- To the Cable News Network (CNN) who in their exposure of The Venezuelan Conspiracy unknowingly played a significant role in the government's capitulation and settlement of the lawsuit.

- And to the late Myles Jay Tralins, Esq. the Miami lawyer who in addition to being my mentor and dear friend through due process insured that truth and justice prevailed.

CONTENTS

Langley, Virginia – September 1991

* * *

The CIA believes that to insure the unimpeded flow of
Venezuelan oil to the United States it is necessary to install a
puppet government in the Miraflores Palace in Caracas. They
determine that this new government should be lead by a charismatic
socialist revolutionary and former paratroop commander who the
Agency believes will follow Washington's agenda.

The Central Intelligence Agency with the assistance of the
US Coast Guard embarked on a clandestine mission to
destabilize the elected government and install Hugo Chàvez
as the President of Venezuela.

After assuming control of the government, Chàvez
double-crosses the CIA and begins to actively support the
anti-American policies of Fidel Castro, Muammar al-Qaddafi and
the late Saddam Hussein. Hugo Rafael Chàvez Frias remains
today the President of the Bolivarian Republic of Venezuela.

FORWARD

As a single parent with professional pursuits as a marine surveyor and maritime fraud investigator, I enjoyed a comfortable life living in the lush ambiance of the Caribbean. Pursuing the belief that success should be viewed as a *journey – not a destination* allowed me to develop a thriving marine practice while raising a fantastic son who in growing up also became my best friend. Being interested in military history particularly the Cold War period during the 1950's and 1960's I read a lot and frequently recalled the words of the late President, John Fitzgerald Kennedy, "do not ask what your country can do for you, but what can you do for your country". In 1980, clearly influenced by the late president's thoughts I accepted a personal invitation from Washington to enlist and become an officer in service with the United States Coast Guard Auxiliary at which time I was commissioned and charged with the responsibility to form and organize an Auxiliary unit in St. Thomas, U.S. Virgin Islands. Due in part to the personal involvement of Benjamin Stabile then Vice Commandant of the United States Coast Guard the St. Thomas Flotilla soon prospered and flourished. During this same period I expanded my private marine practice to Sint Maarten in the Netherlands Antilles where I soon was appointed the government's shipping inspector which lead me to the creation of the Antilles Sea Rescue Organization, another volunteer search and rescue unit modeled after the US Coast Guard Auxiliary. Unfortunately two years later due to the lack of schooling past the 6th grade on Sint Maarten my son and I were forced to relocate to the island of Puerto Rico where Jason continued his education while I remained active as an officer in the Coast Guard Auxiliary. It was not until British insurers subsequently instructed me to investigate the loss of a catamaran in Venezuelan territorial waters that I would again be called upon by the United States Coast Guard, this time to introduce a re-organization and training program for the Coastguard Command of the Venezuelan Navy. When accepting the assignment I had no idea of how deep I would become entwined in espionage and a covert US government conspiracy to destabilize the government of the Republic of Venezuela; a conspiracy whose sole objective was the installation of Hugo Chavez as president to insure the flow of oil to the United States. What you are about to read is that story.

PROLOGUE

Before the creation of the Department of Homeland Security the United States Coast Guard was under the control of the Department of Transportation, a domestic sea service charged with protecting the coasts of the United States and her territories. However, following exposure through federal court proceedings of the US Coast Guard's espionage activities against the Venezuelan military establishment it was discovered that Coast Guard missions were not solely domestic in nature. The subsequent investigation revealed that the US Coast Guard was receiving covert orders from Langley, Virginia and working under the direction of the CIA better known as *The Company.*

This particular CIA/USCG escapade began to unfold when I was targeted as a potential CIA asset in the CIA conspiracy to install a subservient government in Venezuela, a government lead by Hugo Chàvez. During the fall of 1991 I was approached by the United States Coast Guard Attaché at the American Embassy in Caracas, Venezuela who asked that I undertake a mission to assist in the training, development, and deployment of the Venezuelan Coastguard Auxiliary and Reserve forces.

As an 11 year veteran with exemplary service to the Coast Guard, training in the field of maritime fraud and a background of successful liaison with a number of governments and law enforcement agencies in the Caribbean and Latin America unbeknownst to me at the time had made me the ideal choice for recruitment as a spy.

Following my refusal to engage in espionage all hell broke loose. The saga you are about to read brought about an abrupt end to my Coast Guard career, almost cost me my life and resulted in a lawsuit being filed in the United States District Court in Miami, Florida. The case was settled in May 1996 but at the request of the Government for reasons of national security the court proceedings were sealed and a gag order was imposed. On February 8, 2004 the seal and gag order was lifted on case number 95-0323 CIV-NESBITT allowing the story of the Venezuelan Conspiracy to be told.

The Venezuelan Conspiracy and the media[1]

1   Yarbro, Stan, "Coast Guard aide say's CIA tried to sink him," *The Daily Business Review*, Miami, Florida. March 7, (1995)
    Reyes, Gerardo, "CIA quiso infiltrar Armada Venezolano, asegura demanda," *El Nuevo Herald*. (1995) ("CIA wanted to infiltrate the Venezuelan Navy, lawsuit assured," *The New Miami Herald*.(1995)
    International Television News, Cable News Network (CNN) Atlanta, Georgia. March/April 1995
    Noreen Marcus, "Maritime expert settles dispute with US for refusal to spy" *The Daily Business Review*, Miami, June 8, 1996

THE CENTRAL INTELLIGENCE AGENCY

The CIA has a well deserved reputation for poorly planned, ill-advised, and illegal activities throughout the world particularly in Central and South America. Published reports show that the Agency has played an active role in the overthrow of democratically elected governments, murder and has repeatedly been identified as the organizer and security shield as well as the bankers who provide funding to facilitate narcotics smuggling throughout the region. As the bankers they covertly reaped huge profits from narco-trafficking in addition to their unknown level of financial support from taxpayers courtesy of the US federal government that provided funding to finance their illicit and clandestine activities – without congressional oversight.

One well publicized case involved the late Barry Seal, a CIA agent operating between the United States and Central and South America, who is said to have smuggled over $3 billion worth of drugs into the US during his tenure with the Agency. The modus operandi or MO of the CIA has remained somewhat consistent since its creation shortly after World War II when President Truman signed the National Security Act of 1947 which established the Central Intelligence Agency and the National Security Council. Under the direction of a Wall Street lawyer named Frank Wisner the newly born CIA created a covert action section that according to its confidential charter had amongst other responsibilities, the dissemination of propaganda, economic warfare, sabotage, subversion against hostile states, and assistance to underground resistance groups. Over the years the CIA has frequently been referred to as America's terrorist organization. As a covert branch of the President's foreign policy advisors the CIA's primary function is to support presidential policy. Once a foreign government is identified as a target and this is generally a democratically elected government that resists American influence over its internal affairs, the CIA then begins its subversive activities and employs every tactic in the book. The CIA's book of dirty tricks for Latin America was initially conceived and refined at the infamous 'School of the Americas' originally based in Panama then later moved to Ft. Benning, Georgia.

Some have nicknamed this infamous institution the 'School of Dictators' and the 'School of Assassins'; so named for its training of Latin American military officers in the skills needed to successfully conduct a coup and the use of interrogation, torture, and murder. The Agency's long and repulsive history of corrupt and illicit activities throughout the world in recent years has with increased fervor been focused on Central and South America. The following timeline of alleged illicit CIA activities were monitored and reported by American and foreign journalists and international civil rights groups.

- The **Dominican Republic:** after supporting the murderous dictator Rafael Trujillo whose reign of terror began in the 1930's his businesses which grew to almost 60 percent of the economy began to threaten US business interests. The CIA earns credit with having the dictator assassinated. In 1963 when the socialist policies of the democratically elected Juan Bosch become intolerable Bosch is over-thrown and the CIA installs a right wing military junta. Following a popular rebellion that breaks out to re-install Bosch US Marines crush the rebellion. American journalists in Santo Domingo report that the Marines were covertly directed by the CIA lurking in the shadows.

- **Ecuador:** CIA backed military officers force the democratically elected President Jose Velasco to resign after which the Vice-President Carlos Arosemana assumes the presidency. Arosemana is said to have been hand-picked by the CIA. Later a CIA backed military coup overthrows President Arosemana because his policies have become unacceptable to Washington. A military junta assumes command, cancels the 1964 elections and begins abusing human rights.

- **Bolivia:** In the early 1970's a CIA backed military coup removes the leftist President Juan Torres from power replacing him with Hugo Banzer a CIA lackey who, as the country's dictator has over

2,000 political opponents arrested and jailed without trial followed by reports of torture and summary executions. The CIA is now pressed to deal with the recent election of Evo Morales a socialist reformer who enjoys the support of Hugo Chàvez and Fidel Castro. Chàvez and Castro are clearly interested in expanding their socialist agenda and Cuban/Venezuelan duo into a trilogy and beyond.

- **Brazil:** in 1964 a CIA backed military coup over throws the elected government of Joao Goulart. The new military leader, General Castelo Branco finds favor with the CIA especially when he creates the continents first death squads. Investigative journalists later discover through sources inside the military that the CIA trained the death squads.

- **Chile:** 1973, the CIA supports the overthrow and assassination of Salvador Allende the country's and Latin America's first elected socialist leader. The CIA replaces Allende with General Augusto Pinochet who even up to his death remained the focus of prosecution for fraud and the murder of thousands of the country's citizens during his reign of terror.

- **Panama:** General Manuel Noriega was installed by the CIA and on its payroll beginning in 1966. The Agency protected and sustained his involvement in narcotics trafficking throughout the 1980's. When his independence and obstinacy became untenable he was removed in a US military operation orchestrated by the CIA ostensibly for the good of the country – which country was never defined.

- **El Salvador, Nicaragua, and Honduras:** as their history is quite well documented little more need be said about CIA atrocities in these countries. Media exposure of the military aid funded by Iranian arms sales gave us the Iran-Contra Scandal. When a transport plane carrying supplies to the Contras is shot down over Nicaragua the lone survivor Eugene Hasenfus and the two dead pilots are identified as employees of the infamous CIA. The aircraft belonged to Southern Air Transport a front company owned by the CIA, which of course means that it was paid for by the US taxpayer. In 1983 the CIA provided Honduran military officers with the 'Human Resources Exploitation Manual'. The manual

THE VENEZUELAN CONSPIRACY

shows how to torture people and is put to use with CIA guidance by the army's notorious Battalion 316. Sandinista leader Daniel Ortega ousted as Nicaragua's president in 1990 was returned to power in 2006 with over 38% of the popular vote, in spite of strong US opposition. Ortega, backed by Venezuela's Hugo Chàvez adds another piece to the socialist puzzle being assembled in the anti-American Latin America Alliance.

- **Haiti:** In 1959 the US military facilitates the installation of 'Papa Doc' Duvalier as the dictator and President for life. Soon after 'Papa Doc' creates a private police force known as the Tonton Macoutes who terrorize the country. After the ignominious reign and death of 'Papa Doc' the CIA was concerned that the new President for Life, 'Baby Doc' Duvalier may have a limited life span. The CIA doesn't fancy instability in a country ruled by a despot of their choosing and begins closely monitoring the day-to-day situation. When Baby Doc displays too much of his excesses and wavers from negative international attention he was quickly removed. Within hours he and his entourage of cronies are flown from Port au Prince to the US Naval Station Roosevelt Roads in Puerto Rico on their way to a comfortable retirement in the South of France. The CIA quickly creates the National Intelligence Service or SIN to suppress the increasingly restless populace. The CIA then orchestrates elections in favor of another right-wing military strongman who has a budding business in the transshipment of narcotics to the United States. Even though Jean-Bertrand Aristide had only served eight months as the elected President he too is removed by a military insurrection and replaced by Raoul Cedras. The CIA and President Clinton confronting a public relations nightmare have Raoul Cedras the military dictator removed, and sent off to a rich retirement. The CIA returns Aristide to the Presidency on the condition he accepts the agenda prescribed by Washington. When Aristide falls from favor he is again removed. Haiti today continues to remain in chaos.

With its highly successful record of overthrowing democracies and establishing and supporting self-serving dictatorships that are subservient to the United States the CIA is frequently referred to as America's terrorist organization. Over the last twenty five years there have been repeated print and electronic media reports of the CIA's involvement in heroin smuggling from Asia and cocaine trafficking throughout Latin America. In the mid 1980's it was reported that the CIA in addition to the Iranian arms sales, used its profits from narcotics to organize and finance the activities of the Contras in Nicaragua in an effort to disrupt the economy and destabilize the Sandinista government. When this was revealed the United States was condemned in the World Court for engaging in international terrorism, it later rejected a U.N. Security Council resolution calling upon it to observe international law.

An important element of the CIA's covert activities involves the recruitment of American citizens who as external NOC *assets* [2] are used in the gathering of intelligence in foreign countries. These individuals' may be journalists, military attachés, priests or missionaries, businessmen and others who are well placed to observe and report sensitive information to their CIA handlers. Their recruitment may be the result of blackmail, such as the business executive who is inclined towards the services of prostitutes or the excessive use of alcohol, financial reward, the supply of narcotics to a known user or rapid promotion in the case of military officers. In most cases these external assets are generally recruited under the status of NOC which simply means if they are exposed or get caught they're on their own.

One of the CIA's more recent transgressions involved the United States Coast Guard in Venezuela and was focused on insuring Venezuela's continued supply of oil to the United States. In the early 1990's because of the political pandemonium being experienced throughout the country the CIA embarked on a program that they believed through destabilization of the elected government would allow US manipulation and control of the country's natural resources.

In May 1993 the Venezuelan Supreme Court ruled that there were sufficient grounds for an indictment on charges of corruption against then President Carlos Andres Perez frequently referred to as CAP as he was known throughout the country. This ruling resulted in the decision by the National Congress to remove and place CAP under house arrest so he could be brought to trial. During this period of chaos the CIA believed that those in power were not demonstrating

---

2   Spies with No Official Cover

a willingness to *follow the line* dictated by Washington unlike CAP who was a crony of George H. W. Bush. The Agency was concerned that the weakened political foundation of the Venezuelan government rendered the chaotic administration a perceived danger to the security of the United States due to the possible disruption in the supply of **oil**. Having been placed under house arrest and stripped of his power CAP was the subject of ongoing criminal investigations relating to his pilfering of the national treasury and money laundering amongst a host of other charges including unlawful financial support to the Violet Chamorro government in Nicaragua.

It was public knowledge that CAP was a deviant thief who had misused at least $17 million in a security fund for personal election debts and his extravagant inauguration. Early diplomatic reports from Martin Skol, the US Ambassador to Venezuela during the tenure of President George H. W. Bush confirmed that Carlos Andres Perez was clearly a criminal who was supportive of US interests, but in view of the corruption surrounding his administration and growing civil unrest throughout the country was no longer in control. After being impeached CAP fled the country in August 1993.

Rafael Caldera, was a well known politician with aspirations that included an interest in the presidency. In 1993 Caldera split from the right-wing Venezuelan Christian Democratic Party also known as COPEI, Comité de Organización Politica Electoral Independiente, which he had originally founded in 1945 to form a new political party. The support of Caldera's newly formed *Convergencia*; a coalition of small leftist parties enabled him to gain the presidency in the December 1993 elections. Rafael Caldera was inaugurated as president on February 2nd 1994. The CIA was not pleased and deemed Caldera to be an aging, ineffective, and lame-duck leader who would resist and dismiss American influence in favor of following his own nationalistic agenda; it was at this time that gaining influence and control of the government was considered of vital importance and became a top priority because of Venezuela's position as one of America's largest suppliers of oil.

In November 1993 CIA agent Joseph J. Velling imbedded under the guise of a second secretary and commercial attaché in the American Embassy in Caracas told me that in spite of previous failures *they* were committed and that their only option to gain control was to install their own man in the Miraflores Palace. Velling said that their man was Hugo Chàvez. Chavez had been arrested, tried, and incarcerated for Operation Zamora the first bloody CIA engineered, yet unsuccessful attempt to overthrow the government of Carlos Andres Perez which had taken place on February 4th 1992.

On November 27, 1992 15,000 rebel forces reportedly organized by Chàvez' from his prison cell but lead by General Benito Visconte of the Air Force, Rear Admirals Hernan Gruber Odreman and Antonio Cabrera Aquirre of the Navy, and Colonel Orlando Suarez Galeano of the Army had staged the second CIA backed coup attempt, but it too had failed. While the two attempted coups in 1992 were unsuccessful, they had boosted Chàvez' status as a folk hero with the country's poor; his growing popularity was considered a favorable enhancement to future US interests. The CIA's Inducements of personal wealth through offshore bank accounts and covert NED[3] funding of Chàvez's political action groups found favor with the aspiring revolutionary. In response to the growing support of the country's poor, which was over 80% of the population CIA operatives within the administration were able to convince Caldera, who had only assumed the presidency in February 1994 to consider a pardon for Chàvez and his early release from prison the following month.

In addition to the commanders of the National Guard, Army, Navy, and Air Force the CIA was particularly interested in Rear Admiral Jesus Enrique Briceño Garcia, who at the time, was the Commandant of the Venezuelan Coastguard and one of the shining stars of the Venezuelan Navy. Through the U.S. Coast Guard attaché and their government informants the CIA knew that Briceño would soon move to headquarters where he would be named the Commander of Naval Personnel and ultimately be appointed the Commanding Admiral of Naval Forces whose command included the Venezuelan Coastguard. Briceño Garcia also had the backing and the support of his close personal friend, Carlos Presencia Jurado who was a powerful politician and a leader and key player in the COPEI political party. COPEI and the Democratic Action (AD or the Acción Democràtica party) were the dominant political parties in Venezuela from 1958 to 1993. Because of his political connections Carlos Presencia Jurado had earlier held the position as the vice minister of transport; he was

---

3   National Endowment for Democracy

also a close friend of Andrés Antonio and Juan José Caldera the sons of President Rafael Caldera. As well as being a powerful politico Carlos Presencia was a polished gentleman, an accomplished civil engineer, and a Captain in the Para-military Venezuelan Coastguard Auxiliary. I respected Carlos Presencia as a skilled administrator and a savvy mover and shaker in the political arena. Through our work together we became good friends and shared a mutual interest in the expansion of the Coastguard. Briceño as Commandant of the Coastguard had appointed Carlos Presencia to the rank of Captain and National Coordinator of the Auxiliary about the same time that he had promoted me to the rank of Captain and his National Policy Advisor on Auxiliary Affairs. Briceño Garcia's rapid rise to prominence was in part a result of the intervention and behind-the-scene influences applied by Carlos Presencia Jurado.

The plan created by the Central Intelligence Agency with the assistance of the United States Coast Guard was to compromise the integrity and neutralize the leaders of the military like those dissident commanders in 1992 that had previously prevented Chàvez from taking control of the government. According to the CIA's Velling the officers who couldn't be compromised and convinced to fall into line would be disposed of, the method of disposal wasn't disclosed. If there were some who still might be in opposition to Chavez, as was the case in the 1992 coup attempts the Agency was prepared to overcome these remaining obstacles through *slush-fund* payoffs to numbered bank accounts and if necessary resident alien status with *Green Cards* for any hesitant officers and members of their immediate families to live in the United States. Chàvez' February 1992 coup attempt had relied on rebellious commanding officers from a number of army units in other parts of the country who after Caracas had been secured were to seize control of key government installations in other areas of the country. Lieutenant Colonel Chàvez also believed that he would receive support from other military units that included a General of the Fuerza Aereas[4] and a Colonel of the Guardia Nacional[5] who both had assured Chàvez and the CIA of their command's support of the coup. However, at the last minute the officers reneged and in the heat of battle challenged the Chàvez followers in the streets and

---

4   Air Force
5   National Guard

on the steps of the Miraflores Palace. Two months later the Guardia Nacional Colonel who had strayed from his commitment to Chàvez and the CIA backed coup mysteriously disappears after he and his family board their 65′ Hatteras motor yacht and were seen leaving from a marina near La Guaira. They never returned. Whether they chose to disappear or were disposed of is never determined. There is never a report of the incident; the Colonel and his family simply ceased to exist.

Before dawn of the 1993 New Year the other dissident conspirator, an Air force General, his wife and two children are reported missing from their home in an upscale Caracas suburb, they never returned. Soon afterwards an unconfirmed report said that they had relocated to Peru. In February 1993 officers at naval headquarters in Caracas warn me of another possible coup said to be in the making that their intelligence reported was to be surreptitiously directed by Chàvez. During a subsequent training visit to Caracas Coastguard Auxiliary Captain Nicholas Goschenko warned me of yet another coup which was reportedly being planned by top ranking Venezuelan Air Force Officers. When the attempted coup by the Air Force is thwarted the government keeps information about the coup quiet and it silently drops from the radar screen.

During this period of unrest and political instability the CIA began to question the reliability of their limited resources within the Venezuelan government and was aggressively seeking an alternative and trustworthy individual that was well placed who could provide reliable intelligence. As an American citizen with intimate knowledge and close friendships that had been developed within the Venezuelan military establishment I was offered generous incentives to insure my commitment and participation to operate as a spy and *NOC asset*. Velling told me that my involvement could provide essential and critical information for the benefit of the US government in its plan to destabilize and oust the government of Venezuela. The inducements, unbeknownst at the time had included my earlier promotion by the USCG to Captain, further elevation to Flag Rank, payments from a secret slush fund, and CIA assistance in opening an off-shore and tax free bank account. When I declined to become involved in espionage I found myself with a dishonorable discharge from the service and the removal of all my records from the US Coast Guard database.

The illicit actions of the CIA and the US Coast Guard were undertaken against me personally because I had refused to spy and betray the trust and loyalty of my Venezuelan friends.[6] With my official records removed and virtually dissolved, in effect I no longer existed as a Coast Guard officer. The ensuing lawsuit in the US District Court in South Florida exposed a nefarious conspiracy against the Republic of Venezuela which had been initiated with the full knowledge and involvement of the Commandant of the US Coast Guard, Robert E. Kramek and James Woolsey, the Director of the CIA. Following an investigation by Michael W. Sheehy, Esq., chief counsel of the Senate and Congressional Oversight Committee on Intelligence, CIA operative, Joseph J. Velling, previously assigned to the CIA mission at the US Embassy in Caracas mysteriously dropped from sight. Inquiries through the State Department's Foreign Service personnel office by an investigative journalist with the Miami Daily Business Review confirmed that Velling had been assigned as a political officer in Caracas from July 1993 until September 1994. The State Department Foreign Service personnel office said that Velling had resigned in September 1994; the records do not show the reason for the resignation. The journalist traced Velling to Seattle, Washington but he did not return a phone call to his home.

Well into the litigation which was hampered by the US Attorney's claims of National Security and Privilege, a Watergate type DEEP THROAT emerged who provided critical and confidential information that enabled Myles Tralins, my lawyer to prevail in the lawsuit against the US government. The CIA's clandestine plot specifically targeted government ministers, the Admirals and General officers of the Venezuelan military and had no relationship to the security of the United States. The scheme orchestrated by the CIA was not only reprehensible but potentially dangerous. Having refused their enticements of promotion and substantial cash payments from the CIA's secret *slush fund* the two agencies were infuriated when I declined their offer.

The Venezuelan Conspiracy provides a real-life example of the illicit workings of these two US Government Agencies who through manipulative practices operate solely on their own agenda and do

---

6   As the Chàvez regime continues in power some names in the book have been changed to conceal the identity of the participants who still reside in a country where disappearance and assassination is not unusual.

so without any oversight or control. The CIA's unlawful activity in Venezuela clearly demonstrates how they can compromise and corrupt other agencies such as the United States Coast Guard, but it doesn't stop there. Through regular training visits to Caracas and to the Venezuelan island of Margarita (considered an Islamic terrorist and narcotics hot-spot) I am made privy to the complicity of the Maritime Groups of the National Guard who were assisting the CIA and the Colombian drug cartels in the transshipment of narcotics through Venezuela.

In one particular case a National Guard General on the CIA payroll was incarcerated for his complicity in the transshipment to the United States of a consignment of cocaine with a street value estimated at over $20 million. The shipment transited through the Caracas' Simon Bolivar airport (Maiquetia); after a Boeing 707 aircraft was loaded and departed Maiquetia the plane and the cocaine were never seen again. This case of CIA bungling and lawlessness was the subject of a CBS News 60 Minutes documentary. In 1991 the US Customs Service intercepted a large shipment of cocaine and through their investigation found that the cocaine was part of a failed CIA operation that had originated in Venezuela. The story was the subject of an article published in the Wall Street Journal in November 1996.

During the year 1992 and in the fall of 1993 after receiving a number of awards and commendations from the Venezuelan Navy and the US Coast Guard I learned that my activities in Venezuela were being monitored with increased fervor by the CIA as a possible NOC asset. Following the Agency's unsuccessful attempt to recruit me as a spy during surreptitious meetings at the US Navy Base Roosevelt Roads CIA agent Joseph J. Velling became furious. As America's National Security was not at stake I told the CIA's Velling that I was not willing to betray my military colleagues in Venezuela and would not participate in the CIA's clandestine scheme to subvert the elected Government of Venezuela.

The CIA appears to have overlooked or dismissed as irrelevant significant background information about the enigmatic Chàvez; and in spite of unforeseen setbacks was ultimately successful in bringing the leftist leader to power in December 1998. While being a disgraced former commander of an elite Venezuelan Army paratroop unit their pawn and instrument of deception had also been the founder and leader of the Revolutionary Bolivarian Movement 200 also known by its Spanish acronym, the MBR-200 (Movimiento Revolucionario Bolivariano). Following his release from prison in 1994 Chàvez founded the socialist and left-leaning MVR (Fifth Republic Movement) the dominant party of his PP or Polo Patriotico and the electoral arm of his Movimiento Revolucionario Bolivariano. Together with smaller left-wing parties the coalition had produced a strong civil-military alliance with an extensive social and political reform agenda that was in opposition to the traditional Venezuelan political parties.

THE CUBAN CONNECTION

After being released from prison for the 1992 coup attempts Chàvez visited Fidel Castro in Havana on December 13th and 14th 1994. His visit was undertaken as the leader of the Movimiento Revolucionario Bolivariano. In spite of their past intelligence failures the Agency would soon learn that Chàvez had double-crossed his CIA handlers, but this shouldn't have been surprising considering the Agency had ignored his acknowledged socialist sympathies, friendships, and loyalties to Fidel Castro, the late Saddam Hussein, and Muammar al-Qaddafi.

Fidel Castro who was not trained as a soldier received his education in Law and is an ardent admirer of Jose Marti (1853-1895), a renowned writer and revolutionary known for his opposition to colonial rule. Marti had painstakingly organized the war for Cuban independence but died in one of the first skirmishes. Conversely the charismatic Chàvez who some say believes that he is a reincarnation of Simón Bolivar obtained a College-level degree in Military Sciences and Arts from Venezuela's Military Academy. On July 5th 1975 he received a commission as a Second Lieutenant. During his military training Chàvez' passion for the ideals of Venezuela's great liberator, Simón Bolivar began to be formulated which ultimately led to the creation of the MBR-200.

The MBR-200 was founded in 1983 by Captains of the Army, Hugo Chàvez Frias, Felipe Acosta Carles, and Jesus Urdanta while they were instructors at the Military Academy; the MBR-200 was so named for the initial 200 officers and senior ranking NCOs that supported Chàvez' pursuits of a Bolivarian Revolution. The MBR-200 was the forerunner of the political arm of the Movimiento Revolucionario Venezolano or Fifth Republic Movement.

A short time after his visit to Havana Chàvez visited Iraq and Libya and reportedly returned with a large amount of money. An army Colonel who had been a supporter at the time said that Chàvez had received generous contributions from Tripoli and Baghdad to supplement his political movements' war chest. In addition to money he received from Baghdad and Tripoli the CIA had unwittingly been providing cash that enabled Chàvez to fund his Movimiento Revolucionario Venezolano.

Following his popular election informed management sources within Petroleos de Venezuela (PDVSA) say Chàvez began providing oil to Havana at well below market rates. Being pleased with his new revolutionary friend Castro dispatched scores of doctors, nurses, engineers, and other technicians to Venezuela to assist Chàvez with his aspiring 'Bolivarian Revolution'. Chàvez, Castro and their followers continue to entrench the socialist reform programs of the Bolivarian Republic throughout the country.

It's troubling to think that in their early dealings with Chàvez the CIA would be so naive to have disregarded his socialist agenda and well known allegiances to anti-American leftist regimes. In spite of his socialist sympathies the CIA pressed on and continued with their scheme to install him as the President of the Republic of Venezuela. On the other hand Chàvez was clearly paying attention and once installed as president promptly and silently ended his CIA connections. After his inauguration in February 1999 it didn't take the American government long to realize the dreadful mistake that had been made. It was at this time that the CIA with the NED lurking in the shadows developed a renewed interest in president Chàvez but the interest was now focused on how to get rid of him. Through CIA engineered coups attempts and NED funded opposition groups the US government has and continues to actively wreak havoc in an effort to discredit his administration and remove him from power. Much to the dismay of the US administration Chàvez continued to grow in popularity and soon gained the reputation of being the Fidelito, or little Fidel of South America. While garnering the backing and support of a number of American celebrities Chàvez continues his anti-American rhetoric while promoting his socialist reform programs which he claims have been successful allowing him to take center stage and gain global recognition.

 **RETALIATION**

Only a few days after my meeting with CIA agent Joseph J. Velling and refusing to act as a spy I received a letter from Captain A. A. Sarra dated November 15, 1993 stating that the Venezuelan Initiative and the training and reorganization program didn't fit within the mission profile of the Coast Guard Auxiliary. Captain Sarra followed up with another letter dated November 26, 1993 advising that my appointment as Department Chief would be discontinued and notifying me that I was to be demoted as the Coast Guard was withdrawing its support of the program. In response to Capt. Sarra's termination letter I appealed to Captain Sarra's superior officer, Rear Admiral William Ecker, USCG, Chief, Office of Navigation Safety and Waterway Services requesting a review and explanation of my demotion and the termination of the Coast Guard's sponsorship of the Program. On December 18, 1993 Rear Admiral Ecker unsympathetically confirmed the termination of the US Coast Guard's sponsorship of the Program and that my demotion would be effective on December 31, 1993. In his letter Rear Admiral Ecker further suggests that, "the proper channel for [his] my efforts is with and through the attaché in Caracas, CIA operative Joseph J. Velling; adding that all matters concerning the Venezuelan Auxiliary Program were now the responsibility of the CIA and its embassy attaché Joseph Velling." I appealed to a number of individuals and agencies in Washington for help including a personal plea to the Senate and Congressional Oversight Committee on Intelligence but nothing happened. On December 22, 1993 I sent a personal letter to President Clinton requesting executive intervention from the White House. In my refusal to carryout espionage for the CIA I had indelicately and perilously stepped on a number of *big* toes. With classified and insider knowledge of the Venezuelan Conspiracy I became something more than just a potentially dangerous nuisance.

My direct approach to President Clinton and later to Michael W. Sheehy of the Intelligence Oversight Committee had made me even more unpopular. I continued my appeals by taking the initiative to write a letter jointly addressed to Vice Admiral Robert E. Kramek, Commandant of the Coast Guard and James Woolsey, Director of the CIA. The letter dated August 11, 1994 requested their intervention with details of their agencies combined transgressions against me personally, the Venezuelan military, and the people of Venezuela. No doubt when this very pointed communication crossed the Commandant's desk the US Coast Guard considered I was overdue to walk the plank or possibly more covertly disposed of by their cohorts – the spooks at Langley. On September 27, 1994 the CIA's assistant director, James V. Hirsch in a nondescript single paragraph letter responded denying that the CIA had undertaken any attempted character assassination of *Geary*.

"The CIA has not initiated any action which would adversely affect his (Geary's) personal or professional life."

Admiral Kramek didn't answer the letter; his response was to dishonorably discharge and dismiss me from the Coast Guard Auxiliary. My letter of December 22, 1993 to President Clinton fell on deaf ears possibly in part due to his ongoing dilemma in explaining his *non-sexual affairs* with White House interns. As a 15 year veteran of the US Coast Guard Auxiliary I had carefully followed the chain of command, but the Commandant and the less than luminous Rear Admiral William Leahy, the US Coast Guard District Commander in Miami felt they had been embarrassed in the exposure of their dirty deeds and malicious collusion with the CIA. As I was assigned to the 7th U.S. Coast Guard District Admiral Leahy was named in the US District Court case in Miami (95-0323 CIV-Nesbitt) which exposed the joint CIA and Coast Guard conspiracy that had taken place in Venezuela. In spite of corroboration of the CIA/USCG conspiracy by the Senate and Congressional Oversight Committee on Intelligence and Rear Admiral Ecker's letter instructing me to work with the Agency, the nefarious CIA and the Coast Guard were able to continue unimpeded in their program to destabilize the government of Venezuela while attempting to silence me through character assassination. I had refused to compromise my integrity and ethics in refusing to engage in espionage for the CIA and the US Coast Guard against the citizens of a friendly foreign country and even though the national security of the United States was not an issue I became a CIA target.

On October 14, 1994 I was summarily dismissed from the U.S. Coast Guard Auxiliary without the required notice, hearing or an appeal mandated by Coast Guard protocols. The dismissal letter stated:

- **"This action is being taken based upon actions that you have taken to embarrass the Commandant and the U.S. Coast Guard. In your letter of 11 August 1994, you wrote to the Director of the Central Intelligence Agency and the Commandant of the Coast Guard. Your letter addressed internal Coast Guard and Coast Guard Auxiliary business, by-passed the established chain of command, contained unsubstantiated accusations, inappropriately involved an outside government agency in the internal procedures of the Coast Guard...."**

The Disenrollment Letter conspicuously omitted any reference to or acknowledged the recruitment attempts by the CIA to entice me to engage in espionage against the Venezuelan military or to the several written requests I had made to those involved or the communications with my direct superiors including Rear Admiral William Ecker and Captain Al Sarra. The disenrollment letter did not charge me with any violations of the Manual or of the Auxiliary or US Coast Guard Rules and Regulations. I was told that the decision ordered by Kramek was final and not subject to further review or appeal in spite of the order being a violation of my due process rights and in direct violation of US Coast Guard Regulations.

It was at this time that my close friend the late Miami lawyer, Myles J. Tralins, Esq. took an interest in the case which he deemed to be a blatant abuse of power, arbitrary and capricious, and a flagrant violation of my rights under the law. Shortly after their disgraceful actions were revealed in court the government's lawyers embarked on a campaign of *stone-walling* and refused to respond to the interrogatories under the guise of national security. While it took over a year to reach a settlement the emergence of a Deep Throat and far-reaching media coverage expedited the capitulation of the CIA and the Coast Guard. In spite of having incurred substantial personal expenses, enduring the CIA and Coast Guard attacks on my character, and attempts on my life I did not seek monetary damages. My objective and goal was not to profit monetarily but simply to reveal a clandestine plot by these two government agencies who had attempted to intimidate and force an American citizen to commit espionage. The lawsuit demanded that the Coast Guard restore my unblemished and hard-earned service records and allow me to honorably retire at my rank of Captain to which I had been promoted and earned through a commitment to my country and the United States Coast Guard.

It had been a treacherous and hard fought battle but after the Conspiracy was exposed by the print and electronic media the U.S. Government quickly agreed to all the conditions made in the lawsuit. In acrimoniously agreeing to settle the case their last shot was to file a motion that the final settlement agreement was to be sealed and carry a gag order. The pleadings and the final resolution were thus sealed, including a Stipulation that the court records be closed to insure that the media or others with an interest in the CIA, U.S. Coast Guard, and other dubious and surreptitious US government agencies who were engaged in deceptions against other nations would be denied access.

Semper Paratus…

ONE

It was a clear and cloudless day in the fall of 1991 with Puerto Rico being cooled by light breezes from the southeast. The Atlantic to the north and Caribbean Sea to the east were blessed with calm and virtually flat seas. While enjoying my morning coffee on the balcony of my condominium I gazed out over the Villa Marina Yacht Harbor and watched Ms. PIGI gently tugging at her mooring lines in anticipation of the 80 MPH run to the British Virgin Islands. Our custom built Magnum offshore racer with her high-powered engine would whisk Jason and I the 70 miles from Puerto Rico to Village Cay in Road Town, Tortola in just over an hour and in ample time for Happy Hour at the Pub on Wickham's Cay. The incessant ringing of the phone shattered the peaceful serenity and unbeknownst at the time would dramatically change my life; the planned visit to the BVI would have to be postponed.

"Ed, Desmond here. Good morning my friend, how would you like a bit of a get-away in beautiful South America? At the moment I'm not sure of all the facts but have a few notes that Liz took down during a phone call she took this morning while I was in a meeting at Lloyd's. Unfortunately Liz didn't obtain all the particulars other than the assured telling her that they were uninjured and that his yacht had gone aground on the Venezuelan island of Los Testigos. I checked the Policy number and see that the hull and machinery cover is for $400,000.00 with a deductible of 2%. Needless to say I must get someone on the case as soon as possible and you're my man in the Caribbean."

Desmond or Dizzy as he was affectionately known in and around Lime Street, the hallowed ground where many of the marine underwriting syndicates are located in the City of London, was an underwriter who also dealt with claims when he was the Lead on the Slip[7]. Liz O'Brien, Dizzy's secretary was a fiery Irish lady with long black hair and piercing blue eyes set on a dazzling body that could stop traffic. Liz, who had a weakness for Paddy's Irish whiskey had clearly not been hired for her typing, short-hand or office skills. We had become friends in part because of our Irish surnames. Even though she was from Ireland while I was born in California, Liz in her classic Irish brogue would frequently point out that if it were not for Whiskey the Irish would rule the world.

I had first met this stunning female on one of my visits to London when Dizzy had invited me to lunch at the Marine Club and included Liz. The Marine Club, located a basketball court away from Lloyd's was at the time the center of the universe for underwriters, brokers or anyone else who had the inclination or need to mingle shoulder-to-shoulder with the patricians of the insurance world. While his colleagues in the Market considered him to be a lucky chap, Dizzy frequently had to contend with the snide comments rendered by his peers about his less than competent but beautiful and well endowed assistant. The pin-stripe and bowler brigade at Lloyd's was known to frequently mutter that her bountiful bosoms if activated might be sufficient to feed the entire company of Her Majesty's aircraft carrier Ark Royal. Dizzy's wealthy family, a public school education at Kings College in Cambridge where his curriculum had included only rudimentary subjects and a place on the cricket squad had nevertheless opened the doors to a number of opportunities in the City which ultimately lead to his gaining a favored position in the London insurance market.

Being at ease in the good-natured whirl of the City Dizzy took advantage of every opportunity to socialize especially when he entertained his American colleagues at lunch which always included his stunning assistant. When Liz walked through the Club which was always packed at lunchtime, it was akin to biblical times when Moses parted the waters of the Red Sea.

Before the world was blessed or cursed with the emergence of e-mail and the Web which depends on your point of view, my instructions and communications with underwriters in the United

---

7   The Slip as it is referred to at Lloyd's is little more than a single sheet or Slip and the insurance docu-
    ment used by marine underwriting syndicates that reflects the conditions of insurance coverage for
    the yacht. The Slip shows what percentage each participating underwriter shares in the premium and
    any losses incurred as a result of a claim.

Kingdom and Europe were generally received by means of facsimile or FedEx couriers. A personal telephone call from Dizzy indicated that the loss in Venezuela was of considerable importance. Even though Dizzy said he had limited information from the owner he was hoping that the catamaran *Sundowner* might be salvaged. "Ed, I'll fax you what I've got on the loss and the policy information. During the phone conversation the owner told Liz that he and his sole crewman had been taken off the *Sundowner* by the Venezuelan military and flown by helicopter to Caracas. He said that they would be staying at the Tamanaco Hotel in Caracas until they returned to Miami. Because the yacht was documented in the United States the owner reported the incident to the American Embassy where he spoke with the US Coast Guard Attaché, a Lieutenant Commander by the name of James A. McKenzie."

Dizzy, clearly concerned with the loss wanted me to get to Caracas immediately to assess the situation. A short time later the fax machine began churning out the details from London and I was on the phone with McKenzie in Caracas. The coastguard officer at first seemed a bit cold in his demeanor but warmed as he relayed the story confirming that the Sundowner had indeed been stranded on the island of Los Testigos and shortly thereafter had broken up in the pounding surf. "I think I should tell you Mr. Geary that Los Testigos is an uninhabited island with the exception of a Venezuelan Navy radar installation which monitors Venezuela's eastern sea approaches. It is only accessible by boat, but the right of entry first requires approval from the military authorities. I would suggest that you first meet with the owner, Rob Johnson and Bill his crewman and then follow up with a visit to the island if you decide to go. I can obtain the necessary approvals for your visit to the island if you feel it's really necessary." The conversation with McKenzie ended with our agreeing to meet at the Embassy upon my arrival in Venezuela.

Within 24 hours I was on my way to Caracas. It was a beautiful sunny day as the American Airlines flight from San Juan made a wide turn and paralleled the Venezuelan coast in her final easterly approach to Caracas' Simón Bolivar airport. I had been to Venezuela a number of times previously to deal with claims on container ships and cargo losses in La Guaira and Puerto Cabello and had become fond of the country and her warm hearted people. From my window seat I had a good view of the Venezuelan Naval Academy prominently situated in the hills overlooking the industrial area near the port of La Guaira and the cloud shrouded mountains that separated the sea from the capitol city of Caracas. After making my way through the maze of immigration and customs formalities I found myself descended upon by a swarm of taxi drivers all anxious to offer the best rate for the traffic congested journey into the city where they assured me that I would be deposited at the steps of the US Embassy in the center of Caracas.

Pedro an aging driver who I later found had an equally aged Chevrolet sedan appeared to need the fare more than the other aggressive hustlers and after agreeing to a flat $18.00 for the trip he grabbed my bag while pulling me through the crowd. After leaving Maiquetia the local name given to the Simón Bolivar airport, a visitor's first exposure to Venezuela on the drive to the Caracas metropolitan area is the barren hills separated by the carbon monoxide filled tunnels that penetrate the high mountains along the coast. Depending upon the congestion and the degree of bumper-to-bumper confusion the trip from the airport to the city can take anywhere from 40 minutes to 2 hours. During the drive the visitor is soon exposed to the expanse of hillside dwellings known locally as *Ranchos* which clutter the mountains between the coast and the capitol. Literally thousands of Venezuela's poor, estimated at 80% of the population, are crammed into makeshift houses perched precariously on the open hillsides one on top of another without running water or sanitation facilities. Electricity is cleverly and illegally tapped from the power lines that pass through the area. The low price of gasoline and diesel fuel is evidenced by the hundreds of cars and trucks that appear like ants at a picnic and is further confirmed by the massive traffic jams that drivers must tolerate when entering the city center. Having endured the one hour drive from the airport to the United States Embassy I was pleased to see the *Stars & Stripes* flying from a fortress type building just off one of the downtown boulevards in Central Caracas. The cluster of buildings surrounded by high fences and roving surveillance cameras made up the Embassy complex. The building to the left obviously housed the visa section evidenced by the long line of people waiting patiently for their interviews that hopefully would lead to successful immigration status and legal entry into the United

States. To the right of the main complex a large multi-storied building partially shielded from the public eye and equally protected by a high steel fence and a series of checkpoints is where the Diplomatic Mission and the United States military attaché sections were ensconced. This bastion of American power and influence was shrouded and topped with multiple antennas and aerials where the US Army, Navy, Air Force, Coast Guard, FBI, CIA, and a host of other secret spy types clandestinely kept an eye on Venezuela from behind cannon proof glass and reinforced concrete.

After clearing the external security points I found myself inside a bullet proof enclosure explaining to a Marine guard the purpose of my visit was to see the US Coast Guard Attaché Lieutenant Commander James A. McKenzie. I underwent a short interrogation and identity check by a Marine who identified himself as Lance Corporal Billy Larrabee from Little Rock, Arkansas. After a phone call advising McKenzie I was waiting downstairs in a slow southern drawl Larrabee looked at me saying, "I see from your driver's license that y'all are from Puerto Rico. I know Puerto Rico because I was stationed at Rosy Roads before I received orders to report for Embassy duty in Venezuela. I really liked the island especially the pretty ladies and the cheap rum. I've only been in Venezuela for a couple of weeks, but it sure beats the hell out of wading through the water after being pushed out of a LCU[8] and crawling around the sand on Vieques Island."[9] The congenial corporal then escorted me to the 4th deck where I was introduced to Jim McKenzie. While the other services, Army, Air Force, and Navy have Captains or full Colonels as their attachés I was surprised to find that McKenzie was of such a low grade. As a lieutenant commander he had only achieved the minimum rank that permitted him to be posted as an attaché. McKenzie apparently had a mentor somewhere in the government that had been instrumental in his appointment to embassy attaché duty. Even though the new kid-on-the-block; he clearly had friends in high places. His uniform was crisp and well tailored but displayed few military ribbons that are awarded for missions and accomplishments in the Coast Guard.

Motioning to a chair for me to sit his shifty eyes darted round the room and seemed uncomfortable with direct eye contact. "Good

8   Landing Craft Utility
9   The Puerto Rican Island used by the Navy for live-fire training exercises

Morning Commander, I'm Ed Geary the marine investigator assigned to the *Sundowner* case. A few days ago we spoke on the phone about the US flag catamaran that had stranded at Los Testigos and the possibility of meeting up with the master and crew before they returned to the States." Leaning back in his chair to gain access to a file drawer to his left McKenzie withdrew a folder placing it in front of him, "Of course, I remember our conversation but unfortunately Mr. Johnson and his Mate Bill Miller had an opportunity to catch an earlier flight to Miami and left yesterday. I took their notarized statements and made a copy for you." After a few minutes reviewing the statements and looking at a number of photos that had been taken by the Venezuelan Coastguard, I realized that a visit to Los Testigos wouldn't be necessary as the only remaining part of the catamaran was a small piece of one of her transoms showing a portion of the vessel's name *Sundown….* The statements that McKenzie had taken appeared to be straight forward and contained the information of the *Sundowner's* last few minutes as a whole boat with her last plotted position, date, time, speed, and the other normal boiler-plate navigational details. The report indicated the cause of the stranding had been because Bill Miller who was at the helm at 0200 hours on the morning of the stranding didn't know the vessel's actual position. Miller, being off course by some 2 NM miles caused the Sundowner to go aground on the out-lying reef at Los Testigos Island. The statement indicated that they had attempted to back-off the reef with the main engines and then tried to kedge the vessel free using her anchors but were unsuccessful in the heavy seas. Clearly the owner had tried to save the vessel after the stranding and mitigate the damages. There wasn't anything left of the vessel to inspect and as the loss was apparently due to a navigational error unless some other evidence to the contrary surfaced, a claim of a total loss was clearly covered under the hull and machinery insurance policy. Getting up from his chair McKenzie slowly meandered around his desk while momentary glancing at a photograph of President Bush on the office wall, "You know in my speaking with the two they appeared to be genuine in spite of being a little embarrassed in not paying attention to the course they had set from St. George's, Grenada to Margarita. My reading of the two based on a number of years in the Coast Guard which was on board everything from a Point Class up to a Medium

Endurance Cutter is that there wasn't anything suspicious in the loss of the catamaran. The Venezuelan Coastguard in Los Testigos reported that they searched the remains of the wreckage for drugs or other contraband, but didn't find anything. I asked our LEGAT, the Legal Attaché who's an FBI guy here at the Embassy to run them through EPIC [10] and their Local and State law enforcement agencies, both came back clean. The owner of the boat and his crew apparently were pillars of the community – no problems with narcotics, no records and no warrants." Returning to his desk McKenzie turned and with a smirk said, "The only item in the owner's background check that might lead me to question his honesty and integrity was a mention that he was a friend of George Bush, but as George Herbert Walker Bush is my Commander-in-Chief, I'll leave it at that."

I stood up and was preparing to leave when McKenzie held up his hand to stop me asking if I might have a few minutes to discuss another subject? Returning to my chair I told him to fire away. "Yesterday while speaking with Washington concerning the *Sundowner* and preparing a SITREP [11] I mentioned that you were coming to investigate the loss and learned that you've got quite a reputation with the Flags [12] at headquarters. I spoke with Captain Bill Griswold, the Director of Auxiliary, who told me that for a number of years you've been actively involved with the British Coastguard and the US Coast Guard and her Auxiliary and were instrumental in developing an intelligence pipeline for the Coast Guard with a number of other foreign law enforcement agencies in the Caribbean and Latin America." I smiled with obvious satisfaction and replied, "You guys are quite thorough. Yes, I've been a member of the Coast Guard Auxiliary since 1980 and because of the nature of my work as a marine investigator have on occasion had the need to cooperate and assist international law enforcement which in turn has, shall we say opened some doors for the US Coast Guard. Why do you ask?" McKenzie stood and again briefly gazing at the picture of Bush said, "The Venezuelan Navy and Coastguard could really use your skills and expertise in organizational and management development. They're one of our biggest suppliers of oil and if we can assist and strengthen their military establishments they might become an even

---

10 El Paso Intelligence Center
11 US Coast Guard Situation Report
12 Admirals

stronger ally and a better friend of the US." Turning in my chair for direct eye contact with McKenzie, "But what's this got to do with me?" "You've got a proven track record in organizing and the training of the Coast Guard Auxiliary units in the US Virgin Islands and early on pushed for the creation of search and rescue units in the British, French, and Dutch Caribbean Islands. You then followed through with some top-notch liaison with the various governments to obtain their backing and support for the United States. I understand that in 1983 the Dutch government even made a recommendation to the US State Department that you be appointed the Honorary Consul of the United States for the Dutch Caribbean islands of St. Maarten, Saba, and St. Eustatius. What you've done has proven to be an unquestionable benefit to the United States and particularly to the Coast Guard. Would you be willing to consider a similar mission for the US Coast Guard in Venezuela?"

"That's a big order commander. The work I've done in the past has been supported by some pretty influential people and I couldn't have accomplished anything without their support. Derek Ancona, a retired British Royal Navy Commander and the Chief of Her Majesty's Coastguard in London helped in by-passing the red-tape to get me the training materials needed for the British islands. Admiral Ben Stabile Vice Commandant of the US Coast Guard and Capt. Bruce Beran who was later promoted to Admiral and Pacific Maritime Commander were my mentors with the Coast Guard training efforts in the Caribbean. Ben told me to prepare a *wish-list* for what I needed as the founder and first Commander of the USCG Auxiliary in St. Thomas and was able to by-pass the normal procurement channels to get me everything on my wish-list. Bruce was the motivation behind the Antillean Sea Rescue Foundation in Sint Maarten and he and his wife Connie actually came to Sint Maarten for the commencement ceremonies. After the ball got rolling it took countless hours of preparation and work with the Coast Guards and Marine Police Commands of the area to get everyone reading from the same page. What you're asking would be quite a task with even greater responsibility considering a country the size of Venezuela. If I were to agree to accept the mission what help would you be willing to provide?" Pondering his reply McKenzie then said, "Whatever you need we'll get it for you. Please think about it and if you've got the time I'd like you to meet with

Nicholas Goschenko. Goschenko is a Captain in the Venezuelan Coastguard Auxiliary who regularly bugs me to death about having the US Coast Guard provide training and support to the Venezuelan Coastguard. He's also a close friend of Rear Admiral Briceño Garcia the Commandant of the Venezuelan Coastguard.

Goschenko was born in Venezuela but his Hilton-father was an officer in the Czar's army. His family later moved to Bulgaria where his father who was trained as an engineer became an officer in the Red Army. After World War II the family immigrated to Venezuela. He works for MARAVEN which is a subsidiary of PDVSA, the Venezuelan National Oil Company; I think the best way to describe Nicholas is that he's a mover and shaker. He's very close to the Commandant and through some distant family ties is also related to a number of the navy's admirals. Goschenko is trying to develop a Venezuelan Coastguard Auxiliary based on the US Coast Guard Auxiliary with one exception. The Venezuelan Coast Guard Auxiliary is actually a Para-military arm of the regular Coastguard which is a branch of the Navy. Even though the ranks are made up of volunteer week-end warriors they have a high level of law enforcement authority. If you would be willing to organize and restructure their auxiliary units the Coast Guard and the US Government would have someone that, let's say is on *the inside* with a direct link to the military. You'd be able to develop a close and very beneficial connection for us with the Venezuelan Navy. I'm in a position where I could provide you with whatever help you needed. Here, I've made a note of how to contact Goschenko, think about it and let's keep in touch."

Out of curiosity to see exactly what Captain Goschenko had in mind after leaving the embassy and checking in at the Eurobuilding Hotel I called him at his office in the Chuao section of Caracas. "Captain, it's so nice of you to call. Lieutenant Commander McKenzie told me that you were in town and would be telling you of our needs in the area of training and organization. I was hoping to hear from you. I'm only 5 minutes from your hotel which is also in Chuao; would it be possible for you to come to my office so we might speak?" His accent was thick and heavy confirming McKenzie's comments that Captain Goschenko's origins were that of a White Russian family from the former Soviet Union. "Yes, McKenzie and I did indeed speak briefly of your work for the Coastguard and how I might be able to assist you. What you're doing for the naval forces is quite commendable. I'm here on a marine loss and thought that I'd be traveling to Los Testigos today or tomorrow, but now find I don't have to go after all. Where exactly is your office located?" Hoping that I wouldn't change my mind, Goschenko quickly responded, "Please come to the front desk of the Eurobuilding hotel and I'll send a car and driver to collect you in 10 minutes, if that will be convenient." "Fine, I'll wait at the concierge desk and look for your driver."

The meeting in Goschenko's office started at 3:00 and didn't finish until after 7:00pm. He showed me a number of maps and charts where Navy and Coastguard bases were positioned along the Venezuelan coast with a description of patrol vessels and the personnel who manned them. The charts also indicated the number of navy and coastguard officers and sailors that were deployed at each station. He said that he had attempted to introduce training programs but without the proper audio and visual aids or training materials the program was in difficulty and virtually at a standstill. After our lengthy meeting we enjoyed an excellent dinner at La Estancia, an outstanding Argentinean restaurant in Chacao in central Caracas. Goschenko was an enthusiastic 45 year old oil company executive clearly of Russian extraction who had spent the last 5 years attempting to create and develop a Venezuelan Coastguard Reserve and Auxiliary, but with limited success. Goschenko's appeal was strong and he clearly needed help and support.

In late September 1991 at the request of the US Coast Guard attaché and under the direction of US Coast Guard headquarters in Washington I agreed and accepted the assignment for the mission to assist the Venezuelan Coastguard in the reorganization and the training of its Auxiliary and Reserve forces. Two weeks following our initial meeting Goschenko called me in Puerto Rico asking when I would be returning to Caracas. Goschenko said he had spoken with the Commandant of the Coastguard, Rear Admiral Jesus Enrique Briceño Garcia who was anxious to meet me and had assured Goschenko that he would make himself available whenever I was able to come back. After our call I made arrangements to return to Venezuela the following week. In anticipation of my meeting with the Commandant I prepared a general outline and proposal of what I believed would work as a model for the Venezuelan Initiative involving reorganization and training.

After booking the flights I called Goschenko to provide him with my arrival time, he told me that he'd be waiting for me outside the arrivals area at Maiquetia airport adding that the airport was only a ten minute drive to Coastguard headquarters in La Guaira. When I arrived I found Goschenko waiting for me in full Class A uniform. After the traditional Russian bear hug which promptly bent the frames of my Ray Ban sun glasses hanging from a light cord around my neck, Goschenko smiled saying, "Captain, you're going to get on just fine with the Admiral, Briceño is a pure navy type who doesn't tolerate any loose ends. He works by the book and has a passion for excellence, even though he's an admiral he wants his people to work with him not just for him. The Venezuelan Coastguard was only created a few years ago as a branch of the Navy and that's why we need help. Briceño has virtually transformed the Comando de Guardacostas from a rag-tag non-descript branch of the Armada[13] into a well disciplined and proud sea service. I've been working with him trying to form a Coastguard reserve and auxiliary command modeled on those in England and in the United States. Your help could make the difference in making our dreams come true for Venezuela. Last year I was able to attend the US Coast Guard Auxiliary national conference in the States and brought back some good ideas. From what I've seen I think that the British Coastguard Auxiliary is a bit different to what we need in Venezuela, but maybe a combination of the British and the US Coast Guard Reserve and Auxiliary would be better for us. What do you think?" I smiled and looking at Goschenko's crisp white uniform with its glistening gold shoulder boards and other appointments felt ever so humble. "Nicholas, I believe the first goal should be to determine what the admiral wants as to the precise purpose and mission of his reserve and auxiliary forces. Based on what I've learned from you, McKenzie and my experience elsewhere, I've put together a draft proposal for the admiral and you to consider. Once the admiral tells us what he is trying to achieve and reviews the proposal we can work out the details together. As I see it the first step in the program would be the preparation and the approval of a detailed organizational and management structure with various levels of command and groups covering search and rescue, vessel inspection, aids to navigation,

---

13 Spanish for Navy

training and so on. I have also prepared a critical path analysis of the program with a proposed time frame for accomplishment of each task. Each step we take and before we take it, should be approved by the admiral or his XO"[14] Briefly looking at the outline with a quizzical look on his face said, "Vessel inspection – what's that?" "Nicholas, the vessel inspection program is designed to educate the recreational boating public on what they and their boats should be equipped with before they go to sea. The US Coast Guard and the auxiliary have developed an outstanding proactive program that involves safety inspections and vessel examinations which has been very effective in reducing boating casualties." Pulling a brochure from my briefcase, I fanned through a number of pages covering a variety of subjects including vessel inspection, fire extinguishers, life jackets, and flares. "We can go over all the requirements in more detail later and maybe think about producing a local version in Spanish for the reorganized Coastguard reserve and auxiliary units to use throughout the country."

As Goschenko's Mitsubishi Trooper turned into the Coastguard base at La Guaira the gate opened as the duty officer came to attention and saluted smartly, an acknowledgment that was promptly returned by Goschenko. The headquarters administration building was painted in the blue and gray colors of the Guardacostas while the national flag of Venezuela and the Comando de Guardacostas fluttered in the fresh easterly breeze. The admiral's office was located on the third deck; as we approached the admirals yeoman rose from his desk and snapped to attention rendering a crisp salute. "Captain, please come this way the admiral is expecting you, may I bring you refreshments, would you prefer coffee or a cold drink?" "Some of your excellent Venezuelan coffee would be just fine, black please." Rear Admiral Jesus Enrique Briceño Garcia, Commandant of the Venezuelan Coastguard was a handsome, lean, and self assured officer who had the bearing of one accustomed to being in charge. Rising from his desk he extended his hand in welcome. His neatly tailored white uniform was complimented by shoulder-boards decorated with the gold embellishments of those of flag rank. The admiral had neatly groomed gray hair, a tanned face and smiled as we entered his office. "Nicholas, it is a pleasure to see you how is your wife and daughter?

14 The Coastguard Command' Executive Officer

And your son Nicholas, how is he progressing with his studies at the Naval Academy?" "Thank you for asking admiral, the family is well and Nicholas Junior is still struggling with the intricacies of celestial navigation. Admiral, please allow me to introduce Captain Ed Geary an officer of the US Coast Guard Auxiliary in Puerto Rico. Captain Geary is the gentleman that the US Coast Guard attaché Jim McKenzie at the American Embassy spoke to you about." The admiral smiled and with an outstretched hand said, "Welcome to the headquarters of the Venezuelan Coastguard, it is our honor to have you here. After learning of your work for the US Coast Guard in the Caribbean I have been looking forward to your visit."

After shaking the admiral's hand we all sat down. "Sir, it is I who is honored to have been asked to participate in helping the navy in their endeavors in the organization and training of the Coastguard's Reserve and Auxiliary forces. I understand that you personally know our Commandant Admiral J. W. Kime and therefore are well informed of the benefits that a strong reserve and auxiliary can provide to the regular forces. In the United States the number of reservists and auxiliary actually outnumber the regular Coast Guard. Without the assistance of the reserve and auxiliary the US Coast Guard could not fully perform or carryout their increasing number of missions." Briceño stood up and walking to the window overlooking a row of ex-US Coast Guard Cutters donated by Washington, turned and said, "Yes, I have spoken with your Commandant as well as with Admiral Paul Welling, the Atlantic Maritime Commander and have been impressed with your work in the Caribbean and especially with the auxiliary. Captain, from your experience and professional training in the maritime field and the leadership and organizational skills you have demonstrated within the US Coast Guard, I hope that with Captain Goschenko's enthusiasm and support, you can do the same for my command."

The admiral radiant with enthusiasm carefully detailed his ideas of the programs that he would like to introduce and adapt for the Venezuelan Coastguard and her Auxiliary. He clearly had done his homework as many of the ideas mirrored those of the US Coast Guard. In anticipation of the meeting in La Guaira, I handed the Admiral a letter of introduction and the proposal which I had prepared suggesting an organizational structure of the Venezuelan Coastguard

Auxiliary and Reserve forces. The proposal included a synopsis and general overview of the program and a CP[15] of the timetable which detailed how I believed the mission could be accomplished within a given time frame. In expressing his pleasure and appreciation of the proposal the admiral was ecstatic, "Captain, this is outstanding."

The admiral then summoned his yeoman and asked that he call Capitán de Fragata[16] Bravo Mayol and request that he come to his office. Bravo Mayol, the Executive Officer (XO) reported directly to the admiral and was responsible for Coastguard Operations. "Capitán, please allow me to introduce Captain Ed Geary of the US Coast Guard Auxiliary in Puerto Rico. Mr. Geary will be working with us at headquarters in the development of a reserve and auxiliary to enhance the effectiveness of our regular forces. I would like you to work out the details of implementation with Nicholas and Captain Geary and keep me informed. Mr. Geary will work with my full authority and is to have the full cooperation of all members of the Comando de Guardacostas."

Two weeks later I returned to Venezuela. Goschenko and I had frequently communicated by phone and fax during which time arrangements had been made for me to speak at the next joint dinner meeting of the *Asociación Nacional Marinos Deportivos* (ANMD[17]) and the Coastguard Auxiliary Group Picua. Picua while headquartered in Caracas had their operational facilities in the port city of Carenero, a two hour drive to the east. In attendance were twenty auxiliaries from the Grupo Picua and another fifteen men who were officers in other units of the Coastguard Auxiliary; all those assembled were members of the ANMD. The ANMD was a maritime organization made up of individuals and companies whose support and goal was to make available and provide basic educational programs to the boating public of Venezuela. The Venezuelan Coastguard Auxiliary and the ANMD had parallel and overlapping objectives which at the time provided both organizations with a blended membership. The meeting began with a short welcome speech by the ANMD's President Edwin Neufeld, who then turned the podium over to Goschenko. While Goschenko was speaking Neufeld whispered to me that in addition to his responsibilities with the Coastguard Nicholas was also

15 Critical Path Analysis
16 The US Navy equivalent of the rank of Commander
17 National Association of Sport Mariners (English Translation)

the ANMD's National Operations Director.

Capitan Goschenko was eloquent in his dissertation elaborating on the progress made in the last year while emphasizing the need for a strong and well organized Auxiliary. Goschenko then delivered my introduction. "My friends and colleagues, I am pleased to introduce Captain Ed Geary an officer of the United States Coast Guard Auxiliary in Puerto Rico who has offered to help us bring our dreams of a professional, well trained Auxiliary and Coastguard Reserve to reality. Mr. Geary and I have met with Contralmirante Briceño Garcia who has ordered the full cooperation and support of the Armada". I stood and raising my right hand to my forehead saluted the group then turning slightly, saluted Goschenko. Obviously pleased, Goschenko smiled and started clapping, the group rose and followed Goschenko's lead with applause to the level of a closing performance by Placido Domingo at the Metropolitan Opera in New York. After two hours of intense questions, answers and a continual flow of La Selecta, the premier Venezuelan rum, the pressures of a motivated and enthusiastic audience began to take its toll on me. Back at my hotel Goschenko pressed for a last night-cap, I politely declined opting instead for a cappuccino.

TWO

Upon my return to Puerto Rico in addition to the demands of my marine practice I continued drafting the text of a short test and preparing the format for the various subjects that would be covered in the Venezuelan Auxiliary training manual. Nelly Ortiz, my dependable and ever reliable secretary in spite of her other duties tirelessly translated the test and other materials from English into Spanish, both of us hoping that the fractured Puerto Rican Spanish would reasonably resemble the Spanish spoken and written in Venezuela. Goschenko and I were of the same mind that before starting with the training in Venezuela we should first determine the level of knowledge and skills of our new students. It would be foolish to start classes at the 6th grade level when the students may be ready for post graduate work. The Coastguard Commandant, Contralmirante Briceño Garcia or Capitán de Fragata [18] Bravo Mayol the XO were always available when I needed advice or had to consult with them on technical matters relating to course subjects or compliance with existing governmental or naval regulations. Both were overwhelming in their continued support of the mission. This support was first evidenced and began when the Admiral authorized the use of the Escuela de Guardacostas, the Coastguard School at headquarters in La Guaira for the auxiliary and reserve training sessions. The Admiral almost apologetically asked if he could also include a select group of petty officers of the regular Venezuelan Coastguard in the classes. Subsequent training classes were carried out either at the Coastguard School in La Guaira or other naval installations throughout the country.

During subsequent training in other parts of the country classes were held at naval facilities in Maracaibo, Punto Fijo, Puerto Cabello,

---

18 Venezuelan Naval Grade of Commander

Puerto la Cruz, and Isla Margarita. Those in attendance included a minimum of thirty auxiliaries and reserves in addition to a dozen or so regular service members. The first tests administered in La Guaira and later throughout the country revealed a sound level of knowledge and comprehension of basic nautical skills while exposing an overwhelming eagerness and enthusiasm to learn. The passion to learn and the thirst for knowledge demonstrated by the pupils was once compared by a Venezuelan journalist who had lived in the States with being on a par with a second year scholarship student at the Julliard School of Music in New York – total commitment.

After the initial testing had been completed the training began in earnest and escalated to a level best described as intensive. The initial efforts were focused on the Coastguards in La Guaira, those in the capital and surrounding cities. I would arrive on a mid-day flight from San Juan and quickly be driven to either the Coastguard School in La Guaira or Caracas where training would immediately commence and many times end well after midnight. At 0600 hours the following morning Goschenko, who was charged with providing transportation, would collect me from my hotel for the drive to Higuerote and the Carenero Yacht Club where on-the-water-training would begin using the fleet of Coastguard Auxiliary vessels stationed at this important port for recreational vessels. The Carenero Yacht Club was a beautiful complex with swimming pools and other recreational amenities surrounded by a modern marina with facilities for over 300 yachts of all sizes, types, and descriptions. The Club's four private meeting rooms, all equipped with audio-visual aids were made available when the weekly training classes were conducted. The only distraction being the bikini clad Venezuelan beauties that lounged poolside or were observed sunning themselves on the foredecks of the large motor yachts moored alongside in the marina. Once the training relating to vessel inspections had been completed it became the favorite mission of the Coastguard as those passing the tests were eager to begin inspecting vessels, especially those adorned with the bikini clad beauties.

On December 5th 1991 in recognition of the successful training efforts the Junta Directiva (Board of Directors) of the ANMD presented me with a Diploma of Excellence for my collaboration in educational support of the Venezuelan Maritime Services. During the second week of January 1992 I found myself busy training the Coastguard group Sabalo in Maracaibo, located in the eastern region of Venezuela. This heavily guarded Coastguard Base on Lake Maracaibo provided secure dockage for a number of Auxiliary vessels which actually out numbered the Coastguard's regular patrol boats. Lake Maracaibo was an important region due to the oil terminals located on the eastern shore of the lake and because of the increase in narcotics trafficking that was known to pass through the area. The sectors west and north of Maracaibo were also important military regions because of the penetration of rebels loyal to Colombia's National Liberation Army (ELN) and the Revolutionary Armed Forces of Colombia also known by its Spanish acronym FARC, who frequently crossed into Venezuela near the border post of San Antonio. The ELN and FARC narco-guerillas were also known to use stolen boats for drug trafficking and the movement of arms in and around the city of Castilletes in the Gulf of Venezuela. From their naval intelligence sources senior Coastguard officers believed that certain National Guard officers were involved with narcotics trafficking and selling arms to the Colombian rebels. However, because of the involvement of senior and influential National Guard officers in Caracas the intelligence could never be acted on.

Training continued at a non-stop pace as other Coastguard and Auxiliary commands throughout the country patiently waited their turn for the opportunity to participate in the basic training courses which had now been ordered as mandatory by the Commandant. On February 4th 1992 a meeting was scheduled at naval headquarters in the San Bernardino section of Caracas to further expand and enhance the training programs that were planned to continue throughout 1992 and 1993. In early February the first mission of the expanded training program was scheduled for the largest Auxiliary Group in Venezuela, Grupo Picua in Caracas. Unfortunately, the training was forced to be rescheduled when tanks and ground forces under the command of Lieutenant Colonel Hugo Chàvez attacked the Miraflores palace in an attempted coup focused on the overthrow of the government of Carlos Andres Perez.

Following his surrender on February 4, 1992, Lieutenant-Colonel Hugo Chàvez spoke on Venezuela's national TV, his words translated from Spanish read: *"First and foremost, I would like to say good morning to the People of Venezuela; this Bolivarian message is directed to the valiant soldiers of the Parachute Regiment of Aragua and the Armored Brigade of Valencia. Comrades at arms regrettably for now, our objectives and goals in the capital city were not accomplished, That is to say, we here in Caracas were not able to take power. All of you did very well, but it is now time to reflect. There will be new opportunities as our country definitely needs to head towards a better destiny. So hear my words, hear Commandante Chàvez who gives this message so that you may please reflect and lay down your arms because now honestly our planned objectives on a national level are impossible to accomplish. Comrades at arms listen to my message of solidarity. I appreciate your loyalty, I appreciate your bravery and courage, and I before the country and before all of you assume the responsibility of this military Bolivarian Movement."* The bloody coup was unsuccessful but immediately gave Chàvez folk hero status with the country's poor.

On March 5th 1992 when I returned to Caracas to continue the training I was surprised to learn that the Commandant of the Venezuelan Coastguard had awarded me a permanent commission as a Captain in the Venezuelan Coastguard and had appointed me to the position of Senior Policy Advisor to the Commandant – Auxiliary Affairs – Coastguard Command of the Venezuelan Navy. In a subsequent conversation with Captain Griswold at US Coast Guard Headquarters I was surprised when I was told that *Washington* had not objected and approved my Venezuelan officers' commission and the appointment as the Commandant's policy advisor.

After accepting the commission, briefly discussing the appointment and receiving the Admiral's personal congratulations I walked briskly to the Coastguard office of Personnel Records where I was given a medical examination, had a blood sample taken to determine blood type and was photographed, and fingerprinted. I was then given my new identification card as an officer in the ARMADA DE VENEZUELA. Returning to the third deck and to continue the momentum I presented Admiral Briceño Garcia with a copy of the newly completed Coastguard Auxiliary training manual that I had brought with me from Puerto Rico. Copies of the Auxiliary manual were reproduced by the Navy and within two weeks had been distributed to all Coastguard Commands throughout Venezuela. Also in March 1992 Rear Admiral Robert E. Kramek then Commander of the US Coast Guard's Seventh District in Miami who later became

Commandant of the US Coast Guard, sent me a Certificate of Appreciation, 'For your continuing support of Coast Guard programs and missions during Operation Desert Shield and Desert Storm.'

During my training visit in June 1992 I found that Admiral Briceño Garcia had another surprise in store for me. On June 12th 1992 the Commandant awarded me the *HONOR AL MERITO – Order of Naval Merit – First Class* for my services to the Venezuelan Navy and Coastguard. Not normally being at a loss for words I struggled for the proper terminology to adequately express my appreciation and gratitude. Mere words seemed inadequate for this immeasurable honor that the Minister of Defense and the Commandant had bestowed upon me during the formal presentation ceremony. Because the award had been given to an American citizen the event was covered by the national press and the Venezuelan television networks. Because the commendation was unique the Ministry of Defense and the Venezuelan Navy's public affairs officers had publicized and garnered the interest of the print and electronic media in my acceptance of this prestigious naval citation and uniform decoration. The reason for the increased attention was because this military meritorious service commendation is normally only awarded to citizens of Venezuela who are serving members of the Venezuelan armed services. When Jim McKenzie, the US Coast Guard attaché in Caracas who I was surprised to find had not been invited to the formal ceremonies at navy headquarters learned of the citation he phoned me that evening at my hotel, "Ed, congratulations on receiving the naval commendation. You know that's on a par with our Navy Cross, I don't think anyone outside of the Venezuelan military has ever received the medal." In the same breath McKenzie said, "I'd like to ask you a favor. Next time you're with the Admiral maybe you could suggest that he might consider me for the decoration. I know you've got a lot of pull with the Venezuelan flags and if I were to be awarded the medal it would really look good in my personnel records." Being a bit surprised and flattered by the request, "Jim, that's a big order, I don't know what the Admiral's reaction will be but I'll mention it if the opportunity presents itself."

The following month at a cocktail party in Caracas attended by the Commandant and a gaggle of Admirals and Generals who commanded the Army, Navy, Air Force, National Guard, and a sprinkling of government ministers I waited until Briceño Garcia had consumed his two drinks, (during private and public functions I found that the Admiral never consumed more than two scotch and waters) and believing at the time that McKenzie was a friend, I casually asked if Jim McKenzie had ever been considered for the Order of Naval Merit – First Class? The Admiral smiled and gently placing his arm over my shoulder said, "Captain, this Citation is only awarded to exceptional sailors and marines who have clearly demonstrated a service to the navy, service that is above and beyond the call of duty. You earned the Citation. When the time comes that McKenzie spends more, or at least the same amount of time helping the Venezuela Coastguard as he does playing tennis, I might consider it. The same goes for John Hill. When Captain Hill the US Navy attaché spends less time with our Navy's junior officers on the golf course and more time dealing with our procurement requests, he too may be considered." Realizing that I had struck a sensitive nerve I knew it was best to drop the subject and let McKenzie do his own bidding. The Admiral then went further, "You know this isn't only a Navy problem, General Martinez the Commanding General of the Venezuelan Air Force tells me he has the same problem with the US Air Force. At least three times a week Colonel Graham, the Air Force attaché is determined to tee off by 1000 hours and immediately after the game he's at the bar. He apparently has a high capacity with low tolerance. I understand that last Wednesday he was so inebriated that his aide had to virtually drag the Colonel to his car." I was to learn later from Goschenko that the admiral wasn't the only person who wasn't overly impressed with Jim McKenzie or the assistance that he was supposed to be providing to the Venezuelan Coastguard. Over lunch one day in Carenero when his name came up Goschenko referred to McKenzie as a *Pippisote,* an unflattering Venezuelan comparison of a man to the male sex organ.

During the following summer Renaldo Perez, Commander of the Tiburon auxiliary group on Margarita Island asked if I would be available to visit and provide some basic introductory training for some new members of their auxiliary unit. "Ed, if you could schedule a visit I'd be very grateful. As school is out please feel free to bring your son with you. My daughter Jenetta is also out of school for the summer so Jason would have someone to keep him company while we were involved with the training. We also have plenty of room so while you are here you're more than welcome to stay in one of our guest rooms." In civilian life Renaldo after gradating from college in the United States, became a certified public accountant with a very successful tax practice. Renaldo lived on Margarita Island with his wife Eva and their two children Jenetta who was 16 and Hector age 14. Their home was a large magnificent penthouse over looking the Caribbean near the Hilton hotel. Jason having met Jenetta and Hector on a previous visit was more than anxious to accompany me. While Jason liked playing video games with Hector he was more inclined to spend time with Jenetta, a tall blonde and beautiful young lady who with her parent's permission at the age of 16 was frequently engaged in modeling assignments for cosmetics and bathing suit advertisements. She was also a regular in television commercials. During the period of the training visit Renaldo said that Jenetta was having a piano recital and would like Jason to come. Packing for the trip included our Levi's, my uniforms, and Jason's dark blue blazer and tan trousers.

The training of the new members of the auxiliary group proved very successful while Jason had a great time at Jeneta's piano recital and even more fun later during visits to the beach. While we were both clearly prejudiced Renaldo and I agreed that his beautiful daughter on the arm of a tall well mannered young gentleman from Puerto Rico looked quite impressive. Afterwards Jason always insisted that he travel with me on subsequent training visits to Margarita. Because of Jennetta's limited English he told me he would always be grateful that he had become fluent in Spanish.

The visit to Margarita and later to Caracas had been successful and a happy time except for the untimely death of Fermin Yanez. Fermin was an active member of the ANMD and the Coastguard Auxiliary Group Picua in Caracas, because of our mutual interests we had become good friends. He was a successful businessman and a creative soul who owned many or most of the motion picture theaters in Caracas. During training visits to Caracas he would frequently invite me to dinner at La Estancia, his favorite restaurant where Venezuela's film directors, producers, actors, and financial backers were regulars and would mingle with the upper crust of Venezuelan society. The diminutive entrepreneur while small in stature, he was no more than "'4" and probably 120 pounds when soaking wet, was a giant intellectually. In addition to Coastguard matters we would often discuss the growing political problems facing the country and the government corruption that was increasing at an alarming rate. Along with over a hundred of his friends, business colleagues, and fellow coastguards I said good-bye to him at his funeral in Caracas. I will always miss his wisdom, his laughter, and his precious friendship.

In March 1992 having been named Senior Training Officer and National Policy Advisor to the Commandant-Auxiliary Affairs with the rank of Captain I began to direct my attention on the NACON[19] '92 which was scheduled to be held in San Francisco, California. In an effort to further strengthen the relationship between the US Coast Guard and the Venezuelan Coastguard I believed that if I could obtain approval from my superiors in Washington and from the Venezuelan Commandant to involve senior members of the Venezuelan Coastguard Auxiliary in the U.S. Coast Guard Auxiliary's annual conference it could prove to be extremely beneficial. After a number of letters and telephone calls to Washington I grudgingly received the necessary approvals from the vice-commodore of the U.S. Auxiliary to allow Venezuelan participation.

NACON '92 was attended by five Venezuelan Coastguard Auxiliary officers; Captain Nicholas Goschenko and his wife Daniela, 1st Lieutenant Eri Lopez Spies and his wife Beatrice a 2nd Lieutenant, Captain Carlos Luis De Casas Bauder and his companion Veronica, and Captain Carlos Presencia Jurado. While I lead the Venezuelan delegation as the National Policy Advisor to the Commandant I attended the conference in my uniform as an officer of the US Coast Guard Auxiliary. Unfortunately, the aging gang of cronies who made up the leadership of the US Coast Guard Auxiliary was miffed at having their influence and positions of authority diminished by a contingent of Venezuelan Coastguard officers lead by a previously unknown auxiliary officer from Puerto Rico.

Because it was a first, one-of-a-kind international auxiliary support program the Venezuelan Initiative had been placed on center stage. Unfortunately the focus and attention given to the attendance at the 1992 US Coast Guard Auxiliary National Conference by the Venezuelan group wasn't looked upon as positive by the old gang as it had clearly challenged and lessened their importance at this national

---

19 National Conference of the US Coast Guard Auxiliary

gathering. The resentment and loathing of US Auxiliary Commodores and Division Captains at the conference was demonstrated and in evidence for many months afterwards. What these buffoons or I didn't know at the time was that their personal animosity against me was of little importance considering the vested interests and collusion between the CIA and the US Coast Guard. In spite of this animosity and negative reaction by the arrogant clowns who ruled the US Coast Guard Auxiliary, NACON '92 was a great success – at least for the Venezuelan's. In spite of the negative reaction from the geriatric commodores the conference had exposed my Venezuelan friends to the history, goals, and missions of the US Coast Guard Auxiliary and the camaraderie and networking of the auxiliary in the United States which I believed could also be applied in Venezuela. Admiral J. W. Kime, the USCG Commandant at the time made the Venezuelan contingent feel comfortable and relaxed especially in expressing his warm welcome at the opening ceremonies. In his presentation to the general assembly of NACON '92 Nicholas Goschenko relayed a personal message from the Commandant of the Venezuelan Coastguard while expressing the appreciation and gratitude of the government of Venezuela for the assistance provided by the United States in the development and training of their Coastguard Auxiliary and Reserve. The hierarchy of the US Coast Guard and their CIA mentors were also suitably impressed with the accomplishments that had been achieved within the Venezuelan Naval Forces when during NACON '92 I was told that I was to be promoted. On September 18th 1992 Captain William S. Griswold, USCG, Chief Director of the Auxiliary promoted me to the rank of Captain with the designation of Department Chief – Pan American Auxiliary Liaison. I was and have been the only member of the United States Coast Guard Auxiliary ever to hold or permitted to be identified with the rank of Captain.

1992 US Coast Guard Auxiliary National Conference

Back row: Carlos Luis de Casas Bauder, Beatriz & Eri Lopez-Spies, Nicholas Goschenko
Front row: Admiral J. W. Kime, Auxiliary Commodore, the author, Auxiliary Vice-Commodore

THREE

Beginning in October 1991 after the training programs had been implemented and began in earnest, testing and advanced education was expanded at a feverish pace. The regulars, reserves, and auxiliary members of the Venezuelan Coastguard once exposed to the fountain had an unquenchable thirst for knowledge. Thanks to the leadership demonstrated by the Venezuelan Coastguard command and my personal commitment in replenishing this fountain of knowledge the program grew from strength to strength.

In early 1992 the training program was extended to include other coastguard groups in the Venezuelan State of Zulia. The Commandant requested that the training curriculum be increased and expanded particularly in the port city of Maracaibo. The expansion was due to the reported increase in narcotics trafficking and the questionable level of training and expertise of naval personnel at the base which had a close proximity to the open border with Colombia. The Venezuelan Coastguard had two Auxiliary groups operating out of its base in Maracaibo, Grupo Sabalo and Grupo Rescate. Headquarters wanted these groups to be expanded and strengthened through more intensive training. The Commandant said that the Minister of Defense was concerned that the major oil refinery situated along the shores of Lake Maracaibo may become a target of Colombian Marxist rebels who could attack the refinery or the oil tankers that supplied oil to another PDVSA refinery that was located to the east near Carenero. The refinery at Carenero supplied gasoline for domestic consumption and for export. While the training in Maracaibo included search and rescue and statutory and regulatory compliance of recreational vessels and drug trafficking, the primary objective was port security and surveillance focused on the many vessels operating in the area. The advantage of using auxiliary recreational vessels was that most were not marked and could be used covertly whereas the regular Coastguard boats were identified by their multi colored stripes and GUARDACOSTAS painted on their topsides.

In spite of increased FARC guerilla activity in the area the expanded Coastguard and Auxiliary presence was credited with insuring that the refinery or any tankers were not attacked because of the increased Coastguard activity. The surveillance training provided further positive results in the summer of 1992 when after monitoring the movements of a custom built 36′ Intermarine offshore go-fast that had entered Lake Maracaibo through the channel from the Gulf of Venezuela the vessel was boarded and 1,000 kilos of cocaine was found. The resulting investigation found that the cocaine was destined for an anchored Panamanian flagged tanker that was destined to sail for the United States.

In the city of Puerto La Cruz located in the eastern state of Anzoátegui the Coastguard Auxiliary Grupo Delfin was commanded by 1st Lieutenant Silvio Catalano who a dozen or so years earlier had emigrated from Italy. In addition to volunteering more than 30 hours a week for coastguard duty he operated two schools one of which taught computer skills the other languages. Silvio's fluency in a number of languages never ceased to amaze me. In spite of running a successful business enterprise he was totally committed to his adopted country and its Coastguard. Under his command the Coastguard Auxiliary in Puerto la Cruz went from strength to strength during which time his language school became so successful that it caused the local Berlitz franchise to close.

As the Aeropostal 727 jetliner circled for its final approach at Barcelona, the airport that serves the eastern Venezuelan city of Puerto La Cruz, I was fascinated by the dry and desert like topography of the eastern sections of Venezuela considering the lush tropical countryside found in the country's interior and jungles to the south. "Eddie, Eddie, over here." The voice was unmistakably that of Silvio Catalano calling amidst a crowd of people waiting to meet the flight from Caracas. The handsome, olive skinned Italian at 5′10″ and a trim 160 lbs had a charismatic personality. While he could have easily been a movie star (an opportunity he had declined in his early years) his engaging and cheerful manner had instead lead him into sales. After first completing his college studies in Rome Silvio had successfully applied his people skills as a door-to-door encyclopedia salesman. Within a short period of time his employers, the publishers of the Encyclopedia Britannica recognizing his management skills elevated him to the position of general sales manager. After a number of years working 12 hour days and making a pot full of money he decided to set out to seek his fortune in the new world and in spite of having relatives in the United States chose to move to Venezuela.

"Eddie, let's first get you checked into the Hotel Melia then I've scheduled a meeting for us with Capitán de Navio Saùl Pérez Altuve, the commanding officer at the Coastguard base at Guanta. The Capitán is anxious to get the training programs started so the auxiliaries can help his regulars with their coastal patrols. He told me that he's got a growing problem with illegal drugs moving along the coast to Trinidad, but just doesn't have the manpower to keep his patrol boats at sea for extended periods."

Puerto la Cruz, surrounded by a lush landscape similar to Marbella and the Costa del Sol in southern Spain is a beautiful city built much along the same lines of Fort Lauderdale, Florida with numerous man-made canals that fringe the coast adjacent to the tranquil Caribbean Sea. The canals are bordered by lavish and expansive condominiums, villas, and Five-Star hotels. The Melia, a luxury hotel located on the eastern side of Puerto la Cruz is a favorite of business executives and senior military officers because of its peaceful ambiance and excellent selection of restaurants and bars.

"Let me see G-E-A-R-Y oh yes Capitán we have your reservation for five nights at the official military rate." Silvio and I proceeded to the 5th floor room that I would call home for the next few days. The 'room' was actually a suite that provided a spectacular view of the harbor and the out-lying islands located a short distance offshore of the city's white sand beaches. Putting my bags on the bed I turned, "Thanks Silvio, the room is magnificent I do appreciate you making the arrangements for me. Okay, let's go see Capitán Perez and get things rolling." The Coastguard base was less than a ten minute drive due east along the coast on the edge of the city and situated near the PDVSA's LAGOVEN oil terminal.

"Capitán Pérez, may I introduce Captain Ed Geary the coordinator of training that the Commandant spoke to you about." Pérez stood and with a broad smile extended his hand, "Captain, welcome to my command. I have been anxiously awaiting your arrival and looking forward to meeting you. If we can increase my effective manpower through the use of the auxiliary I will be eternally grateful." Capitán Pérez Altuve, a 30 year veteran of the Navy was clean shaven no more than 5'4" and weighed probably 300lb. The congenial Captain's abundant body mass appeared to be desperately trying to release itself from the captivity and restraints of an undersized uniform that was tightly buttoned. Observing professional courtesy in anticipation of my arrival he had worn his Class A dress uniform and in the oppressive heat of the day was red-faced and perspiring profusely. With the exception of his bald head, clean shaven face and white uniform rather than red, a visitor's first impression was that of Santa Clause in a sub-tropical environment. Much like the legendary Mr. Clause he had a warm smile and a kindly disposition that immediately produced a pleasant atmosphere. I immediately liked him. Slipping my now wet hand from his perspiring grasp, "Capitán, as I'm sure Silvio has told you the training programs have achieved a very high level of success in Caracas, La Guaira, and Maracaibo. I see no reason why, with your support, the efforts of Silvio and, the Grupo Delfin we can't do the same for your command." The Captain smiled then looking at Silvio said, "When do we begin?" That evening at 1900 hours in a classroom provided by management of the LAGOVEN oil terminal, 20 members of the Grupo Delfin and 10 regular coastguard sailors assembled to begin intensive basic training. For the next five days instruction commenced at 0800 and lasted until 1800 hours. On the last day of training we reviewed the subjects that had been presented while discussing reading assignments from the training manual. I asked that the reading assignments be completed in the interim period before I was scheduled to return to Puerto La Cruz at which time we would continue the training. When I departed on the sixth day I left behind 30 individuals who had successfully mastered the basic skills of seamanship. On the drive back to Barcelona airport Silvio and I discussed what we had covered and the subjects for the next training sessions. "Silvio, it's important that all the students complete their assignments so we can move on to the next step." "Eddie, you can count on me. I'll see that your orders are followed to the letter. When will you be back?" Looking at my agenda I told Silvio, "In two weeks."

In returning to Puerto La Cruz two weeks later we continued the classroom training and then began the on-the-water exercises which included man-overboard drills, towing, firefighting, first aid, and vessel inspection. For the fire fighting exercises the LAGOVEN oil terminal provided us with a number of fire extinguishers and one of Silvio's friends a local fisherman, offered us the use of his aging 20′ wooden outboard boat for the training. The basic principles of fighting a fire began in the classroom with an explanation of the essential elements of a fire; heat, fuel, and oxygen and in eliminating one of the elements how a blaze will be extinguished. Pointing out that the extinguisher nozzle should always be directed at the hottest point which is the base of the fire. Initially the fire fighting training involved the use of a small derelict and abandoned sailboat allowing each trainee to take turns in putting out a fire on the beached boat.

When the time came to move to a real-life scenario we then used the fisherman's 20′ wooden outboard boat that was floating. As the flames intensified I shouted at the now panicking coastguard trainee, "Point the fire extinguisher at the base of the bloody fire not at the flames on top!" To simulate an on-board fire we had tethered the wooden outboard boat to the dock with two coastguardsmen sitting at the bow. A bucket with a small amount of gasoline had been placed near the stern and ignited. Unbeknownst at the time when the gasoline had been poured into the bucket from the boats portable fuel tank a small amount had dripped into the bilges.[20] When the bucket was set alight a slight breeze blew the flame which ignited the fuel that had dripped into the bottom of the boat. Luckily we had more than one fire extinguisher that was used to extinguish the flames which had quickly spread to the hull. We didn't lose the boat in the ensuing blaze but the fisherman didn't offer the use of his boat for subsequent fire fighting training. With the one exception when the man that was to be rescued was almost run over by the rescue boat, our man-overboard and recovery drills at sea were carried out without incident. I was pleased that we hadn't dismembered or drowned any of our *man-in-the-water* volunteers.

The training paid off when in the fall of 1992 a German flag sailboat that had come to Venezuela to stay during the hurricane season caught fire while at anchor in the harbor at Puerto La Cruz.

---

20 The lowest point inside a boat

Seeing the smoke from the burning boat the Coastguard auxiliary vessel *Rescate Uno* quickly responded rescuing the two persons in the water and extinguishing the fire which saved the yacht. I was pleased, Silvio was pleased, and the German who owned the yacht was pleased even more.

The Auxiliary Training Manual which had been prepared in both Spanish and English and submitted to the Commandant of the Venezuelan Coastguard on March 5th 1992 was promptly approved by the Venezuelan Ministry of Defense and the Commanding Admiral of the Venezuelan Navy. It proved to be a positive element and a valuable tool in the subsequent training programs that were carried out throughout the country. The Coastguard Command reproduced the required number of copies that were then used by all the Coastguard and auxiliary commands throughout Venezuela.

Due to a significant increase in recruitment and growth of manpower levels it was necessary to reprint additional copies of the training manual for the various navy and coastguard commands throughout the country. Grupo Picua in Caracas, Grupo Sabalo in Maracaibo, Grupo Galapago in Maracay, Grupo Orca in Puerto Cabello, Grupo Rey in Falcón (Puerto Fijo), and Grupo Tiburon in Nuevo Esparta (Isla Margarita) soon received copies of the training manual for each member of their group. It wasn't long before all the auxiliary groups throughout Venezuela had completed their basic classroom and on-the-water training and were then considered to be fully operational units within the Coastguard Command. In appreciation of the training they received each Auxiliary Group presented me with a personally engraved trophy or wall plaque in recognition to express their gratitude.

On July 28th 1993 Grupo Tiburon in Porlamar, Isla Margarita appointed me their honorary Group Commander. I particularly enjoyed working with the men and women of Grupo Tiburon on Margarita Island because they were an interesting collection of souls and as well as being dedicated to safety at sea they were also just plain nice people. During the training of the group over a 12 month period I don't recall ever having to pay for more than two or three meals. It was very flattering that each day during the training exercises one or more of the auxiliaries would insist that I join them and their family for dinner at a restaurant of my choosing. On many occasions rather than slight one over another we would end up with 15 or more sitting around the table. I ate a lot of Wonton and Pork Fried Rice during this period because the local Chinese restaurant was the only place in town that had tables that could seat 15 or more people. I enjoyed some great meals with some even greater people while also having the satisfaction provided by an intensive training regimen with a dedicated group of volunteers who learned fast.

After less than three months we were conducting advanced training exercises which included safety inspections at sea, drug interdiction, and surveillance. The continued training paid off handsomely when in the summer of 1993 the Venezuelan flag passenger ship 'Los Roques' had mechanical problems ten miles offshore and the Coastguard Auxiliary rescued 78 passengers from the floundering vessel. Drug interdiction training was a subject of great interest, but had to be presented with extreme care and considerable attention. Most of those who are involved in drug trafficking are usually a nasty bunch that carry big guns and have no reservations about shooting their way out of a problem. The last thing I wanted was someone being hurt or worse yet being killed because of carelessness. In early 1993 the Coastguard asked that I include training of Detachment 76 of the Maritima Unidad[21] of the Venezuelan Guardia Nacional who were based at Porlamar on Margarita Island. It was during the initial training of the Maritima Unidad that I first became acutely aware of the extent of the CIA's involvement in drug trafficking in Venezuela.

In scanning the horizon through my binoculars while on a routine surveillance patrol on board a Detachment 76, 45' patrol vessel some ten miles to the west of Porlamar I observed a 150' general cargo ship with a rusted and faded blue hull flying the national flag of Honduras. The aging tramp steamer clearly had seen better days but was still engaged in some type of trade. The days training exercise was to look for vessels to ostensibly conduct boarding's for vessel safety inspections. For this reason the Honduran ship became our target. She was riding low in the water steaming at 12 knots on a north easterly course and was the type of vessel that fits what is known as an EPIC[22] profile in US maritime law enforcement circles.

I was soon to learn why the commanding officer of the local

---

21 Maritime Patrol Unit
22 El Paso Intelligence Center

Guardia Nacional lived in a beautiful home, drove an expensive car and never wanted to openly discuss drug interdiction training. I suggested to the commander of the Guardia Nacional patrol boat that the target ship be contacted by VHF radio and told to stop her engines and hove-to[23] as she was about to be boarded. The commander of the patrol boat, Lieutenant Carlos Sabatini, pulled me aside and quietly said that this would not be a good idea as this was a protected ship that was authorized to transit through Venezuelan territorial waters. According to Sabatini these *authorized* vessels regularly transited the waters in and around Margarita Island and from what he had learned from his superiors were normally from Cartagena or Barranquilla in Colombia. Sabatino said he didn't know where they were going and really didn't want to know. "With all due respect Captain it's best not to ask anymore questions." Showing me a clipboard holding a sheet marked Standing Orders he pointed to the 7th line about half way down the page which contained a dozen or so names, the Lieutenant went on, "You will see this ship the Lady Dianna registered in Honduras is shown here. This and the other vessels have been given clearances and are under protective orders. Certain people have made *arrangements* with my commanding officer at the Maritima Unidad of the Guardia Nacional in Porlamar and the regional commander in Caracas that these ships are to be allowed to pass unchallenged as they are part of a classified operation." I was now really curious, "Certain people, what certain people Lieutenant? I don't know who the other people are but I do know in some cases the American government tells the Guardia Nacional that they must not board certain ships in Venezuelan waters." Sabatini looked at me while softly uttering the letters, "C-I-A."

It became clear that the Guardia Nacional didn't need training in drug interdiction as they already knew in advance what ships were transporting drugs. The patrol boat commanders had orders not to interdict certain ships because the CIA had the Guardia Nacional on its payroll. I doubted the CIA had an interest in exporting Colombian coffee but now knew they were involved in the business of transporting something illegal with the protection of the Guardia Nacional.

According to my intelligence sources within the Coastguard, over

---

23 Stop

the last few years because of the *American Connection* the commanding officer of Detachment 76 in Porlamar and his superior in Caracas had become wealthy individuals. In view of their active involvement in the drug trade and until I could quietly terminate the narcotics interdiction training of the Guardia Nacional and delete it from the curriculum, the training would be revised to focus only on fire fighting, search and rescue, and towing. I also wondered how I might get a copy of one of these *Standing Orders*.

In subsequent coastguard training exercises held with Grupo Tiburon on Margarita Island I learned that the island, as well as being a focal point in narcotics trafficking was also home to a number of Islamic terrorist organizations. The town of Juangriego located on Margarita's north western coast was inhabited predominantly by Arabs who, according to their false identity cards claimed to be Syrians. A confidential source that had access to classified files of Venezuela's internal security service, Direccion de Intelligencia Seguridad y Prevencion (DISIP) later told me that while some were Syrians other nationalities which included Afghans, Iraqis, Lebanese, Jordanians, and Egyptians had paid to be issued with false Venezuelan identity documents that concealed their countries of origin as many were wanted by the authorities. In concert with their brethren in South America, particularly the Hamas Movement and Hezbollah in Cuidad Del Este in Paraguay, the *Arabs* of Margarita were channeling funds laundered through the Banco Confederado in Margarita to terrorist organizations in the Middle East. According to a DISIP informant, Margarita Island was the center of an extensive terrorist financial network that was the conduit for laundered funds from South America, Panama, and the Cayman Islands; funds that ultimately ended up in Lebanon.

It was bizarre, on one side of the coin we had drug traffickers and terrorists with Middle East interests and on the other side we had the CIA. Not surprisingly the Agency was not only involved in narcotics trafficking by sea but also by air; General Jorge Castillo Davila a National Guard officer in Caracas had been arrested, tried, and convicted for working with the CIA when he was caught using his soldiers to provide cover for an abortive plan to ship Colombian cocaine by air from Maiquetia to Miami. In view of the CIA's cooperative program with the notorious Detachment 76 of the Maritima Unidad in Porlamar I determined that as they were obviously committed to CIA funded narco-trafficking it would be counterproductive and possibly unsafe to continue coordinated training of the units of the Guardia Nacional with the Coastguard in Isla Margarita.

Considering the US government's abortive Andean Strategy in South America and maneuvers such as the fiasco surrounding Operation *Blast Furnace* and Operation *Snowcap* in Bolivia the CIA's manipulation and disruption of governments within Latin America was believed to have been curtailed but this was not the case. I don't know who first said it but it's definitely true, *the more things change – the more they remain the same.* In discovering the Agency's secretive activities involving the Guardia Nacional it confirmed that the CIA was still up to its infamous dirty deeds in Venezuela and Colombia. It also wasn't the last time I was to hear of the agency. Having confirmed what was happening in and around Margarita Island and from reliable reports heard *on the street,* the Maritima Unidad unit based in Puerto la Cruz shouldn't be trusted either. In checking with my sources in Caracas I found that all the units of the Maritima Unidad of the Guardia Nacional had apparently been corrupted by the CIA. After I learned of this under the guise of having inadequate time I tactfully discontinued all the training programs that were in the works for Puerto La Cruz that jointly involved the Venezuelan Coastguard and the Maritima Unidad of the Guardia Nacional. Determined to continue the drug interdiction training but without the involvement of the Guardia Nacional I had the officers of Coastguard Grupo Tiburon on Margarita Island travel to Puerto La Cruz where Grupo Delfin was based and Grupo Sierra travel from the city of Cumana for the advanced educational sessions.

The ongoing training exercises that were conducted in the eastern provinces during 1992 had been closely monitored and carried out under the watchful eye of the Commandant and his headquarters staff. At the conclusion of the training of the eastern units the Coastguard command hosted a reception at the CORPOVEN oil installation in Puerto La Cruz. During the reception in appreciation for my efforts I was presented with a bronze trophy and citation of merit from the Venezuelan Coastguard Regional Commander, Capitán de Navio Juan Manuel Gómez Montilla.

The year 1993 continued with new challenges and with increasing demands for complex and more specialized training. The advanced training covered a myriad of subjects including, comprehensive inspections on larger vessels, statutory and regulatory compliance, drug enforcement, search and rescue, first aid/CPR, towing, and fire fighting. During the first of a number of vessel boarding's off the Venezuelan coast near the Macuto Sheraton hotel and the nearby Carabelleda Marina a French catamaran was hailed and told to lower her sails and hove-to in preparation for a boarding party. Although it was only an educational exercise one Coastguard Auxiliary credited his training when during the boarding he found a hidden compartment containing 15 kilos of white powder that tests later found to be high grade Colombian cocaine. According to papers found on board the catamaran had sailed from Cartagena and was bound for Fort de France in Martinique. The occupants of the catamaran were arrested and turned over to the naval authorities and the boat was seized. Jason who normally attended the training sessions when he accompanied me to Venezuela on this occasion had decided to remain at the Eurobuilding hotel to enjoy the swimming pool. Back at the hotel while showering and preparing for dinner he was fascinated when I relayed the story about the cocaine found on the catamaran and was sorry that he hadn't come along. That evening Jason and I had been invited to dinner at Goschenko's home in the La Trinidad section of Caracas; Goschenko said he'd pick us up at 6:30pm on his way home from the office. While we waited for Goschenko in the hotel lobby we had a father and son discussion about the growing problems with drugs and how it was ruining the lives of so many people both young and old.

"Hi Ed, hello Jason I'm really pleased that you're able to come to my home for dinner. My son and daughter Nicholas and Alexandra have heard a lot about you and are looking forward to meeting you. Nicholas is 17 and Alexandra is 16." I looked at Goschenko and with a slight grin said, "Nicholas and Alexandra, hmm I guess there's no question of the Russian origins of this family." A beaming Goschenko acknowledged the comment, "That's for sure. But I want you to meet my mother she too is a real Russian. We'll stop by her house on our way home so I can introduce you and Jason. I've told my mother a lot about you and she's looking forward to meeting you."

The home of Goschenko's mother was a large house situated in a beautiful suburb on the outskirts of Caracas. "Captain Geary, it is such a pleasure to finally have the pleasure to meet you in person, Nicholas has often spoken about you and your work with the Guardacostas. I would like to introduce my sister Katrina, Nicholas's aunt." "It's is a pleasure to meet you both and please allow me to introduce my son Jason." "Madame Goschenko, Nicholas has often spoken about you and I too have been looking forward to having the opportunity of meeting you personally." "Mother I think it would be a good time to sample a bit of your vodka." With a sheepish grin on his face Goschenko continued, "My mother makes her own vodka in the cellar which is the best outside of Mother Russia and the smoothest in the world. I'm sure that if I were to ask her kindly she will give me a bottle or two to take home." "Nicholas, of course you may have a bottle but first let us enjoy a drink together with the Captain and his son." Jason declined a sample of the best and smoothest opting instead for orange juice. Pouring plentiful doses of the clear liquid from a former wine bottle into three whisky glasses Mrs. Goschenko raised her glass, "As the British say, Cheers." And with that the charming 80 year old matron knocked back about 4ozs of the high-octane spirits with Nicholas only seconds behind. Deciding to err on the side of caution I slowly sipped the potent fluid, "No, no, Ed, good Russian vodka is not meant to be sipped but taken all at one time." "Nicholas, if I were to swig the contents of the glass you'll have to carry me out to the car." "But in the movies John Wayne always knocked his whisky back in one swig." "You're watching too many movies Nicholas."

After exchanging some small talk about our visits to Venezuela and what life was like in Puerto Rico Nicholas stood saying, "Mother I'm sorry, but we must be going as my wife the lovely Daniela has prepared a sumptuous dinner for our guests and we must not be late." Expressing our thanks and Nicholas, with two bottles of his mothers Vodka held tightly in his hand we left. At Goschenko's home, turning the key in the lock while pushing on the door, "Daniela, Daniela, we're here." From the kitchen Daniela emerged wiping her hands on a towel as she approached. "Where are the children?" Kissing her husband on the cheek she responded, "In the bedroom playing games on the computer. Alexandra, Nicholas, please come your father's home." Alexandra was a striking girl with long black hair and beautiful eyes that belied her 16 years. Young Nicholas too was a handsome lad with tussled hair wearing a t-shirt emblazoned with the logo of the New York Yankees.

After the introductions were made Jason, Alexandra, and Nicholas disappeared into the bedroom. The three quickly became immersed in a video game concentrating on a super hero that was taking out all the bad guys with what sounded like a battery of AK-47's that had a never-ending supply of ammunition. With a limited command of English Daniela called on Nicholas to translate, "My wife says she hopes you like pork as she has prepared a lovely roast." I responded, "Gracias Senora Goschenko, cerdo asado es muy bueno." She gracefully replied, "Please, my name is Daniela there is no need to be formal amongst friends." Daniela was clearly a warm person who in spite of her exhaustive chemotherapy treatments for breast cancer made everyone around her feel welcome. She declined joining Nicholas and I for a round of his mother's vodka choosing instead a glass of Argentinean Concho y Toro Chardonnay.

The dinner was excellent with the exception of some unidentified root vegetable that had the taste of partially cooked cardboard. The distortion of Jason's face when he tasted the brownish vegetable quickly vanished upon receipt of my subtle kick under the table. On the drive back to the hotel Jason was quiet while Goschenko and I conversed about the usual Coastguard business and the degrading state of affairs caused by Carlos Andres Perez.

"Captain, I'm very pleased that you could come to my home for dinner tonight. It really means a lot to me. Daniela is very sick and has been weakened further as a result of the chemotherapy treatments. With me being away so much because of my job and coastguard business it's nice that she has now had the opportunity to meet you and Jason." Putting my hand on his shoulder, "Nicholas, it was our pleasure to have dinner with your family and I do know what you're talking about in being away so much which is why when I travel I try to bring Jason with me as much as possible. I don't have a wife to consider but children grow up too fast and I think it's necessary for parents to be around as much as possible during their formative years." "Captain, I can see you are a good father, all of us in Venezuela greatly appreciate all the time you give to help us with the Guardacostas. Yesterday I learned something at headquarters that you will find most interesting. You must however keep this confidential. Briceño told me in private that after the Coast Guard in Washington had received his letter commending you on your work in Venezuela for the Navy he was told that you were going to be promoted to commodore." "That's great news Nicholas and for sure it will go no further."

Back in our hotel room Jason was less restrained. "Dad, that's great news isn't a commodore like an admiral with the gold things on your shoulders?" "You got it kid, a commodore is indeed equivalent to a rear admiral, the *things* on the shoulders are called shoulder boards and in the auxiliary they're not gold but silver with a single star." "Wow, my Dad is going to be an admiral!" "Hey, not yet, that is good news but for the moment I just need to concentrate on being a good captain." "Dad, there's something else, that brown stuff at dinner was awful. Do you know what it was?" "No, it was pretty dreadful but as guests we don't complain about the food." "Ok Dad, but please don't ever again ask me to eat something that's likely to make me sick." From the gargantuan breakfast he consumed the next morning Jason didn't get sick and we agreed that no permanent internal damage had been done.

Members of the Picua group in Caracas and Grupo Tiburon from Isla Margarita became enthusiastic coastguards who flourished from classroom and on-the-job training. Even though they were all volunteers they loved learning and somehow even enjoyed the heat of the blazing sun in the regulation work uniforms that headquarters ordered be worn during our training exercises. The occasional fall into the sea when mishandling a tow-line or while conducting man overboard drills didn't diminish their enthusiasm. The members of the group took the training seriously, but also had the courage to laugh at themselves when they made a mistake. They all worked hard and played hard and were just fun to be around especially after a few rum and cokes at the end of the day.

The average age of the Venezuelan Coastguard Auxiliary in the mid 1990's was about 46. Its officer corps which at my insistence now included a growing number of women came from all walks of life, accountants, doctors, dentists, engineers, oil men and women, woodworkers, and fishermen. The boat crews were made up of volunteers that ranged from professionals to construction laborers each providing the brains or the brawn that was needed to complete the varied missions. The common thread that was woven into this interesting tapestry was the bond of enthusiasm and a willingness they each demonstrated to serve their country's Coastguard and maritime community.

The US Coast Guard Auxiliary was created in 1939 and continues to serve the country and the regular Coast Guard with its ever increasing number of missions. Similar to the Venezuelan Coastguard Auxiliary the US Coast Guard Auxiliary in its earlier years was a motivated and well managed group of volunteers who successfully completed their missions and always got the job done. Unfortunately, in recent years the US Coast Guard and her Auxiliary have become politicized and changed for the worse.

Over the years Auxiliary membership has steadily declined as a result of the lack of motivation, apathetic leadership and complacency. The decline and deterioration of the organization became increasingly evident as this middle-aged matron descended ungraciously into old age. Much like a malignant growth, the decline manifested itself because those in positions of power within the US Coast Guard Auxiliary had ensconced themselves in ivory towers far removed from the rank and file membership who actually carried out the ever increasing missions of the Coast Guard. Auxiliary members frequently voiced their grievances and criticism of decadent Auxiliary leaders who played musical chairs in an effort to retain their positions of power. Unfortunately, the privileged few weren't listening.

I personally bore witness to this power play when a local auxiliarist with over 20 years of service to the US Coast Guard was denied promotion to command of the Puerto Rican US Coast Guard Auxiliary. The promotion to Division leadership was denied for two reasons. First because she had refused to engage in the local political games or engage in the musical chairs that had become entrenched and accepted practice within the Puerto Rican Auxiliary Division management. The second reason and maybe the most important, was that she was a woman. The general attitude was that no self-respecting *muy macho* Puerto Rican male could ever imagine taking orders from a female. Even though having been shunned and locked-out from the local Auxiliary leadership this gallant lady continued devoting countless hours to auxiliary missions and work in support of the US

Coast Guard. Knowing full well of the sleazy tactics being engaged by the musical chair gang in Puerto Rico and after being apprised of the situation you'd think that the Chief Director of the Auxiliary in Washington would have addressed the problem and promptly done something about it, right? No way Jose, the Chief Director or maybe better described as the Wimp-in-Washington simply wanted to go with the flow and not rock the boat; some say because he was too close to retirement.

The position of Chief Director of the Auxiliary is a back-water appointment where the US Coast Guard deposits Captains or Commanders who generally haven't graduated from the US Coast Guard Academy and therefore haven't got a hope in hell of further promotion. These near-do-wells normally have three or four stripes on their shoulder-boards and are apathetic, lukewarm bodies that the Flags at headquarters just don't know what to do with while they bide their time before starting to collect their retirement checks. As these soon-to-be-pensioners didn't go to the Academy they have little chance of further advancement past their current grade and because of this become a perfect match to dump in the job as the Chief Director of the Auxiliary.

There's little pressure on the merry-go-round position as a Chief Director and even less skill required to hold the job. There are however some nice perks and side benefits that allow these emerging senior citizens to bop around the country supposedly to attend conferences, play golf, attend meetings, play golf and engage in the self-serving role as *the big man from headquarters that's here to help you*. Of course all the travel expenses of the Chief Director are paid for by the US taxpayer. As I honestly can't say that all the Chief Directors have been under achievers or aging clowns I'll limit my observations to the ones I've met in the last 15 years or so. Only in the last few years has any attention been given to auxiliary membership retention and while there are still a number of younger and enthusiastic auxiliary members their numbers are in decline. The problem of retention was no doubt magnified because of the increasing number of aging auxiliaries with sight or hearing problems or those being pushed around in wheelchairs. It's admirable that this aging legion of elders still have the will and the desire to serve the Coast Guard, but clearly there comes a time when all good things must and should come to an end. Even a winning race horse eventually has to be put out to pasture or sent to a stud farm. In the case of the Auxiliary's senior citizens putting them out to pasture would be a possible option as the stud farm might be asking a bit too much.

On the other hand the vigor and enthusiasm of the youthful Venezuelan Coastguard Auxiliary proved to be a prime ingredient for the organization's success. Between the years 1991 and 1994 auxiliary membership in the Venezuelan Coastguard increased five fold due in part to an identifiable command structure, accessible, motivated and involved leaders, interesting missions, recognition by the public and the maritime community, opportunities of promotion, challenges offered by the specialized training that was being provided, and the prestige of being directly connected to the Venezuelan Coastguard and its parent the Venezuelan Navy.

Following extensive liaison and planning with the Commandant of the Venezuelan Coastguard, arduous approval discussions with US Coast Guard Headquarters in Washington and Captain Gregory Magee, Commander of the US Coast Guard Greater Antilles Section in Puerto Rico plans were put into place where 52 officers of the Venezuelan Coastguard Auxiliary would, at their own personal expense visit the US Coast Guard Base in San Juan, Puerto Rico. During the visit the Venezuelan's would have the opportunity and exposure to training exercises that included both surface and helicopter operations. The successful training exercises ended with a splendid evening reception on January 29, 1993 hosted by the Honorable Josefina Carrero, Consul General of the Republic of Venezuela. During the reception I was honored when the Consul General presented me with an award and a plaque for my work with the Venezuelan Navy on behalf of the Foreign Affairs Ministry of the Republic of Venezuela. A similar less inspiring afternoon reception was hosted by the US Coast Guard Greater Antilles Section in San Juan.

Unlike previous Commanders who had been admired and respected, the self-centered Captain Greg Magee was looked upon as someone best avoided. I don't recall Magee attending the reception hosted by the Venezuelan government, but if he was there even briefly, he was noticeably silent which wouldn't be unusual considering his serious lack of communicative skills. Initially I had believed that

Magee was a friend, but soon found that he wasn't. Greg Magee was interested only in Greg Magee who had great aspirations of promotion past the grade of Captain. Many of those who served with or under him were able to see him for who he was and hopefully before he'd thrown them to the sharks for his own self-interest. His subordinates viewed him as cold and ruthless in his pursuit of recognition and promotion. Unfortunately, I wasn't one of those to learn of his transgressions until it was too late. Previously I hadn't been aware that on the 23rd of November 1993 Captain Al Sarra as Chief Director of the Auxiliary in Washington had awarded me the Coast Guard medal Award of Administrative Merit, but found during the discovery process of the litigation that Captain Greg Magee, as Commander of the Coast Guard's Greater Antilles Section had rescinded the award on the 28th of November 1993. I guess as his due reward Magee was later moved to a non-descript assignment and owing to his lack-luster performance like any sinking ship soon disappeared into obscurity.

On May 14th 1993 the Venezuelan Coastguard celebrated its 12th anniversary. At a reception at headquarters in La Guaira to celebrate the anniversary Rear Admiral Briceño Garcia presented me with a letter of commendation and wall plaque in recognition of my service to the commands of the Venezuelan Navy and Coastguard. Following the reception and while enjoying the cocktail hour I was approached by two gentlemen who introduced themselves as the Minister of Defense and a senior aide to the Minister of Foreign Affairs. Both expressed their appreciation for my efforts in support of Venezuela's military establishment and suggested that during my next visit to Caracas we might lunch together for a personal discussion. I was intrigued and curious at the reference to a *personal discussion*. In a subsequent meeting with the gentlemen at Naval Headquarters in the San Bernardino section of Caracas the personal discussion I had been intrigued and curious about simply focused on the elevated status and image of the Navy and Coastguard in Venezuela. The Minister of Defense, also an admiral, told me he was impressed with the Coastguard's improved image within the maritime community and the increasingly positive reaction from the public as a whole because of the ever-increasing and favorable media coverage. He believed that the improved reputation of the Venezuelan Coastguard was a result of the enhanced training and the Coastguard's improved professionalism. I acknowledged the admiral's compliments and said I was clearly flattered. He told me I had every right to be. At the time neither I nor the Minister was aware that the CIA and US Coast Guard were involved in espionage and subversive activities in an effort to destabilize and oust the government of Venezuela.

Following the May 14th reception the Commandant asked me to prepare an operational plan for the Venezuelan Coastguard's participation in the UNITAS[24] joint training exercise with the US Coast Guard and US Navy scheduled to be held in July 1993. After completing the planning phase I was congratulated by the Commandant and ordered to oversee and coordinate Venezuela's involvement in the UNITAS exercises on Isla Margarita slated for July 26th through the 29th. The US Coast Guard detachment under the command of Commander James Hass effectively completed the UNITAS mission in Venezuela due in part to the advanced planning and coordination provided by Chief Warrant Officer Wayne Hennessy assisted by my son who acted as a translator for the US Coast Guard officers who didn't speak Spanish. In appreciation the Commandant sent Jason a letter of commendation for his efforts and assistance as a translator. As a result of the UNITAS exercises Wayne and I developed a friendship that has continued over many years.

Rear Admiral Briceño Garcia was a rising star within the Venezuelan Navy and soon after his promotion to COMMANDANT OF NAVAL PERSONNEL at Naval Headquarters in San Bernardino in Caracas he was promoted to vice admiral and the GENERAL COMMANDER OF THE VENEZUELAN NAVY. Following Briceño Garcia's promotion to navy headquarters Rear Admiral Martin Fossa was named the Commandant of the Venezuelan Coastguard.

I didn't look at the clock as I jumped from the shower to pick up the phone when it began ringing in my room at the Eurobuilding hotel, but it was still dark outside. "Ed, Jim McKenzie here. Sorry if it's a bit early but I know you're an early riser. Hey, tonight I'm having a little get together at my place in honor of Admiral Welling's visit to Caracas, as you know Paul Welling is the Coast Guard's Atlantic Maritime Commander and unless you've something scheduled to do for the Auxiliary I'd like you to come." Rubbing a towel over my face I responded, "Sure Jim, what time?" "Things start pretty late here so

---

24 United States Navy joint training exercises with South American navies and coastguards

we're looking to have people come about 8 o'clock. "Later this morning when I get to the office I'll leave the directions to my place on your voice mail at the hotel." The taxi took about 30 minutes to reach the garden apartment of Jim and Kathy McKenzie, ten minutes of actual driving and 20 minutes waiting in traffic getting out of Chuao. I had decided to attend McKenzie's party in my US Coast Guard Auxiliary officers' uniform and was glad I did when I found that the other US military officers were also in uniform. "Hi Ed, I'm glad you were able to make it. Ed, this is my wife Kathy, now how about a drink?" "It's nice to meet you Mrs. McKenzie and thanks Jim; just a Coke would be fine."

With the exception of Briceño Garcia and his aides who were in uniform the other Venezuelan military officers that were present were dressed in civilian clothes. There were also a number of suit-and-collar types from the Embassy with haircuts best described as regulation short back and sides mandated for US federal employees. Possibly for a perceived level of safety the suit-and-collar types were clustered in groups on the balcony of McKenzie's luxurious apartment located in an upscale section on the hillsides overlooking the city. McKenzie was obviously in his niche and in addition to a fondness for tennis, felt right at home being the effervescent host especially when the bill was being picked up by the US government or maybe more accurately the US taxpayer. Colonel Graham of the US Air Force and Captain Hill, the US Navy attaché oblivious to the other guests, were secluded in a corner swinging their arms in an animated display resembling a golf swing. The last swing caused Colonel Graham to stumble throwing him off balance, no doubt not from the weight of his imagined club, but from the excessive levels of Chivas Regal he had consumed. Fortunately Hill caught him preventing his air force colleague from an ungraceful nose dive that would have surely resulted in a crash landing. Other than Kathy McKenzie there were only one or two unremarkable ladies present who appeared to be bored to tears. Obviously this was not meant to be ladies night, but purely a man's *gathering of eagles*. McKenzie later told me that about every month or so each branch of the armed services would find some reason to have a cocktail party that could be charged off to the Embassy. With only a few exceptions when these get-togethers occurred the same people attended, mostly Colonels, Captains (the

Eagles), and a few lower grades of officers like McKenzie. Jim later told me that if you don't invite the Air Force or the Army then they wouldn't invite you to their gathering of eagles – tit-for-tat.

"Ed Geary, what are you doing here?" The high-pitched voice cut through the air like a hot knife through cold butter and unquestionably was that of Paul Blayney. I had come to know Captain Blayney of the US Coast Guard when he had served as the commanding officer of the US Coast Guard's Greater Antilles Section in San Juan, Puerto Rico. Turning as Blayney approached me, "Hi Paul, it's nice to see you but if I may ask, what are you doing here? After you left GANSEC[25] I heard you were warming a desk in Washington." Blayney smiled, "You tell me first." "Last September Jim McKenzie asked me if I'd be interested in accepting an assignment to reorganize and train the Venezuelan Coastguard Auxiliary and Reserves; in March after it had been approved by Washington Admiral Briceño Garcia promoted me to the rank of Captain in the Venezuelan Coastguard and named me his National Policy Advisor, in September '92 the US Coast Guard Auxiliary promoted me to Captain and well, here I am." "But there aren't any Captains in the Auxiliary, the rank doesn't exist." Blayney said rolling his eyes in obvious displeasure. "There is now. I'm the only Captain in the US Coast Guard Auxiliary and now I understand that the Captain's rank may also be improved on when I'm promoted to Commodore." Blayney clearly taken aback picked up the conversation, "While I was in Washington I was given the opportunity to become Chief of Operations for the Coast Guards Atlantic Maritime Area reporting to Vice-Admiral Welling, the Atlantic Area Commander. I don't understand why I or Admiral Welling hadn't been told of this training program in Venezuela or of your promotion to Captain in both the United States and Venezuelan Coastguard." Captain Blayney then introduced me to Admiral Welling who clearly knew more about the Venezuelan Initiative than his Chief of Operations was aware of. From his cool demeanor it also appeared that Welling clearly didn't want to talk about what was going in Venezuela in front of Blayney so I dropped the subject. I knew that the Admiral had been fully informed about the Venezuelan program and was curious why he hadn't told Blayney. It was surprising too that even with Blayney's extensive contacts in Washington apparently no one had briefed him

---

25 The US Coast Guard Greater Antilles Section

on a mission that had been endorsed by two Commandants, a gaggle of admirals and was happening in his own backyard.

A short time later while munching on some finger-food and sipping from a glass of Coca-Cola I watched as Briceño Garcia finished his two whiskies while maintaining a dignified position in preparation for a gracious withdrawal. After the admiral had made his parting remarks I too thanked Jim and Kathy McKenzie for their cordial hospitality and feigning early morning training exercises extracted myself from the party. Anxious to remove myself from this patronizing group of military-politicos I realized in descending the steps that I hadn't arranged for taxi. "How are you getting back to the Eurobuilding?" The voice from the shadows was that of Briceño Garcia. Being a bit startled I quickly turned, "Oh Admiral, sorry I didn't see you. I forgot to order a taxi but I can go back and ask McKenzie to call one for me." Raising his hand the admiral said, "No problem, I can have my driver drop you off at your hotel, it's not that much out of my way."

The traffic was light and the trip to the Eurobuilding only took about ten minutes during which time the admiral spoke briefly about his family and his young son who had recurring medical problems. "You know Captain I hate these embassy parties and my wife dislikes them even more which is why she seldom attends. With the exception of the Spanish and French the rest are boring." I acknowledged the comment telling the admiral that I had only attended at the insistence of McKenzie who said that Admiral Welling had wanted to meet me personally. "You've never met Admiral Welling? I'm surprised at this because in speaking with him last month when I expressed my admiration for the work your doing in Venezuela he appeared to know you very well. I'm surprised to learn you hadn't met him previously. And by the way you're not supposed to know this but Washington is planning to award you the Coast Guard Administrative Merit decoration for your work with my Command." As we approached the hotel the Admiral asked, "How is your son? Please do send my best regards to him when you return to Puerto Rico. I'm sorry he won't be with you but we are looking forward to seeing you for dinner tomorrow night." Opening the car door and turning, I thanked the Admiral for the ride to the hotel saying, "Thank you sir, I'll look for your driver tomorrow at 1900."

Out of courtesy a few weeks later I sent a letter to Admiral Welling expressing my pleasure in having the opportunity of meeting him in person along with a brief synopsis of the training in Venezuela. I received a reply under the letterhead Commander Atlantic Area – United States Coast Guard – New York, New York 10004-5099 the admiral wrote back, "Dear Captain Geary, Thank you for the information on your efforts. I'm glad to hear of the progress you've made since we last met. Just as in the United States, I see great potential for the Auxiliary in Latin America. I look forward to my next copy of EL VOCERO." The letter was signed Paul A. Welling, Vice Admiral, US Coast Guard.

FOUR

During the summer of 1993 following Briceño Garcia's promotion to headquarters, Contralmirante Eliseo Martin Fossa was named the Commandant of the Venezuelan Coastguard. My first meeting with the new Commandant had been arranged by now Vicealmirante[26] Briceño Garcia to insure the continuity of the Coastguard training program. Upon entering the admiral's office I introduced myself, "Good afternoon Admiral, I'm Ed Geary. Please allow me to extend my congratulations on your promotion to Commandant of the Coastguard." "Thank you Captain. I have heard many good things about you from Briceño and from Vicealmirante Carlos Augusto Ramos Flores, the Comandante General de la Armada. Your reputation precedes you."

Rear Admiral Martin Fossa was an imposing gentleman about 5'9", graying salt and pepper hair with piercing eyes that appeared capable of penetrating the steel plate of one of his Cutters. "Captain, I can't begin to tell you the number of compliments I have received from the officers in my command and from the other commanders of the armed forces. Everyone has praised the work you are doing for the navy with particular admiration of our auxiliary program. Last week at a meeting at the War College I was approached by the Chief of Staff of the Army and the National Guard who asked if I might consider temporarily loaning you to their Commands so you might create a reserve force in support of their regulars. Last weekend General Francisco Cortez of the Air Force and his wife were guests at my home for dinner and learning of your experience as a pilot asked if you might be interested in establishing a unit for our Air Force similar to the American Civil Air Patrol. I have explained to my

---

26 Vicealmirante – Vice Admiral
     Contralmirante – Rear Admiral

colleagues that your work for the Coastguard is voluntary and that you pay your own expenses but in any case you simply would not have the time to undertake additional responsibilities for training of the other services. In the short time that I have been commandant I have found that over the last two years you have carried out a major transformation of the Coastguard Auxiliary and Reserve and I do hope that you will continue." "Thank you Admiral, I appreciate your kind words but because I have to make a living I really don't believe I would have the time to begin programs for the other services. However, as Captain Goschenko may have told you we are considering including the Unidad Maritima units of the National Guard in the same classes that are attended by the Auxiliaries, but we aren't yet sure if this would work."

I decided that a first meeting wasn't the time to tell the admiral that the National Guard had been corrupted by the CIA. After glancing at his desk calendar the admiral looked up, "On Sunday I'm having a private luncheon at my home and if you can spare the time I'd like you to attend. The other Generals I spoke about will be coming with their wives and children; it would be a good time for me to introduce these officers to you. If your son Jason is with you on this visit he would be more than welcome to accompany you. And if I may ask on Sunday I'd appreciate if you could speak with the Generals personally and graciously decline their training proposals. I don't want them to think that I'm keeping you to myself, which of course is exactly what I'm doing." I rose from my chair to leave. "Thank you Sir, no problem I'll look forward to Sunday. Because of school Jason is back in Puerto Rico but I can tease him a bit about what he missed at the party." Before leaving I presented the Commandant with his personal copy of the revised and updated Auxiliary Training Manual and the newly created Instructors Examination Manual. "Admiral, to insure continuity I have been training selected officers to act as instructors who will be able to continue some of the basic training classes during my absence. You might call it a Teach-the-Teachers program." I also gave the Admiral a copy of El Vocero. El Vocero known as The Voice in English was a quarterly publication in both Spanish and English that I produced and had printed specifically for the Venezuelan Coastguard Auxiliary. The articles included a mix of US Coast Guard Auxiliary and Venezuelan Coastguard subjects formulated to keep the various auxiliary groups throughout the country in contact with one another by means of networking through a single maritime publication.

The following Sunday the luncheon at the Commandant's home was a pleasurable experience but somewhat intimidating considering that I was mingling with some of the most powerful military leaders in Venezuela. After begging their indulgence in having to refrain from increased training responsibilities for their commands, we all parted friends.

On October 1st 1993 I attended the regular monthly council meeting of the Eastern Puerto Rico Council of the Navy League of the United States which is held in the officers club at Naval Station Roosevelt Roads, Ceiba, Puerto Rico. During the meeting I was surprised and flattered when Hector Nieves, the council president presented me with an engraved wall plaque that was inscribed,

Capt. Edwin S. Geary
A Special tribute to a Distinguished U.S. Merchant Marine
For his numerous contributions to our Nation and
The Navy League of the United States

The Officer's Club at Rosy Roads, the local name given to the Roosevelt Roads Naval Base, is positioned high on a hill overlooking the Caribbean Sea in an area of the Base known as Bundy. Across from the "O" Club the BOQ's (bachelors officer quarters) are situated to provide accommodation to visiting retired personnel and active duty military officers and pilots. The pilots are either temporarily based at Rosy or from the air-wing components of the various carrier groups who are engaged in live-fire training exercises off the coast of the Puerto Rican island of Vieques or in target practice involving drones near St. Croix in the US Virgin Islands. The large circular bar situated in the center of the Club is generally surrounded by VC-8 helicopter and F-16 pilots unwinding from the day's operational exercises or reminiscing about their sorties over Iraq during the Gulf War. Many are still dressed in their colorful emblem emblazoned jump-suits while others relax in shorts and island style flowered shirts.

Local civilian members of the Navy League are always properly attired in long trousers, shirt and tie or open Guayabera shirts. The man I observed who appeared to be lurking in a corner of the Club in a poorly tailored suit clearly didn't fit the normal profile. His narrowed eyes kept darting around the room and when I looked at him he would quickly look away. He was alone and didn't speak to anyone; his peculiar behavior made me curious as to whom he was and why he was here, especially because he appeared to be watching me. As the director of military liaison for the Navy League I had been joined at my table by two navy lieutenants, one the aide to the Base Commander the other the commanding officer of the Sea Cadets unit. The Lieutenants and I were engaged in a conversation concerning an award ceremony for the Sea Cadets that would be hosted by the Base Commander. Being caught up with the planning of the Sea Cadet program I didn't pay much attention, but admittedly did occasionally scan the room for the man who didn't fit. Towards the end of the meeting having moved surreptitiously around the room the man who didn't fit approached from behind and startled me when putting his hand on my shoulder said, "Captain, may I speak with you privately for a moment." The two lieutenants graciously excused themselves and the man sat down.

"My name is Joseph Velling, I'm an attaché and second secretary in the commercial section at the American Embassy in Caracas. The embassy has been observing your work with the Venezuelan Navy and is very impressed with what you have done. Your efforts have had a very positive effect not only on the diplomatic front but also in improving the relations between the military establishments of Venezuela and the United States. I have something to discuss with you, but don't think that now would be the appropriate time. Would it be possible to meet tomorrow say for dinner? What I have to tell you is very important and crucial to your Venezuelan Mission and to the affairs of the United States." "Sorry Mr. Velling, I must say I'm curious at what you need to discuss but unfortunately I'm leaving early tomorrow morning to deal with a case for British underwriters in Panama and won't be returning until next week." Obviously perturbed in finding I'd be away, Velling said, "Okay, when will you be back in Venezuela?" "I've a meeting scheduled at naval headquarters in Caracas in two weeks." With a curt," I'll be in touch" Velling then vanished amidst the throng of naval officers now filling the Club.

I left a short time later and during the drive home felt quite pleased with myself finding that the US Embassy had been observing and was impressed with my endeavors in Venezuela. I particularly liked the bit about having a very positive effect on the diplomatic relations between our two countries. I teased myself a bit and thought, hey; maybe they might even issue me a diplomatic passport. Yeah right.... Arriving home after the Navy League meeting I quickly returned to parental reality when I found the clothes dryer had blown a fuse and Jason hadn't finished his homework.

Following my return from Panama I completed the paperwork for my report to the London underwriters and prepared for a return visit to Caracas. The following week I arrived back in Caracas where Goschenko was waiting for me at the airport. As we drove together to naval headquarters in the San Bernardino section of Caracas we discussed the training and Briceño's promotion to Commander of Naval Personnel at headquarters. Goschenko waited while I went upstairs where upon entering his office Briceño Garcia greeted me. I gave the admiral the two Motorola Star-Tac cellular telephones that he had earlier asked me to buy for him when I had been in Miami. He thanked me while one of his aides reimbursed the $500.00 I had paid for the phones. Goschenko, who had been patiently waiting downstairs and I then departed for Puerto Azul for a meeting with the auxiliary group based at this Caribbean port. Two weeks later specialized training of the Picua auxiliary group was scheduled to take place at the Carenero Yacht Club in the State of Miranda; because his son Nicholas would be out of school Goschenko suggested that I bring Jason along. That night when I returned to my hotel I called Jason to see if he would be interested in coming. "Sure that's great, hey dad do you think we'd have time to visit Margarita so I could see Jenetta?" "Sorry guy, but we've got to be in Caracas and then in Carenero for the training, but maybe the next time I have something going on in Margarita you can come along."

"Geary, Geary, Jason over here." Goschenko was calling amidst the throng of people waiting outside the arrivals area of the Maiquetia airport. "Hi Nicholas, where's your son?" "Oh he's at home helping Daniela but he'll be with us when we drive to Carenero in the morning. How was your flight? It's nice to see you Jason, I'm glad you could come with your father." "Hello Captain Goschenko, it's nice to see you too. My dad tells me that we're going to get to ride in your boat while we're here." "Yes, I want your father to see our aids to navigation that are positioned between the oil refinery at Carenero and Puerto Azul. Daniela will make us a nice lunch and on Saturday we'll make the trip." Saturday morning after an early buffet breakfast Goschenko and his son Nicholas were waiting for us outside the Eurobuilding hotel. After a two hour harrowing ride we arrived at the Carenero Yacht Club. While unloading the car Goschenko turned to the boys saying, "Nicholas, you and Jason take the cooler and the lunch and go to the boat while I park the car." Goschenko's boat was a 30′ Intermarine cruiser fitted with twin Evinrude outboard engines.

After filling the boat's fuel tanks we proceeded out of the harbor on an easterly course before turning to the west and rounding the headland known as Cabo Codera. At about 1030 hours we were about a mile offshore of the settlement of Chinimena cruising at a speed of 20 knots on a westerly course being pushed long by following seas and a current of 1.5 knots. The current in the Caracas channel flows from east to west and is normally minimal before noon increasing in the afternoon to often more than 3 knots. Goschenko had indicated that our time from Carenero to Puerto Azul would be about 3.5 hours, but in fact took us over 5 hours. After slowing to record the positions of the channel buoys situated along the coast near Cabo Codera and those further west we eventually reached Puerto Azul at about 3:30pm in the afternoon.

After a quick visit to the Port Captain's office Nicholas looked at the sea saying, "I'll need to fill the fuel tanks before we leave and maybe we could have a coffee before we return to Carenero." "Nicholas, it's getting a bit late considering we'll be bucking a strong current with increasing seas on the return trip we want to try and get back before it gets dark. I think we should get the fuel and forget the coffee so we can get underway as soon as possible." After filling the fuel tanks we set off on the return voyage. About 30 minutes after leaving the fuel dock at Puerto Azul the starboard engine started to misfire and then shut down completely. While I took the helm Goschenko removed the engine cover to find that the engine cowling rubber sealing gasket was broken which had allowed sea water to splash on the engine shorting the ignition system. "Nicholas, don't you think we should return to Puerto Azul with the port engine and not try to make it back to Carenero with only one engine especially against a strong current." "But my car is in Carenero…" "Nicholas, as it's soon going to be getting dark it's just not wise to continue along an uninhabited coast that's surrounded by reefs especially with only one engine." "Let me see if I can get the engine running again. We've still got plenty of time if we have both engines."

While I maintained the boat on an easterly course and kept it as stabile as possible in the 3'to 4' swells Nicholas dried the ignition and was able to get the starboard engine started. "See, no problem let's go. Let me take the helm, I'll have us back in Carenero before we know it." For the next two hours with Goschenko steering the boat we continued against the current and the seas that were building in what is known as the Caracas Channel. Our speed had been reduced significantly and the sun was beginning to set. "Nicholas, let me look at the chart so I can get our position while it's still light." "I don't have a chart. I know these waters and don't need a chart." Over the roar of the engines I yelled, "No charts! Nicholas, I really hope you're kidding me!" "Don't worry I know exactly where we are, we don't need a chart we'll be back in Carenero before you know it." The next shock came at dusk when Goschenko turned on the navigation and the instrument console lights which illuminated the entire cockpit of the boat. "Nicholas, we can't run with the console lights on because they're much too bright and will destroy our night vision. Please turn them off. Do you have a flashlight?" "There's a box in the forward cabin on the right hand side it's in there."

The boat continued at a snails pace pounding forward on an easterly course as the sun disappeared slowly leading us into darkness. The once prominent outline of the high mountains visible to our right soon faded into obscurity. Only the wake behind the boat was indicative of our movement through the water. "Nicholas, let's try and contact the Coastguard in La Guaira on VHF to let them know we had engine problems and will be late in returning to Carenero. Did you file a float plan with the Coastguard or tell anyone in Carenero that we were going to Puerto Azul and our approximate return ETA? If you did and we don't return before it gets dark they may try and call us on the radio so we can at least give them an approximate location as to our position." At my insistence Jason and Goschenko's son Nicholas were now both wearing lifejackets and sitting quietly in the seats aft of the helm. From the expressions on their faces both were becoming concerned at the slow progress we were making towards Carenero.

The incessant noise, rolling, and occasional spray over the bow of the boat was also clearly taking its toll on Goschenko. Picking up the VHF radio's microphone Goschenko shouted, *"Coastguard La Guaira – Coastguard La Guaira this is Coastguard Auxiliary Vessel Alpha Charlie – Coastguard Auxiliary Vessel Alpha Charlie, Over."* After three attempts at calling the Venezuelan Coastguard Rescue Coordination Centre (RCC) in La Guaira Goschenko placed the microphone back in its cradle. "If La Guaira can't pick us up then there's no way that Carenero will hear our radio call because the yacht harbor is around the headland and behind the mountains." Jason then stood and pulling me close whispered in my ear, "Dad, is everything going to be OK?" In an effort to reassure him even though I was more than a bit concerned, "Hey don't worry big-guy it's going to be a little wet and a bit longer getting back but everything's going to be just fine." Goschenko's son sat motionless in his seat and said nothing.

"Dad, I've been watching our wake through the water and it looks like we've made a wide turn to the right and might be heading towards the shore." With the console lights off and no light on the compass I hadn't checked our course and apparently neither had Goschenko. I grabbed the flashlight and saw that the compass indicated a southerly course towards the shoreline. What I found when I looked at the depth sounder alarmed me even more. If the depth sounder was giving us an accurate reading we had less than 30' of water under the keel then 28'. I shouted, "Stop the engines, stop the engines!" Goschenko then looked at me, "What's wrong, what's wrong?" Pulling the throttles back to neutral and putting the flashlight on the depth sounder I said to Goschenko, "Nicholas, we should be in over 150' of water, look at the depth sounder right now we're in less than 25' of water, we're heading towards the shore." In the darkness and without a compass light Goschenko then realized he hadn't maintained our easterly course and had unknowingly slowly turned to a southerly course moving in the direction of the dangerous shoreline. "Nicholas, please sit down and take it easy. Let me take the helm."

From the darkness a clearly alarmed Goschenko called out, "I think we must be near the reef known as Capitan Abajo. I don't know how I got so close and I'm not certain how far in we are but this reef is particularly dangerous." Taking the helm I had Jason hold the flashlight first on the compass then the depth sounder and slowly turned the boat until we were on a northerly heading. "Jason, I want you to look at the depth sounder and repeat the water depths as it changes." "Ok dad." As I slowly increased speed Jason read off the water depths. "25'- 28'- 30'- 30'- 35'- 40'." "Jason, to save the batteries I want you to turn off the flashlight and then every minute or so turn it on and read me the depth." In rapid succession Jason called out, "55'- 55'- 62'- 72'- 80'- 93'- 100'." After a few minutes I felt a bit relieved, "Ok, that's fine we're outside of the reef line that runs along the coast so I think it should be okay to turn and get back on an easterly course. Jason, please hand me the binoculars from the forward cabin, they're next to the cushions on the left." In scanning the horizon at about 10 o'clock off our port bow I saw a small ship illuminated by her deck lights. She appeared to be a small bulk carrier and was definitely heading east probably to Port of Spain, Trinidad. I slowly increased our speed until I was about a mile off her stern. We maintained this position to keep her in sight and followed the ship for about 3½ hours. "Son-of-a-gun Goschenko, look there at 2 o'clock that's got to be the number one sea buoy for the Carenero oil terminal. Count the flashes."

"Ed, you're right one long and two short that's the buoy." It was now just after 0100 hours and no sooner than Goschenko had confirmed we were passing the Carenero oil terminal buoy the starboard engine stopped running. "Goschenko, please tilt the engine forward so the lower unit doesn't drag and slow us down any more, we'll do the last couple of miles on the port engine." As we pulled into the fuel dock at the entrance to the yacht club we were greeted by six Coastguard Auxiliaries waving and clapping as we came alongside. Stepping off the boat Ed Neufeld, the president of the ANMD and an officer in the auxiliary Picua group was the first to welcome us back. "I can't tell you how happy we are to see you. When you hadn't returned by 2000 hours we started calling on VHF radio but got no reply. We called the RCC at La Guaira and asked them to try and reach you but they said you didn't answer their calls either. The Duty Officer said that they had checked with the Captain of the Port at Puerto Azul who said you had left late in the afternoon and were probably delayed because of the strong easterly current and the wind that had picked up to 20 knots. In any case you're back safely." By the time we secured Goschenko's boat and got to the car it was almost 0300 hours. Goschenko dropped Jason and I at the Eurobuilding Hotel at

0515 in the morning. Jason took a quick shower first and then turned the bathroom over to me. While I was drying myself he pushed open the bathroom door, "Dad, I've got two requests the first is never again ask me to eat that awful brown vegetable we were given at Goschenko's house and the second is please, don't ever again ask me to go anywhere in Goschenko's boat." "Okay, no problem. No brown vegetables or boat rides with Goschenko. Now let's get to bed we've got a plane to catch in a few hours."

Fortunately our return American Airlines flight from Caracas to San Juan left late in the afternoon because we didn't get up until almost noon. Towards the end of October I returned to Venezuela to meet with the Coastguard's Executive Officer, Capitán de Fragata Bravo Mayol at headquarters to prepare for a presentation I was scheduled to give at the Naval War College. The presentation was important because along with the Minister of Defense all the admirals of the navy would be in attendance. My presentation would focus on the benefits, cost effectiveness, and increased efficiency that was being attained by the Coastguard as a result of the support provided by the enhanced reserve and auxiliary training programs.

The presentation at the Naval War College was very successful in that it garnered even more support from Venezuela's military hierarchy. The day was uneventful until I returned to my hotel and found a white envelope that had been slid under the door of my room. The envelope was addressed and written by hand to Captain Geary, the return address printed in bold type on the upper left corner indicated a return address of the Venezuelan-American Chamber of Commerce – Caracas. Inside the envelope on stationary of the Venezuelan-American Chamber of Commerce was a hand-written and unsigned message, *I will be in Puerto Rico on November 5, 1993 and would like to meet you at the Navy League meeting to finalize our arrangements.* At the time I thought to myself – what arrangements?

After speaking briefly following the Navy League meeting on November 5th 1993 Velling, who again had been lurking in a corner approached me and suggested we meet for dinner the following evening for a discussion of our mutual interests in Venezuela. The next night Joseph J. Velling who a month earlier had introduced himself as a Second Secretary in the Commercial Section of the American Embassy in Caracas was sitting at a corner table in the officer's club picking at a bowl of peanuts. "Hi Captain, I'm glad to see you, how was the trip to Panama?" "Just fine, I got your note when I was in Caracas and have been looking forward to meeting with you again. I'm curious as to the *arrangements* you made reference to in your note." With a mouthful of nuts he began to speak as pooled saliva drooled from the corner of his mouth, "You know our ambassador has been closely monitoring your accomplishments in Venezuela and is impressed with the promotions and the accolades that you've been awarded by the Venezuelan Navy for the training and unit reorganization of the Coastguard. What you have done has been a great service to the United States and is a very positive move in fostering our good relations with the Venezuelan government." I wondered why Velling was repeating himself but in any case was pleased with this apparent praise and that my efforts had not gone unnoticed by the US Embassy. "We are particularly interested in learning more about the military, especially the country's naval forces and would like to enlist your help. The ambassador has spoken a number of times with McKenzie and Jim's replacement Commander Gary Sooy who both said that you're the guy who really knows what's going on."

Believing at the time that as Velling's introduction had come through the Coast Guard attaché and the American ambassador it appeared that whatever *they* needed must be official in nature. Velling, chewing on another handful of nuts he had crammed into his mouth coughed and then began to speak. "I think I need to level with you. I'm not really a commercial attaché, I'm with the Central Intelligence Agency assigned to the Caracas embassy. I use the cover as an attaché and second secretary in the commercial section of the embassy for obvious reasons, reasons I'm sure you understand. Because of Venezuela's position as a major source of our oil Washington feels that it's essential that we keep a close eye on what's happening in the country to insure that there's no disruption shall we say, in the *pipeline.* Since the impeachment of Carlos Andres Perez there's been a growing dissatisfaction with the current administration and the problems brought about by the FARC guerillas that are moving back and forth across the border with Colombia." Looking over at the buffet table Velling then said, "Let's get something to eat, the dinner is on me." Taking large quantities of food which he piled high on his plate and to prevent it from falling to the floor began to eat with his fingers while returning to the table. Considering his gluttonous attack on the food buffet it appeared that he may not have eaten for many days. After sitting down he stuffed a handful of prawns into his mouth causing the cocktail sauce to drip onto the red gingham table cloth. Wiping his mouth while still chewing," You are really lucky to be able to live so close to the Roosevelt Roads Navy Base and be able to have the benefit of such great food at such a low price. Good restaurants in Caracas are really expensive." Gasping for a breath of air between bites he went on, "Please tell me a bit more about what you're doing in Venezuela." Taking a sip of iced tea I explained, "After each visit I prepare a detailed report of the training which includes a list of who attended, where the training took place, and the subjects covered. The report is sent to the Commandant of the Venezuelan Coastguard with a copy to Captain Griswold, the Chief Director of the Auxiliary in Washington. Captain Griswold and I assume others at Coast Guard Headquarters review the reports which as well as the details of the training exercises, includes details of staff meetings with the Venezuelan Coastguard, the admirals at naval headquarters in the Comandancia De La Armada in San Bernardino in Caracas, and my visits to the Naval War College at Mamo. I've brought along some photos and the press clippings of the mission that you might like to see." On the edge of the table and out of range of Velling's drip zone I opened a large red binder and began leafing through the pages. The binder held a photographic record and a document file on the Venezuelan Initiative.

Listening intently Velling repeatedly questioned me on the persons in the photos and where and when they had been taken. Now gnawing on a large cut of roast beef Velling acknowledged that he had seen my reports but wanted to have more specific details. "If you've seen my reports that were sent to Washington I don't see any problem in providing you with additional briefings especially if you're working with the US Coast Guard, but why the duplication?" Almost choking on the large piece of beef he had unceremoniously stuffed into his mouth, "No, no, no, you've missed the point. The information we need is not just about the training but involves private and personal data about the government ministers you know and the admirals, generals, and other senior officers of Venezuela's different military commands. If the United States is to protect its oil interests and in case we need to neutralize the military, the CIA must have detailed and specific information about the admirals and generals, their wives, girlfriends, overseas bank accounts, kids, you know all the personal stuff. I want to know where their children go to school, where they have bank accounts and homes in Venezuela and overseas, personal home telephone, and cellular phone numbers. We know that you have been invited into their homes for private dinners when a lot of the other military heavyweights have been around. We also know that your son Jason is friendly with the kids of the officers and because he reads and speaks Spanish fluently he could prove to be a good source of information." Alarmed at the thought of Jason being placed under surveillance, "You've been watching my son Jason? I doubt very much that what he talks about with the officer's children would have any bearing on the diplomatic relations between Venezuela and the United States." Velling noting my concern shot back, "For some time both you and your son Jason have been persons-of-interest. Hey you'd be surprised what we can learn from the mouths of children. When they are together without mom and dad looking over their shoulders they sometimes can provide a wealth of information. Anyway forget about the kids for now. What we need that is of vital importance is knowing the connection and relationships between the officers who command individual units and the officers of Flag rank in all the armed services; particularly information concerning political party affiliations. I'm specifically interested in exactly what senior officers are involved and what their status is within the Bolivarian Revolutionary Movement which they call the MBR-200, we need to identify those who are supporters and those who aren't. Hugo Chàvez is recruiting a growing number of followers both in the private and military sectors and we need to know exactly who these people are. It's important we know who's for and who's against so we can deal with each case individually."

After devouring the last morsels on his plate Velling stood and returned to the buffet coming back to the table with more food, "Look you should realize that the CIA is all-powerful, if you are willing to work with us I'm in a position to make your cooperation extremely rewarding. The CIA has access to confidential funding and would pay you handsomely if you cooperate and provide the information that's needed." Somewhat taken aback with the subject of confidential funding, "Hold on a minute the confidential funding you're talking about in plain English means the slush fund that the CIA's been identified with in the past and unless I'm badly mistaken your slush funds have been declared to be illegal." "Forget about what you read in the papers. There's a lot of illegal stuff that goes on in Washington but it's only illegal if you get caught. I can assure you that whatever you receive in payment for your services will be confidential, tax free, and deposited in an offshore numbered account that can't be traced. You would have nothing to worry about except how you choose to spend the money."

Now focusing on a plate filled with a collection of deserts Velling looked up, "You needn't be concerned with breaking the law because the CIA is beyond the law. To give you an example the government has a policy that mandates that CIA field agents can't get involved with local men or women while they are posted to overseas stations. When I was working out of our embassy in Mexico City I met this gorgeous Mexican lady whose father was a heavy-weight with one of the Mexican breweries. Well one thing lead to another and we secretly got married and have lived happily ever since. You'll quietly get your money and no one will ever be the wiser." Without looking up from a diminishing piece of Black Forrest cake Velling went on, "How much has it cost you personally to conduct the training in Venezuela?" "Well, I donate my time and pay all my own out-of-pocket expenses. If I would have billed for my time at my normal rate for the hours expended so far the cost could easily be $200,000. Depending on where the training takes place and if it's near a military installation the Venezuelan Navy provides me with accommodation and my meals. But this hasn't happened more than four or five times so most of the costs I've paid for personally, I would guess that so far I may be out of pocket to the tune of about $20,000." Velling smiled, "That's nothing. You'd be paid a lot of money when you start giving us the information we need. In 1991 when you were asked to get involved with the Venezuelan Coastguard you moved quickly and produced incredible results. Less than five months later you had done such a bang-up job to show their appreciation the Venezuelan Coastguard commissioned you with the rank of Captain. You continued as a person-of-interest throughout 1992 especially after you took the delegation of Venezuelan Navy officers to the USCG Auxiliary conference in California. You seem to be under the impression that in September 1992 it was the US Coast Guard who had promoted you to the rank of Captain; not so, the Coast Guard was only the messenger it was the CIA that engineered your promotion."

"How could the CIA get me promoted in the US Coast Guard?" Velling smiled, "Don't ask. A month before in February 1992 we learned that in March the Venezuelans were going to offer you a commission as a Captain in their Coastguard and the Commandant was going to name you his National Policy Advisor. American citizens can't become members of the military of a foreign government so the CIA paved the way. Didn't you ever wonder why you were able to accept an officer's commission in Venezuela's military? If you would have thought about it you should have known that something was in the works when neither the US Government or the Coast Guard had any objection to your being commissioned a Captain in Venezuela."

"I must admit I found it a bit strange that I didn't get any flack from the US Coast Guard or for that matter the State Department after Washington was notified of the commission. When I didn't hear anything, I though it best to let sleeping-dogs-lie especially when six months later I was promoted to the rank of Captain in the US Auxiliary. And shortly after this I learned that I was to going to be elevated to flag rank." Velling smiled. "That's right you are slated to be promoted to Commodore, it's part of the program. But the promotion will not be the work of the Coast Guard the CIA is the moving force behind your becoming a Flag, the US Coast Guard again will only be the messenger. The CIA will pay you from its sources because the Coast Guard can't officially offer you any payment whether you're a Captain or a Commodore. Officially any promotion you receive will actually cost the US government nothing. You've risen to great heights as a Captain but as a Commodore which is considered a Rear Admiral in Venezuela it will add even greater prestige to the Venezuelan Initiative. There's no question that as a commodore or rear admiral whichever you prefer, will definitely put you in a position with greater access to the Venezuelan military's *inner-circle* and the sensitive information we need. If you accept our proposal we would immediately have you promoted. If we can agree and put everything together on what's needed and exactly what you'll be required to do, I can work out the details when I return to Caracas and make the necessary arrangements in concert with the Coast Guard in Washington."

Finally finishing a double piece of Key Lime pie Velling gently placed his hand on my arm, "The CIA and the US Coast Guard know you have done an outstanding job and have been accepted as a trusted member of Venezuela's naval and the other military forces. You enjoy a unique position that permits you to operate covertly within the military as a well placed informant. What you would be doing would be for the benefit of the United States of America and make you one of the country's true patriots." Reaching across the table to grab a large prawn that was remaining on my plate, "Your help and cooperation is vitally important to the Venezuelan Coastguard Auxiliary effort and to the affairs of the United States. In 1992 we backed Chàvez and believed we had all the issues resolved, but now realize we made some serious miscalculations. Since CAP (Carlos Andres Perez) was impeached politically the country is in a mess, we also know that Rafael Caldera is gaining strength and we're pretty sure he will win the December election, but he may not have the support of the military. We know there's discontentment with the current state of affairs and convinced that some your friends in the armed forces are just waiting to see what transpires after the election next month.

If they're opposed to a Caldera government, assuming he wins there could be a rogue attempt to overthrow the government. A government controlled by a military junta that is outside our control would put us in the same untenable position that we are faced with now, or even worse. Based on our information Washington is firmly convinced and believe that another coup will be led by a *junta* made up of the Admirals of the Venezuelan Navy and Generals of the Air Force and the outcome may not be favorable to US interests. Interrupting Velling I began to speak, "But…." "No, please let me finish. The CIA believes that if a defiant military junta were to seize control of the country they could seriously compromise America's interests by cutting off the flow of oil to the United States. Before this happens we need to continue the process to destabilize the present government, neutralize the opposing military, and create chaos which will then pave the way for Chàvez to take power.

Our people on the inside are working with the Caldera camp to arrange for Chàvez' to be released early from prison. If Caldera is elected he'll be inaugurated in February and if we can pull it off we'll get Chàvez released in March. There was a slim chance that we might have been able to have him released before the December 1993 elections, but because of too much opposition that's not going to happen. You should also know that there are other forces working behind the scenes in the country that you wouldn't necessarily know about such as the National Endowment for Democracy. The NED will make a significant contribution to the success of an operation we'll call Deep Six. What the CIA did covertly in the past the NED can now do openly today. This is not the time or the place to tell you about the inner workings of the NED, but the organization is funded, effective, and has the full and unequivocal backing and support of the US government. They [NED] want what we want and have the means to insure that we meet our objective. The military people we had organized to back Chàvez in the February coup backed out at the last minute and blew our plan, we'll not make the same mistakes this time."

According to Velling the CIA may have set the stage and knew exactly when Chàvez was to be released, yet appeared to be uninformed neophytes about the politics in Venezuela. Velling continually emphasized he had collaborated and worked closely with Lieutenant Commander McKenzie and Commander Gary Sooy. Sooy was McKenzie's replacement as the US Coast Guard Attaché in Caracas. I was curious and asked. "Did the CIA arrange for Sooy to be transferred from Honolulu to replace McKenzie?' "Don't ask this doesn't concern you. If you come on board we'll fill you in on a need-to-know basis, you'll get a star on your uniform and become a legendary hero in the Coast Guard while making some good money to boot. I already have everything I need for your security clearance."

"Mr. Velling, I'm flattered by the importance that you feel I have attained in Venezuela but really have no interest to get involved in espionage in spite of your promises of money and promotion. I'm a naval officer not a spy and have no intention in getting mixed up in some absurd clandestine game to discredit the military. If the CIA wants to put Chàvez in the Miraflores Palace they'll have to do it without my help. The Admirals, Generals, and their families are respected friends and even though these officers are clearly concerned with the country's declining state of affairs they are all law abiding citizens who respect and cherish the rule of law and the democratic process." A clearly annoyed Velling started to speak, "But wait...." "No, now it's your turn to wait. In the many official and social gatherings that I have been privileged to attend throughout Venezuela the discussions have been limited only to the deteriorating state of the country's political and economic situation and the upcoming December elections. The senior military officers have always expressed a genuine concern about the welfare of the country's poor, which as you should know represents 80% of the population, but at no time had a possible military insurrection been discussed or even suggested, especially one that involved the Navy and their Marines. Quite to the contrary the Admirals were dismayed at the previous failed coup attempts that involved the Army and the Air Force which has brought about a loss of confidence and a general mistrust of the military establishment throughout the country. I will not get involved in any CIA covert activity that may expose the Admirals, Generals or their families to any personal harm or CIA vengeance; nor will I violate their mutual trust. If it's your desire to Deep Six Venezuela's military leaders you'll have to do it without my help." Velling's pale face turned a glowing crimson color. "You're making what might prove to be a grave mistake in declining my proposal and it could have serious consequences." The serious consequences were not detailed. I stood and dropping my napkin on the chair said, "Goodbye Mr. Velling."

I left the meeting disappointed and troubled by the fact that the CIA and the Coast Guard would ask me to break the law and believed that they could compromise my honesty and integrity for any amount of money. I was under the impression that my efforts in this friendly South American country were indeed appreciated and even though small, may have provided a positive element in improving the relations between Venezuela and the United States. I also had incorrectly assumed that the US government in being pleased with my efforts was planning to reimburse me for the expenses which I had personally incurred to carry out the mission. Velling had falsely lead me to believe that the US government was going to put me on a *legal* payroll for the time expended in return for nothing more than a monthly briefing containing the same information that I was already providing to my US Coast Guard superiors in Washington. Unfortunately, this was a very wrong assumption.

In our final meeting on November 6, 1993 Velling had identified the Coast Guard attaché Lieutenant Commander McKenzie and his replacement Commander Gary Sooy as friends with full knowledge of the *mission*. Working together the CIA and the Coast Guard were involved in the plan to oust the present government and install Hugo Chàvez as the president of Venezuela. In an effort to corroborate the connection between the two agencies the following week under the guise of inviting Velling and the Coast Guard attaché to an IBM corporate party, I made a telephone call to the US Embassy in Caracas and spoke with a secretary who unwittingly verified the *friendly* relationship between the US Coast Guard's attaché and the CIA's Velling. The call satisfied my concern and apprehension that Velling, while being an agent of the CIA was also closely involved with the US Coast Guard who had full knowledge of my work and status within the Venezuelan Naval Establishment. In spite of Chàvez's charisma and growing popularity throughout the country I found it difficult to comprehend why the CIA would even consider a professed socialist reformer in their scheme to gain control of the country's oil. But then again this was the same agency that had given us 'Papa Doc' as the president for life of Haiti and Manuel Noriega as the leader of Panama.

Velling and his infamous CIA apparently knew little about the socialist doctrines of the MBR-200 and clearly weren't aware that in the early 1990's there was only a small number of the military and civilians who were actually committed to the MBR-200 Movement. Those who were initially involved had all been personally recruited by Chàvez to insure their loyalty and commitment to the future Revolution. On the other hand the Revolutionary Movement was indeed growing in popularity particularly with the poor, and the socialists and communists who supported the Cuban governments' hard line extremism. From the early days of 1992 Chàvez made it clear that he was committed to the socialistic principles of his mentor Fidel Castro. While flaunting the name of the great Liberator Simon Bolivar many senior military officers and most of those in the upper and middle classes believed that given the opportunity Chàvez' ultimate goal was the creation of a foot-hold for another communist style Cuba in South America, but wanted no part of it.

In the February 4th 1992 attempt to seize control Chàvez made a number of serious tactical errors in misjudging the support he was counting on from the officers who commanded units of the Navy, Air Force, Guardia Nacional, and Army who he trusted and believed were loyal to him. Had Caracas fallen with little opposition as planned, his military cohorts in the other parts of the country would have seized control of key government installations with minimal resistance. In spite of the CIA's backing the wavering support of the military in the heat of battle is why both 1992 coups attempts had failed. In my casual discussions with various government ministers, admirals, generals, captains and colonels, the general consensus was that 10% of the military favored Chàvez, 10% opposed him and 80% could go either way. Even though the purported policies of Hugo Chàvez were clearly to the left, the CIA was of the opinion that he was hungry for power and if the Agency satisfied his appetite he could be bought and manipulated.

In addition to the unsuccessful coup attempt on February 4th personally lead by Chàvez, the second attempt on November 27, 1992 while orchestrated by Chàvez from prison was lead by a small group of senior air force officers with MBR-200 sympathies. When the coup failed the officers fled to Peru in a commandeered Air force C-130. Velling confirmed that both the unsuccessful 1992 coup attempts had been planned and engineered by the CIA. The intrigue deepened further when a few months after the CIA had coordinated his release Chàvez flew to Havana to meet with Fidel Castro.

FIVE

In November 1993 the Venezuelan Coastguard Auxiliary held its first national conference at the Naval Academy at Mamo, a short drive up the coast from Coastguard headquarters in La Guaira. Hosted by the Commandant Rear Admiral Martin Fossa the meeting proved to be a great success that gave the newly expanded Coastguard Auxiliary the proper recognition it rightly deserved. Those in attendance included Coastguard Auxiliary officers from throughout the country, three retired admirals who had commanded the Venezuelan Navy, and cabinet ministers from a number of defense related government ministries.

Following the national conference I returned to Isla Margarita for the continued training of Grupo Tiburon and Grupo Delfin who had traveled by ferry from Puerto la Cruz on the mainland. After the plane's normal intermediate stop in Barcelona I arrived at Margarita's international airport where I was to meet Javier Augusto Soto. Originally from Buenos Aires, Argentina Javier had immigrated to Venezuela where he established a successful business as an interior designer on the prosperous and duty-free island of Margarita. Immediately outside of the arrivals hall I spotted Javier. "Captain, welcome back to Margarita, how was your flight?" With a broad smile and shaking Javier's hand, "It's great to see you Javier, the flight was fine and I'm pleased it was mas-o-menos on time." In Venezuela just because your flight is scheduled to leave at a certain time doesn't necessarily mean it will leave at that time. In Spanish the term, *mas-o-menos* translated to English simply means more or less and applies to all flights of Venezuelan airlines. When they say a departure is scheduled at say 1000 hours this generally proves to be more or less at 10:00 o'clock and hopefully on the same day.

The dry barren terrain of Margarita Island is much like the

countryside that surrounds Tangiers in Morocco but without the camels trekking along the road. "Would you like to stop for something to eat or maybe have a drink? I have a client who had me design a new upscale restaurant in Porlamar and I'm taking some of my fees as part of a barter deal. The Blue Topaz has great seafood and it's not out of our way. I told Jose Soto, and by the way he's no relation, about the problems you found with Detachment 76 and their drug protection activities that I'd call him when you arrived. If it's okay we'll meet him at the Blue Topaz. Jose is an agent with the DISIP[27] who has some information that you will find interesting. He suggested that you visit Juangriego to see what's going on before meeting to discuss something of mutual interest."

The Blue Topaz was magnificent and clearly everything that Javier had described. Situated on the main street in downtown Porlamar, the commercial center of this holiday island the bar-restaurant had become the favored watering-hole of the local up-scale crowd. It was also a popular rendezvous for wealthy Venezuelans who flew in from Caracas to spend long weekends in the many beautiful condos that fringed the island's numerous white sand beaches.

Two steps down from the street the restaurant's imposing entrance allowed customers to pass a magnificent Italian renaissance water fountain fashioned in hand carved granite. In the center a small pool was adorned with a life-size marble statue of the goddess Diana. The over-sized plate entry glass door was tinted in azure blue which shielded the restaurants subdued interior from the piercing rays emitted from the eternal sun of this Caribbean isle. Javier opened the door cautioning, "Watch the first step." The warning was just a moment too late as I stumbled to regain my balance in missing the darkened first step. With the exception of the rays of the sun penetrating the darkness through the open door and a number of soft iridescent lights over the bar, the interior was shrouded in obscurity. After momentarily adjusting to the darkness I followed Javier to a corner table illuminated by a single Tiffany lamp. Jose Soto, a strikingly handsome man with tousled hair showing a touch of gray was wearing a sports jacket emblazoned with the logo of the Tampa Bay Buccaneers. Standing as we approached, "Hey Javier, what's happening my man." Shaking his hand Javier smiled, "Good

---

27 Direccion de Intelligencia Seguridad y Prevencion

to see you Jose and how is Terre doing, has she fully recovered from the accident?" Terre, Jose's sister had been run down by a hit and run driver a month before and while she could have easily been killed suffered only a broken arm. "She's a tough lady, the arm is still in a cast but hopefully she'll be back to normal in a couple of months."

Jose, I'd like you to meet Captain Ed Geary. Ed's been doing the coastguard training and in July was made the honorary commander of the Tiburon Coastguard Group here in Margarita." "Pleased to meet you Jose, Javier has told me that you work for the DISIP and I'm curious about what you have that I may be interested in." His eyes quickly darting around the room Jose began speaking in a hushed tone, "I understand from Javier that you can be trusted but must insist that whatever we discuss will be held in the strictest confidence." "No problem, whatever we speak about will go no further." "As Javier told you I'm with the DISIP and work both here in Margarita and in Puerto La Cruz, I have a proposal that I'd like to discuss. Javier tells me that you have good connections with the DEA, the US Customs Service and the American Coast Guard. Because of my work in the DISIP I have let's say, been retained by the Arabs in Juangriego. They're all Arabs but to launder their true identity are shown as *Syrians* on their Venezuelan identification cards. My job is to provide them with information and advance warning of any government moves that could damage or compromise the activities of their import-export business which involves narcotics from Colombia. They make a lot of money from the business which is laundered through banks here in Margarita and in Aruba, Curacao, Panama, and the Cayman Islands. They have family connections in Paraguay and in Beirut who are involved with and support Hamas and the Hezbollah factions in the Middle East. Sometimes the money is transferred to Hezbollah in Paraguay through the Banco Confederado in Margarita while other times it's taken to Cuidad Del Este in cash. I've watched their activity in the drug trade grow by leaps and bounds. It's unstoppable.

In the last two months alone there has been at least ten large consignments transshipped through Margarita to Sint Maarten and Trinidad. The Arabs are working independently and paying the Guardia Nacional for protection while at the same time the Guardia Nacional has a separate arrangement with your CIA for protection of their shipments. The Guardia Nacional commanders in Caracas are simply double-dipping."

In hushed tones, absorbed in the subject and conversation we were all startled when from the shadows the tender voice of a demure waitress asked, "Would you like to order something?" Javier, looking up inquired, "Ed, I assume you'll have the normal cappuccino. I'll have a Polar. Jose, what would you like?" Turning, Jose smiled at the Venezuelan beauty and said, "What I'd really like is to see you for dinner sometime but for the moment two Polars[28] and a cappuccino." The waitress tilting her head back in a provocative fashion smiled, "I'll get your order while you write down your phone number." Javier smiling at Jose said, "Wow. You don't waste any time amigo." Obviously amused by his own possible success, "You know Javier I once heard of a man in Caracas who was known to have stopped many beautiful women on the street to ask them if they would like to go to bed with him. The story goes that he got his faced slapped many times – but he also went to bed with a lot of beautiful women." Jose's prospective new love returned with our drinks after which the phone numbers were exchanged. Javier, either through envy or disapproval said, "Can we get back to business please." Apologetically Jose tendered, "I'm sorry Javier, but hey your married, I'm not."

With his eyes once more darting around the darkened room Jose looked directly at me, "Ed, I'm ready for a change. I've been with the DISIP for 15 years and the only way I can live the way I do is because of a small inheritance that my late wife received when her uncle died and the money I make on the side, I want to make some *big money* and then retire to Florida. I believe the big money can come from what I know is going on in Margarita and particularly in Juangriego and Porlamar. What I'm looking for is to be paid for the good and reliable information that I can provide. Exactly how close are you to the DEA and US Customs?" "Jose, what's the purpose of the question? " Again looking quickly around the bar Jose put his elbows on the table and brought his fingers together tip to tip against his mouth. "I know from my brother-in-law in Clearwater that Customs will pay informants up to 10% of the street value of seized narcotics. He told me that he saw a story in the Tampa Tribune where a confidential tip lead to the seizure of drugs with a street value of $20 million, at 10% the tipster would have received a lot of money. If your contacts can be

---

28 A popular Venezuelan beer

relied upon I can produce the information that would make the $20 million seem like petty cash and do it more than once. Of course, it will be very dangerous for me and for my children and something I could only to do for a short time. I'd be willing to take the chance if I could be guaranteed a percentage of the seizures and when I decided it was time to leave I would want to be assured of resident alien status for me and my two children in the United States."

"Jose, tell me what route and method do they use for the drugs destined for the US?" "It depends on the size of the shipment. In the case of a large load they use coastal freighters that first sail to Haiti or the Dominican Republic. In Port au Prince, Santo Domingo, and Puerto Plata the containers are transferred to ships bound for ports in Florida and the east coast of the USA. When crossing the Caribbean 95% of the ships get through without being boarded. There's never a problem between Colombia and Margarita because the Arabs have the Colombian authorities and the Guardia Nacional on the payroll. The Guardia Nacional doesn't interfere with the ships as they pass along the coast and stay in Venezuelan waters. In other cases when ships arrive in Margarita which is the central distribution point, at night they transfer the drugs from the freighters which are anchored offshore to a warehouse in Juangriego." "Do you know where these freighters originate?" "Most come directly from either Cartagena or Barranquilla and from what I've heard it's high grade cocaine from labs near Medellin. In Juangriego the shipment is broken down into smaller lots made up of 5 to 10 kilo packages. The smaller packages make it easier to conceal on go-fasts and the smaller island boats that are destined for places like Sint Maarten, Martinique or Guadeloupe. Last year they set up an arrangement with a Frenchman who lives in Saint Lucia for local distribution in Fort de France, Pointe ó Pitre, St. Barth's, and St. Martin. It's been a very smooth operation; the Frenchman sends triple engine go-fasts from St. Lucia that meet up with larger ships from Margarita. The drugs are transferred at sea and then the Frenchman handles the distribution with his own people.

The consignments that are destined to Europe are normally concealed in the floors or ceiling panels of 40' containers. In the case of smaller amounts destined for Europe they sometime use mules.[29] With help from employees of Air France or KLM who are

---

29 Individual men or women who act as couriers

paid according to the quantity involved they can safely send 10 or 20 kilos in pre-screened baggage or hidden in compartments inside aircraft destined for Schiphol, Orly, and Charles de Gaulle. There were probably more but on at least three occasions that I know of they sent 1000 kilos hidden in false keel-coolers and half-round cylinders that were welded to the hulls of containerships sailing to La Havre and Marseilles in France.

The Arab's also have people in the ABC[30] islands that employ swallowers[31] who as passengers leave from Curacao on direct KLM flights to Holland. They have also sent swallowers from Caracas on direct flights to Miami and New York. Cocaine is tightly packed in a condom sleeve that reduces them to a pellet about 5cm x 2.5cm which are then swallowed. Depending on the physical size of the swallowers which are usually young women, they are made to swallow anywhere from 30 to 60 pellets. If they get through they are met and after they let's say, drop their load into a bathtub they get paid and then return home. The swallowers were fairly successful in getting through until one time during a flight to Holland a pellet broke and the woman died of a cardiac arrest. The medical examiner reported the cause of death to the Dutch police at Amsterdam's Schiphol airport who started doing random X-rays of passengers arriving from the Dutch Caribbean islands."

"Jose, I thought we were only talking about shipments to the United States. While I have some good contacts with the Dutch INTERPOL[32] bureau and friends in the French Narcotics Task Force in Caracas, I don't know if the Dutch or the French have a program like the United States to pay informants. I believe I can make the right contacts with US Customs but how do we keep your identity anonymous and if you're nameless how will you be able to receive any money? If you're nameless and resident alien status is to be part of the deal it would only work if Customs would agree to put you in the witness protection program. To get approval for Green Cards you would have to provide a lot of information right in the beginning to make sure everything you ask for can be agreed to. I think it might be best to delay direct contact with the Dutch or the French and first concentrate on the US. If something can be worked out you could funnel your

30 Aruba, Bonaire & Curacao
31 Men and women who will swallow condoms filled with cocaine
32 International Police Organization

information through US Customs who could then act as a go-between with the others. I know from a French narcotics officer working out of the US Coast Guard Base in San Juan that there is a high level of cooperation between the US and European drug enforcement agencies. If they were to receive actionable information through the DEA or US Customs and the French were able to make a couple of good busts and be satisfied that you're for real the Europeans would be much more inclined to deal. One of the problems that the US Customs Service has experienced with unknown informants is that the information they provide is many times questionable. There have been a number of cases where Customs has received information on something that's coming down but after they have organized a team involving boats and sometimes helicopters find that the information was bogus. The traffickers are very smart. Based on information from bogus informants Customs have set up an operation in one place only to find that a shipment has gotten through somewhere else. This happens because the false information is provided to have law enforcement in one place when the actual delivery is taking place somewhere else. While I haven't personally been involved I have heard of problems where an informant provided good information, Customs made a bust then reneged on paying. It's something to think about. I have a connection on Dutch Sint Maarten who had access to critical information on shipments to Puerto Rico and the Virgin Islands and was close to the Colombian drug king-pins who had successfully set up shop on the island. After he gave me a rundown on what he had to offer I put him in contact with Customs in San Juan. As a test case to establish the creditability of the informant the deal was that he would provide information on a shipment of 1000kg of cocaine that would be on a particular twin engine outboard boat that would leave Sint Maarten at a specific time. The informant agreed to provide a full description of the individuals on board, the name and number on the boat, the make and horsepower of the engines, and the amount of fuel they carried. Based on the sea state, weight of the boat, the weight of the cocaine which in this case was 1000kg, and the horsepower of the engines, I calculated the time the boat would take to reach Fajardo and gave the information to Customs. This would be viewed as a test case only to prove that he was for real. If the information was good and the specific boat and contraband was seized while the informant wouldn't receive any payment his credibility would be established for future shipments. US Customs agreed to pay the informant 10% of the street value of any narcotics that were later seized based on his information. It's the same scenario that your brother-in-law told you about and the procedure you'd have to follow to make it work. Give Customs a freebee and then you'd get on the payroll." Jose briefly pondered his options which in fact were zero. "Okay Jose, we've discussed the generalities let's get specific.

"Ed, like I said the shipments sent to the United States travel in a number of different ways. The Arabs are meticulous and pay close attention to their methods of packaging and concealment to avoid detection. Their methods are under constant scrutiny and subject to change depending on the perceived danger of discovery at a particular port. Hassan knows that only a small percentage of containers are inspected when they arrive at mainland US Ports and virtually have a free ride when they are transshipped through Trinidad and the other Caribbean ports like Haiti and the Dominican Republic. I'd need to be careful but I could get the destinations and the container numbers that would make them easier to track. In some cases they have used a dozen or so 40' containers going to the same port where they pack the floor cavities and the roof, but stagger them so they get loaded on different ships. While one or two may be detected the others get through. When they have containers that are being transshipped through one port like Port of Spain, Trinidad, bound for say Miami and they want to leave a small quantity of drugs in Port-of-Spain they have devised a method of being able to open a container without breaking the customs seal. Hassan knows that the standard practice in shipping is to place the custom's seal only on the right door of the container. When the container arrives in Trinidad; by slightly bending the center plate between the doors they are able to open the container's left door; the narcotics are removed and the door is closed without damaging the seal on the right door. Customs in Trinidad aren't aware the container was opened nor are Customs in Miami because the seal is still intact. The 'tool' they use is quite simple, but very effective.

Hassan likes to use Trinidad for shipments to the USA and Europe because he's got reliable people working for him on the island. Some of the European consignments in containers that are transshipped via west African ports are loaded on trucks that then go overland to Tangiers in Morocco and then cross the straights of Gibraltar to Algeciras in southern Spain. I've also heard them mention that some of these shipments have been cut down and loaded in cars and small trucks that cross from Tangiers to the Spanish port of Tarifa on the fast ferries. Hassan believes this is a good route because no containers move through Tarifa and the Spanish customs in Tarifa aren't as thorough as they sometimes are in Algeciras." "Jose, I think it's important to focus on the shipments to the US. You've obviously got a lot of information that sounds very useful but for now let's first concentrate on the shipments that go north to the US. What's the next step?" "It would not be wise for me to be seen with two strangers driving around Juangriego as all the police and the Arabs know me. Javier, your Ford Bronco has dark tinted windows could we all travel in you car? After Javier cleared the back seat of the Bronco which was piled with sample books used to display tiles and wall coverings to his clients; Jose positioned himself low in the back while I slid into the seat on the passenger's side.

About halfway to Juangriego while passing through the town of La Asuncion Jose reaching over the seat, taped me on the shoulder, "Ed, Javier tells me that you're originally from California how did you end up in Puerto Rico?" Without turning, "My son and I were living on Sint Maarten in the Dutch Caribbean and after he had finished the 6th grade we were faced with the problem of his education. When children in Sint Maarten finish their first level of schooling which is the 6th grade the parents usually pack their bags and send the kiddies off to a boarding school in Holland. Even though as a single parent the idea was tempting I just feel that young children should be brought up by their parents not a disinterested headmaster that's 6,000 miles away. I really didn't want to move to the States so I began looking around Latin America and the Caribbean. My searches lead me to Puerto Rico and a particularly good private school in Fajardo located on the eastern end of the island so we pulled up the anchor and sailed to Fajardo. The pulling up the anchor is actually what happened because at the time we lived on a 43' Hatteras motor yacht.

Over the years I've met a number of truly wonderful people in Puerto Rico, but early adjustment to the island's banana republic attitude is important to maintain your sanity. Even though the Island is part of the United States with Commonwealth status the local politicians act as if Puerto Rico were a sovereign country. The Puerto Rican government once tried to sign a bi-lateral trade agreement that included Castro's Cuba, but when Washington found out about it they told the mental dwarfs in San Juan to drop the idea. There's a high level of unemployment because many Puerto Ricans can get more money from government hand-outs than they can from holding a job and having to work every day. The humorists' have a number of Puerto Rican jokes but one of the favorites asks the question, what's the difference between a Puerto Rican and a Dominican? The answer, 'one get's welfare – the other doesn't.' But much like anywhere else you have to weight the good with the bad." "Okay, so the Puerto Rican government and the politicians aren't honest or too bright but what in actuality is the truly bad side?" "Crime and corruption; the per capita murder rate, armed robberies, muggings, and car theft puts Puerto Rico in the top ten in the United States. And crime isn't limited to the lower classes. Many of the islands politicians are either in jail or under indictment for fraud or embezzlement of government funds. The investigations involving fraud and corruption keep the FBI and other federal law enforcement agencies busy. The US government attorneys always have a full case load bringing the bad guys to justice.

Strangely it doesn't seem to bother the locals too much who appear to believe that a bit of graft and corruption should be the norm for Latinos. Based on past experience the locals know too that when the local coffers run dry Washington always just sends more money. The state and local police are really a joke. At least half of the cops in the eastern and southern parts of the island are in jail for transporting or selling drugs, stealing cars or receiving stolen property." "Sounds pretty bad, Okay then what's the good side?" Still looking forward I said, "An average year round temperature of about 75°, Roosevelt Roads Naval Base and thanks to American Airlines a first class airport with connections to anywhere in the world." Jose now with a grim look on his face, "If the local government and the cops are crooked how does that leave me if I'm providing let's say, sensitive information?" "Jose, if something can be arranged it wouldn't involve any contact with the Puerto Rican police. In any case because of the high level of corruption the federal authorities seldom share or trust them with important intelligence. If the Customs Service is interested in what you have to offer you'd work directly with their agents. The Feds have such a distrust of the local cops that they don't let them in on anything that's coming down. In many of the cases the Feds are the ones that arrest the Puerto Rican cops and sometimes even the judges." With a heavy sigh Jose then looked directly at me, "Ed, I'm going to have to rely on you to put me in touch with the right people if not I could quickly be dead meat."

Turning into the main square of Juangriego Jose poked Javier with his finger, "Make a turn at the next corner and go slow." The Bronco maneuvered around a stalled car and slowly passed a number of tourist shops with gaudy displays of t-shirts and inflatable beach toys hanging from improvised wire mesh racks. As Jose slid lower in his seat he told Javier, "Okay slow down, see the red Mercedes parked on the left? The guy next to the drivers door is Johnny Hassan, he and his brother Mohamed Abbas the guy sitting down, are the ones who run the show. Both drive new Mercedes 450s which doesn't come from selling t-shirts and the other cheap shit they offer to the tourists. I don't know how he got the name Johnny it was probably just a nickname he picked up along the way. Both Hassan and Abbas were born in Lebanon and have close ties with the large Lebanese community in Cuidad Del Este in Paraguay."

Johnny Hassan was a dark skinned man of about 45, slender in build and short being no more than about 5'2", was wearing a plain white shirt with blue trousers. Slowly driving past the two Arabs they appeared little more than unremarkable shopkeepers simply discussing the business of the day; not the treacherous drug lords described by Jose. Hassan, his eyes squinting from the smoke rising from the cigarette dangling from his mouth was flaying his arms in the air in an animated explanation. Abbas looked a bit like Yasser Arafat but without the traditional head scarf. His bald head had some nasty scars and he too was smoking as he rocked back and forth in a plastic garden chair resting on its two back legs. Neither of the men appeared to pay much attention to the Bronco as it slowly passed them. "If you should ever come to Juangriego and pass their shop, never drive by more than once. Hassan has a photographic memory and if he thinks someone looks suspicious or appears to be watching him he'll have me run the license plate to see who the person is and why they're in Juangriego. Johnny Hassan is a very nervous person who distrusts everyone except maybe his brother Abbas. Javier, continue down the street and at the gas station take a left turn. I'll show you the warehouse they work out of." On an unremarkable side street leading to the waterfront we found a two story concrete block building set back about 100′ from the road. The entire perimeter was surrounded by a ten foot cyclone fence. Situated about thirty feet from the building was an inner enclosure protected by an eight foot high steel cyclone fence topped with barbed razor wire. Surveillance cameras and large spotlights were mounted at each corner of the outer fence. Two guards in green uniforms and holding sawed-off shot guns were sitting in chairs positioned on each side of the wide entrance door of the building. The door was of a sufficient height and width to accommodate a large truck. Directly above the door a sign announced in English that this was the building of VENEZ Import-Export. Below the English name was a collection of letters in Arabic.

"Jose, what happens here?" "When a shipment arrives it's taken off the ship by the small boat, which I'm going to show you in a minute and brought to the warehouse. See the black truck parked along the side of the building? The driver and three armed guards watch while six to ten guys transfer the boxes from the pier to the truck, after it's loaded the truck then returns to the warehouse. Normally Abbas and another Arab by the name of Ahmed always monitor the transfer. Hassan, Abbas and Ahmed are armed and carry 9mm weapons. The municipal police are on Hassan's payroll and when something is coming down which is usually after midnight, they watch from a respectable distance to make certain everyone stays away and there are no prying eyes. My job is to make certain that the local cops stay honest and that there's no interference from the authorities in Caracas. Hassan pays me purely for information; I'm his eyes and ears with the federal authorities. He keeps me on the payroll to let him know if there might be any chatter that could effect his operation." Further down the road we came to the Bahia de Juangriego and a small pier where we found an aging 40′ ex-crew boat that had obviously seen better days when she had been servicing the oil rigs out of Morgan City, Louisiana. Jose with a smirk on his face, "That's what Hassan calls his Dream Boat; when I asked him how he picked the name he said, because of that boat all his dreams would come true." Taking a last look at the boat as we continued along the road away from

Juangriego towards the village of La Galera I asked, "And how often does our Mr. Hassan use his Dream Boat?" "Depending on the number of ships at least three or four times a week. The warehouse is only that, a warehouse. Once the drugs come off the ship if it's necessary the consignment is quickly repackaged before it moves on. Everything is planned carefully so the consignments never remain in the warehouse more than 24 hours. In the last two years there was only one case where a ship had engine problems after she had been loaded and was delayed for two days while they did the repairs.

Hassan is a nervous type and always keeps his gun handy in an ankle holster. He's left handed so the holster is under his trousers and buckled to the inside of his left ankle. There are always two guards with shotguns at the bottom of the stairs leading to his office who are there to protect him because he keeps a lot of money in a safe in the office over his shop. Abbas is the courier. When he takes cash to Paraguay for their friends in the Hezbollah organization he carries it in a briefcase from Maiquetia to Sao Paulo and then flies on to Foz do Iguaçu in Brazil. At Foz do Iguaçu Abbas normally stays at a hotel called the Bourbon where he is met by their Lebanese contact and driven across the open border between Brazil and Cuidad Del Este, Paraguay. When Hassan transfers large amounts of money by wire he normally uses the Banco Confederado in Margarita, but not exclusively. Last month I was in his office to get paid and overheard him speaking to someone in the Cayman Islands about money being transferred to a bank in Beirut. On another occasion while he was in the toilet and I was alone in the office I saw wire transfer instructions on his desk for the transfer of $2 million to the BNP bank in Paris." "Jose, I know of the connection between the Guardia Nacional and the CIA, but how does Hassan fit into the picture?"

"Ed, from what I've learned the CIA has connections in Caracas with the General in the Guardia Nacional who commands the Maritima Unidad. The General arranged for the Lieutenant Colonel who commands Detachment 76 in Margarita to be put on the payroll which is actually two payrolls. The Guardia Nacional gets paid by the Arabs and also by the CIA, in return the General gets a piece of the pie and the local commander gets a slice for allowing certain ships to pass or enter Margarita without being boarded. Hassan didn't know of the Guardia Nacional double-dipping until I told him; I learned what was going on after a meeting in Caracas last year. Hassan wasn't pleased and promptly arranged a meeting with the General in Caracas. Once the CIA connection was known I'm not sure but I think the General used the opportunity of the meeting to get more money from Hassan. According to Hassan the General acknowledged that the CIA was paying him but said it was irregular. He said the Americans may have a shipment once every six weeks or so or maybe nothing for two or three months. When the CIA needed him they would give him the name of the ship and when it would sail from Colombia to insure it was on the list to be *overlooked*. The General said that his involvement with the CIA was small in comparison and assured Hassan that he was his biggest customer. Hassan has never let on about how much he pays the General but it's got to be a fairly sizeable amount. After meeting the General in Caracas Hassan never again brought up the subject and everything appeared to return to normal. Nothing's changed it's just like it's always been. Hassan hates the Jews and I think as a dig towards the Israelis I heard him once refer to the list of protected ships as *the chosen few*.

Venez Import-Export does a monthly distribution and always wires the General's commission in US dollars to his bank account in Aruba. I don't know what the commission is, but it has got to be pretty good considering the number of movements involved. Hassan told me that there hadn't been any conflicts and as far as he knew the CIA wasn't aware of his arrangement with the Guardia Nacional. He apparently wasn't worried about the Guardia Nacional's involvement with the Americans so long as it didn't effect his operation. He said the information was something he might be able to use as blackmail if he ever had a problem with the General. He also told me that if the General ever got too far out of line he'd have him killed. I think this was a subtle message meant for me as well. The only problem occurred last year when Hassan really got really pissed-off when he learned that the CIA had used a stolen sailboat to move a small quantity of narcotics through Venezuela. He was furious that the Guardia Nacional and their CIA clients had done such a stupid thing and couldn't understand why the General would compromise a very profitable business enterprise for the sake of a side business that couldn't have amounted to much. Hassan told me that in any case he thought the CIA was little more than a bunch of stupid cowboys.

Javier was shaking his head while I was frantically trying to write everything down and knew it was time for a break, "Wow, that's quite a story. Let's stop somewhere and have a cold drink." "Okay but let's wait until we are well away from Juangriego, it would be too dangerous for me to be seen with two strangers when I hadn't let Hassan know I was here. Let's go to the Bodega Tampico in Pampatar. It's on the way back."

Located on the outskirts of town the Bar Tampico was like a caricature out of a Hemmingway novel. Six plastic tables and matching chairs emblazoned with faded red and white Coca-Cola decals fronted a bar counter that had been fashioned from a display counter which had obviously been long over used by a now closed supermarket. The establishment was empty accept for an aging, toothless proprietor who struggled to balance a tray carrying the three Polar beers to our table. While sipping on the lukewarm beer I finished writing down the information that Jose had offered. I assured him that when I got back to Puerto Rico I'd quietly make some inquiries, but would not release his name or any details that could be traced back to him. If I could arrange something I'd let Javier know and Jose could take it from there if he was interested. Shielded from any prying eyes we let Jose out of the Bronco in a back alley a block away from the Blue Topaz.

The next day the training of the Grupo Tiburon continued, but after the previous day's activities in Juangriego I found it hard to focus on the subject of the Basic Principles of Towing. Two days later I returned to Caracas. The Venezuelan Coastguard's chief of operations called me at the hotel to ask if while I was in Caracas I could meet with the commanding officer of the auxiliary group in Valencia located in the Venezuelan State of Carabobo. If this was acceptable he said he would arrange for one of his staff, a Navy lieutenant by the name of Armando Aguilar to drive me. The commander called the night before to confirm the arrangements, "Ed, because of the traffic and the driving time to Valencia if it's okay I'll have Aguilar pick you up in front of the Eurobuilding at 0530 hours," "Sure, that's fine. What kind of a car will he be driving?" "He's asked if he could use his personal vehicle and put in for mileage reimbursement and I agreed. He has a dark green 2-door Mitsubishi Trooper." The following morning before leaving the hotel's lobby I picked up two go-cups of coffee, one for me and one for the lieutenant. At precisely 0530 the dark green 2-door Mitsubishi Trooper drove around the hotel's entrance circle as the passenger door swung open. Saluting, the lieutenant said, "Good morning Captain." "Good morning lieutenant, here have a coffee. I'm not certain how you take it but it's got milk in it and here are three sugars." The traffic was light along the highway that passed by the University and the Plaza Venezuela on the freeway to the west. "You know lieutenant this is probably the only time I've ever driven through Caracas where the traffic has been bearable." Smiling he replied, "Most people don't get up this early". Traveling at a high speed we made good time getting out of the metropolitan area. As the sun began emerging on the horizon behind us we were just outside the city of Maracay.

"Lieutenant, do you mind if I smoke?" "No, carry on sir." In reaching over the back seat to get my briefcase where I carried my pipe and tobacco pouch I saw a large dark colored Chevrolet sedan about 100' behind us that appeared to have tires hanging alongside the passenger doors. Before I had a chance to look away the car increased its speed and had positioned itself in the passing lane immediately to the left of the Mitsubishi. I was then able to confirm that the dark colored sedan did have two tires tied along its passenger side. "Lieutenant look…." But before I had time to have him look at the car to our left to tell him about the tires the car had slammed into the driver's side of the Mitsubishi. The lieutenant shouted, "Coño! Pendejo!" While trying to release the holster clasp and take hold of his weapon the lieutenant struggled to maintain control of the Mitsubishi as the Chevrolet repeatedly slammed into the side of our car trying to force us off the road. At the speed we were traveling had we been forced from the right lane we would have ended up in a deep ditch that paralleled the road; because of the trooper's high profile we would have most likely landed upside down. The large dark sedan kept moving to and fro as the driver repeatedly slammed into the side of Mitsubishi. No more than maybe 300' ahead was a slip road to our right leading to a gasoline station, "Lieutenant, look try and make it to the gas station!"

We entered the forecourt of the gas station at maybe 70 mph barely missing one of the pumps before bouncing over a curb and coming to a stop. With the two tires still hanging along its passenger side the dark sedan sped away and continued down the highway. "Lieutenant, are you Okay?" "Yes. I'm fine Captain how about you?" "Yes, I'm fine but I think that somebody out there doesn't like us lieutenant." Clearly shaken we both entered the gas station's shop and while the lieutenant called the police I got us two more coffees. Two police officers showed up about 20 minutes later and the lieutenant told them what had happened. When they saw that we were both naval officers they seemed to have a little more than the normal interest but then said there was not much they could do. Other than a large dark colored car which may or may not have been a mid 1970's Chevrolet sedan with two tires tied along the passenger side there wasn't much more to tell. While the dark sedan appeared to be reasonably clean the rear license plate had been obscured by dirt or mud.

The drivers' side of the lieutenant's Mitsubishi Trooper had a number of black marks from the tires, the driver's door and both fenders were caved in with an assortment of small dents that the lieutenant said hadn't been there before. Looking closely at the damages, other than the crushed fenders and a partially caved in door there was little real evidence of what had happened. The lieutenant gave the police his Venezuelan ID number, produced his driver's license and the registration details of his car. After the two police officers had departed, over coffee we pondered whether to proceed to Valencia or abort the meeting. As we had people waiting for us we decided to continue but agreed we would definitely return before dark. We would also keep a close watch for cars around us, especially those with tires tied to their doors. About two miles further along the highway towards Valencia we came upon the police car which was parked on the side of the road next to two large tires, the cops were waving us to stop. "There's no sign of the car but we found the tires. Holding up some pieces of a light polypropylene line still tied to one of the tires the officer remarked, "They used this rope to tie the tires to the car probably to prevent them from making metal to metal contact with the Mitsubishi and damaging their car or leaving any paint marks. I'm afraid that there isn't much more we can do. We have your contact information lieutenant; if anything comes up we'll get in touch with you."

Albeit a bit delayed we finished our meeting in Valencia and returned to Caracas without being attacked by any other tire adorned

Chevy sedans. Late that afternoon the lieutenant drove me back to the Eurobuilding hotel where I found a hand written note that had been pushed under my door. *Ed, Tomorrow during the day I have some work I must attend to but let's plan to have dinner. I'll pick you up at the hotel at 8:00.* The message was signed by Nicholas Goschenko.

The following morning I took advantage of the free time to catch up on the preparation of the monthly report to Washington when the phone rang. The call was from the Coastguard's Chief of Operations. "I have just spoken with Aguilar who told me what happened yesterday. Are you Okay?" "Yes, I'm fine just a bit shaken from the experience. We were both very lucky. There's no way that a car with two tires tied along its side would coincidentally be driving along the highway at exactly the same time as we were and then attempt to run us off the road by mistake. This was no accident someone had obviously marked our car and tried to hurt or kill us." The coastguard officer clearly concerned picked up the conversation, "I've got an investigation underway and intend to get to the bottom of it. I'll let you know what I find out." With that the commander hung up the phone. I continued with my work until lunch and then went down to the restaurant.

After lunch I stopped at the hotel shop that sold newspapers to pick up a Herald Tribune. Returning to my room I opened the door and found a message printed on the hotels note paper. The time stamp showed 12:15 pm and was from the Concierge: Message from Captain Goschenko. *To save a bit of time I would appreciate if you could meet me at the hotel's entrance on the main road to save me having to enter the hotel's parking area. Please be at the main entrance to the hotel at Las Mercedes at 7:45pm.* At about 5:00pm the phone rang. "Mr. Geary this is the concierge desk did you receive the telephone message from Captain Goschenko about meeting him tonight at 7:45pm? The message was delivered to your room earlier today." "Yes I did, thank you." I straightened my papers and then decided to take a swim in the pool before meeting Goschenko. Dressing in civilian clothes, at 7:30pm I took the elevator to the lobby and started walking down the sidewalk towards the Las Mercedes entrance to the hotel. As I rounded the slight curve in the road that lead to the intersection of Las Mercedes with the main street two shots rang out hitting the pavement in front of me. Because of a concrete wall on my right and the open road to my left there was no place to take cover; I quickly turned and began running up the slight incline leading to the hotel's main entrance. As I ran I looked to my right towards the grassy hillside adjoining the road but couldn't see anyone. Just short of the entrance I dropped behind some cars parked near the doorway. Looking back I saw the road was empty with the exception of the two or three cars that were parked in front of the hotel's lobby entrance.

The silence was deafening, no one was around. Using a car as cover I looked back and could see the only place the shooter could have been was on the small knoll adjacent to a parking area on the left side of the main entrance road. Crouching while using the car for cover I waited another few minutes to watch the area from where I believed the shots had been fired. If a car tried to leave through the main entrance leading to Las Mercedes or by means of a second access road to the left it would have to pass close to the hotel's main entrance. When the owner of the car I was using as a cover returned I went inside the hotel lobby. At the concierge desk I said I was a guest in the hotel and needed to report a shooting that had just happened. "Are you injured? "No I'm not, but please call the police." The flustered concierge said he would immediately summon the police asking me to wait in the lobby until they arrived. Just as I turned away from the concierge Goschenko entered the lobby. "Ed, are you ready to go?" "Hi Nicholas, there's a bit of a problem. Someone fired two shots at me as I was walking down the road to meet you. Fortunately they missed. I received your message to meet you at Las Mercedes and when I was about half-way down the entrance road the shots were fired, I think from the area on the left hand side of the road." "What message? I said that I'd pick you up at 8:00 in front of the hotel why were you walking towards Las Mercedes?" "I got another message where you asked me to walk towards Las Mercedes so you wouldn't have to enter the parking area." "I didn't leave you a second message I only left you one message. I never asked you to walk to Las Mercedes."

A few moments' later three police officers entered the hotel, walked to the reception desk and spoke with a receptionist who pointed towards Nicholas and I who were standing in the lounge area. After the police officers had been told what happened two went outside to look around the area while the third took a statement from me. The police appeared to have little interest while explaining that each week Caracas had between 30 and 40 murders many of which were simply attempted robberies that had gone bad. "No one tried to rob me and there was no one around or near me. The shots were fired from a distance and no one tried to approach me." It was obvious that the police weren't interested even after Goschenko told them that I was an officer in the Venezuelan Navy as well as an American and US Coast Guard Auxiliary officer. Much like the tire incident the day before the cops said they'd file a report with the same run-around, don't call us – we'll call you. "How do you feel Ed? Do you want to maybe forget about La Estancia and have dinner here?" "Are you still buying? If the invitation is still on let's go to La Estancia. I don't and probably never will know who the bastard was that took a shot at me, but I do know he needs a lot more target practice. My only hope is that he'll take his practice shots at someone else. Let's eat." While trying to present a positive appearance the two incidents had been disturbing. That's maybe a wrong choice of words. Better said both incidents scared the hell out of me.

The next day I was due to return to Puerto Rico on the afternoon American Airlines flight. In the morning after breakfast I stopped to speak with the hotel's manager, an affable German who earlier had been made aware of the shooting when he came to work. Introducing myself, "Mr. Kohlberg I'm the guest that was shot at last night, I'd be grateful if you might help me." "Yes, but of course whatever you need please let me know. However, I would first like to offer my sincere apologies for what happened. Caracas is a very violent city with very ineffective police. Our internal security in the hotel is very attentive and we have roving security officers on the grounds and in the parking areas to safeguard our guests. I am very, very sorry for your ordeal." "Thanks, but it's not the shooting incident I need help with. Mr. Kohlberg yesterday after returning from lunch I received a phone message that shows a time stamp of 12:15pm. The problem is that the message was not from Captain Goschenko as it states. I would be grateful if you would allow me to speak to the telephone operator who took this message in case she might have noted the number of the person who called." Reaching for his phone Kohlberg summoned the hotel's assistant manager and asked him to have the department head come to his office immediately.

Marta Cortez a grand-motherly lady who Kohlberg said had been with the Eurobuilding for a number of years appeared terrified as she entered Kohlberg's office. "Ms. Cortez, this is Mr. Geary a guest of the hotel. Yesterday he received a telephone message that had a time stamp of 12:15pm. I want you to find out which of your staff took the message and who the message was from." Handing her the message Kohlberg said, "The message itself is not an issue, Mr. Geary's concern is that there is no return telephone number and the caller wasn't Captain Goschenko. Ms. Cortez, you are aware that the hotel policy is clear that all messages are to include the telephone number of the caller, as you can see the line for the number of the caller is blank. Please bring the person who took this call to my office immediately." Clearly upset Ms. Cortez stood and turned to leave, "I'm sorry Mr. Kohlberg, I don't know what happened but I see that the call was taken by Ms. Sanchez who only joined us last month. I'll be right back."

"While we wait may I offer you a coffee Mr. Geary? The hotel's switchboard is on the lower level so it should only be a few minutes before the telephone operator returns." 'Yes, thank you coffee would be nice." Calling through the open door to his office, "Ms. Delgado, would you please arrange for some coffee." From beyond the door an unseen Ms. Delgado acknowledged her master's request. A few minutes later Ms. Delgado a strikingly beautiful woman in her late 20's gently knocked on the partially open door of Kohlberg's office announcing the arrival of the coffee and that Ms. Cortez accompanied by Ms. Sanchez the recently hired telephone operator were waiting outside. Looking for my approval, "If it's alright with you we'll have our coffee first and then speak with Ms. Cortez and hmm, what was her name...oh yes, Sanchez."

The small cups of the strong espresso were quickly consumed when the two telephone operators were summoned, "Mr. Kohlberg, this is Ms. Sanchez who took the call for Mr. Geary." "Good morning Ms. Sanchez." Handing her the telephone message, "as you know the hotel's policy is very clear that all messages we take for our guests are to have the name and the telephone number of the person calling. Why does this message not indicate the caller's number?" Obviously having never been in the Executive Offices and particularly the office of the General Manager Ms. Sanchez was clearly ill at ease. "I'm sorry sir, but when I received the call the gentleman said he needn't give me his phone number as Mr. Geary already had it. As he said that Mr. Geary already had the number I didn't ask him again. This happens many times and I didn't think it was unusual. I do apologize for any inconvenience that I may have caused the guest." "Thank you Ms. Sanchez. Mr. Geary is there anything else you need from Ms. Sanchez or Ms. Cortez?" "No, thank you Ms. Sanchez I just needed the caller's phone number but now understand the circumstances of why it wasn't obtained." After checking out and on the ride back to the airport I decided that on future visits I'd change from the Eurobuilding and stay at the Caracas Hilton, the Tamanaco or another hotel in the city.

"Hey Dad, welcome home, did you have a good trip?" Not wishing to upset Jason with the details of the incident on the road to Valencia or the shooting, "Yeah, great trip. Goschenko and the Admiral both send their regards. We're really making good progress and the training is moving along smoothly. How about you? Did you miss me? And how was your stay with Poncho and Lucy?"

In view of my frequent travels to Venezuela and other countries in Central America I had made an arrangement with Jason's headmaster that as long as his absence didn't seriously conflict with his studies they would excuse him from school under the condition that he would write a thesis on the visit and his observations of the country and its people that we had visited. He was then required to read his thesis to the class. On those occasions that he didn't accompany me to Venezuela he would stay with our close friends Poncho and Lucy Bird whose home was walking distance from his school, Fajardo Academy.

"They're both fine but still insisting that I'm in bed by 9:30, Yuk. Won't you tell them it's Ok for me to stay up until at least 10:30?" "Hey you're a growing boy and need the rest, maybe next year." "Dad, next year is next month so I'm going to hold you that. Don't forget you told me that a man is only as good as his word." "That's enough Jason."

Possibly in view of my dedication to the Coast Guard Jason had set his goals on attendance at the Coast Guard Academy and after graduation planned a career as an officer in the US Coast Guard. He had been interviewed and was recommended by an Auxiliary review board in San Juan, the first step for gaining acceptance to the Academy. Knowing of Jason's interest in attending the Academy and a career in the Coast Guard in December 1993 Rear Admiral Eliseo Martin Fossa the Commandant of the Venezuelan Coastguard and Rear Admiral Jesus E. Briceño Garcia, Commandant of Naval Personnel both sent letters to the Admiral who was the Superintendent of the US Coast Guard Academy.

The letters praised Jason for his hard work and linguistic skills in acting as a Spanish translator for the US Coast Guard during the UNITAS exercises and included their personal recommendations for his acceptance and attendance at the US Coast Guard Academy. The compliments and personal recommendations of these two outstanding naval officers, both admirals made me a very proud father.

The letters written on the letterhead of the Venezuelan Navy, translated into English read:

Caracas, 21 December 1993

Rear Admiral
<u>Superintendent of the US Coast Guard Academy</u>

It is a pleasure for me to have the opportunity to address you and present to your attention JASON PAUL GEARY. This young man is the son of my personal friend, Capt. E.S. Geary, who belongs to the US Coast Guard Auxiliary Groups.

JASON PAUL GEARY has a firm aspiration and determination to join the prestigious Academy by year 1995.

This young man JASON PAUL GEARY helped in a very unselfish manner with the Auxiliary Groups of the Venezuelan Coastguard performed very efficiently and demonstrated a high vocation for the marine arts.

I would be grateful for whatever is in your hands to do in favor of this recommendation and take the opportunity to wish you and your distinguished family a Merry Christmas and Prosperous New Year.

Sincerely yours
Jesús E. Briceño Garcia, Rear Admiral
Commandant of Naval Personnel

Caracas, December 23, 1993

Rear Admiral
<u>Superintendent of the US Coast Guard Academy</u>

I have the honor to address you, in the opportunity to salute you and wish you and all your family, a Merry Christmas and Prosperous New Year 1994.

The reason for my communication is to bring to your attention and knowledge that citizen JASON PAUL GEARY, son of Capt. Edwin S. Geary, who belongs to the U.S. Coast Guard Auxiliary forces and my personal friend, has manifested his interest in joining the prestigious Academy under your dignified direction, during the year 1995. It should be noted that this young man, JASON PAUL GEARY, has supported and collaborated in an unselfish manner with the Auxiliary Groups of the Venezuelan Coastguard and very efficiently, demonstrated outstanding attitudes for the Maritime interests and Marine Arts. We appreciate the attention you could spare to this commendation of mine.

I remain, to your graceful orders in this noble Command.

Eliseo Martin Fossa, Rear Admiral
Commandant of the Coastguard

Martin Fossa the Commandant of the Venezuelan Coastguard with the author
at Coastguard Headquarters

SIX

It was good to be home but not so good when I saw the stack of mail and faxes which had arrived during my absence. My secretary, Nelly had separated the important stuff from the junk and placed them in two piles on my desk. I didn't have clients personally coming to see me as most of my assignments came by fax, over the phone or by mail. I had determined a long time ago that I didn't need to have an outside workplace or the hassle of commuting to an office where I might only be able to work 8 hours a day. Even though I knew the days would be longer I had converted one of our bedrooms into an office which allowed me to work at home and still be able to care for Jason while attending to my domestic responsibilities as a single parent. Nelly would work in the office between 8 and 5 and would keep a close eye on my marine practice while I was away either working on a case or training the Venezuelan Coastguard.

After sorting out the backlog of work I got a good nights sleep and was glad I did because at 6:00am I received a telephone call from an underwriter[33] in Holland who had called the previous day, "Good morning Ed, it's midday in Amsterdam but knowing you get up with the chickens figured it would be a good time to catch you. I've got a problem." After taking a sip of my first coffee of the day, "Good morning Jan sorry to hear about a problem, but you know I always welcome your problems with enthusiasm, what's up?" "Sometime in the last couple of weeks an Irwin 52' disappeared from her mooring in Simpson Bay Lagoon in Sint Maarten. The German owners who live on the boat and are normally onboard had returned to Munich to spend Christmas with their families. During their absence they had asked friends in Hilton Case on the French side of the island to drive by from time to time and keep an eye on the boat while they were

---

33 Due to possible reprisals the underwriter insists on anonymity

away. Apparently the friends hadn't driven by the lagoon for about a week but once they did they found the boat was gone.

As the lagoon is land-locked and boats can only get to the open sea by going through the channel on the Dutch side when the bridge is open it clearly just didn't blow away." "Jan, do you have any photographs of the boat? I'll also need the hull identification number and any specific information about color schemes or personal items that the owner may have installed that could be used for identification. As you know Irwins in the Caribbean are about as common as bicycles in Holland." "Good idea Ed, I plan to speak with the owners today and will fax you everything I have either later this afternoon or tomorrow morning. And by the way how's the Wheel of Old Amsterdamer cheese holding up?" "It's almost gone. I'll be in touch."

The underwriter and his wife Gretchen knew of my fondness for a particular mature Dutch cheese called Old Amsterdamer. They had a chuckle when after my last visit to Holland they had driven me to Amsterdam's Schiphol airport and later learned that before boarding my flight I had bought a wheel of the cheese in a duty-free shop only to find it wouldn't fit into my carry-on luggage. Amsterdam's Schiphol or Barajas in Madrid have always been my favorite airports to and from Europe because of the excellent flight connections from San Juan. The airlines that serve these airports are also a bit more relaxed when it comes to carry-on bags especially when it comes to those passengers who may carry large wheels of cheese.

The following morning I received a ten page fax containing a photo and the particulars of the missing yacht. I extracted the significant details adding the photo of the yacht to a Stolen Boat Circular which I faxed to a number of marinas and port authorities in the Caribbean and the Bahamas; I then got on a plane to Sint Maarten. After clearing immigration I picked up a rental car from my long-time friend Amin Khan owner of Paradise Car Rental and started to leave the parking area of the Princess Juliana airport. "Hey, Eddie baby, Eddie baby." The voice was unmistakably that of my good friend Ernie Gracetti a former New Yorker who a few years earlier had mysteriously transplanted himself on this Dutch Caribbean island. Because of his happy-go-lucky and good-natured personality along with a seemingly endless supply of cash Ernie had gained the reputation as a high-roller who loved to party. After a few drinks Ernie would occasionally reminisce about his background in New York but generally was reluctant to talk about how he had quietly out-of-the-blue ended up in Sint Maarten. Along with a pit-bull named Killer and a caged parrot called Bernie he lived comfortably on his yacht in Simpson Bay. He soon became one of the islands more popular bachelors. To respect his privacy I never pressed him as to whether his hasty relocation had been to escape from some perceived problem with the Mob or he had just wanted to enjoy a forced early retirement at 40.

Ernie had been in the trucking business with other members of his extended family and once told me of an uncle who was a Capo in the Gambino crime organization. To respect his privacy and my piece of mind I didn't ask or press for any further details. He simply was a good looking Italian guy with a great personality who oozed with charm; everybody who knew him liked him. Ernie was generous to a fault and always was the first to buy a round of drinks at his favorite Italian eatery appropriately named *Good Fellas*. Having helped him with a yacht claim the previous year we had become close friends.

"Hey guy what brings you to Sint Maarten and how's Jason? Does he like the Sonic toothbrush I put him on to?" and in the same breath, "Let's have lunch." I didn't have to ask where as I knew we'd be eating at his favorite located at the Simpson Bay Marina. Over lunch confirming that Jason was fine and enjoying his new high-tech toothbrush we caught up on the local happenings, "Ernie, I'd like you to put the word out about a yacht that's been reported missing, if you hear anything *on-the-street* I'd appreciate you letting me know. Of course there's a 10% reward that the underwriters will be happy to pay for information that leads to a successful recovery." I gave Ernie a dozen of the Stolen Yacht Notices which he said he'd distribute around the island especially the watering holes frequented by the boating crowd. I then drove to the French side of the island where I spoke with the owner's friends who had been responsible for watching the boat and who had later called the owners in Munich to tell them that their boat was missing. Determining that they really didn't know anything more than what they had told the owners previously and after leaving some of the stolen yacht notices at the bars surrounding the Marina Royale I caught an afternoon flight back to San Juan.

Less than a week later after watching the CBS evening news and

Dan Rather had finished telling us what was going on in the world the phone rang. "Is this Ed Geary?" "Yes, this is Ed Geary who is this?" "My name is not important right now. What I have to tell you is what's important, please just listen. I understand that you are offering a reward for the Irwin sailboat that was taken from Sint Maarten earlier this month. I didn't take the boat but I know who did and what's more important I know where the boat is right now. If I tell you were the boat is will you pay me the reward money?" "Wow, that's a lot in one breath. Let me get this straight you weren't involved in the theft of the boat but know where it's at? If you tell me where the boat is you want me to pay you a reward for this information, right? Sorry my man but that sounds like a scam, I'm not interested, thanks for calling." "Wait, wait, don't hang up. I know it may sound a bit funny, but it's true. The boat was stolen to order." "Stolen to order what the hell does that mean?" "Last month I was visiting my girlfriend who lives in Martinique. One night we had gone out to dinner and met these two guys at the bar of La Belle Époque a restaurant on Route de Didier in Fort de France. After a few bottles of wine they got a bit tipsy and started talking. They told me that they had hitched a ride on a sailboat that had recently arrived in Martinique. The sailboat they came in on dropped them off in the marina at Trois Islet. They said they didn't clear in with the authorities because they had French passports and were planning to leave for Saint Martin as soon as they could get a ride. I asked them why they were going to Saint Martin, Emilio said to pick up a sailboat." My curiosity being aroused I asked, "How did you get into a conversation with them in the first place and why would they tell you this; what's your name?" "Forget about my name it's not important right now. I have a pony tail and was dressed like a yachtie, you know shorts, loose shirt, open sandals those sorts of things. They were drinking at the next table and had been eyeing my girlfriend when this big guy who appeared to be in charge introduced himself as Emilio. He looked over and asked me if I had a boat in Fort de France. I told them I had a 46' ketch named the *EVASION* which I lived on in Marigot at the Marina Royale in Saint Martin. Emilio then asked if he and his friend could join us and we began talking about boats, marinas, you know just kind of general boat stuff.

After ordering another bottle of wine he said that he was looking for a couple of people that might be interested to work for about ten days or so as crew. Emilio said the pay would be good but everything had to be kept quite; if we were interested he said the two of us could earn $1,500.00 and our return tickets from Cartagena. Intrigued at the *keeping quiet bit* I asked why this was necessary. Emilio then told me that the guy he worked for was with the US government in Bogotá. After drinking some more wine he said that when he first met the American guy he had told him he used the cover as a commercial attaché but was really with another agency in the embassy. Emilio said he had worked for the American before and after the boats were delivered to Cartagena he was always paid in cash. After the last delivery while sharing a bottle of wine the American told him that the agency in the embassy he worked in was the CIA, but Emilio didn't know if this was true or just bull-shit. Emilio said the American would contact him and tell him that he wanted this or that boat and where it was located. One time last year he said they had taken a 46' Bertram sport-fisherman from the Virgin Islands but usually the boats they picked up were newer sailboats. In any case Emilio said he was told exactly what boat was to be *picked-up* and where it was; all the boats this guy wanted were always somewhere in the Caribbean. Emilio told me that he had *delivered* three boats this year and everything went fine, no problems and he made good money."

The callers' story seemed a bit bizarre but now I was really paying attention. I asked him, "Did Emilio tell you what would happen if he got caught. Would the American help him....?" The caller cut me off, "Look I don't know the whole story right now but Emilio told me it had to be done quietly because if they got caught while taking the boat they'd be on their own, but once they were in Venezuelan or Colombian waters everything's covered and there would be no problem with the US Coast Guard. Emilio said that the American guy told him he had access to confidential information through the embassy in Bogotá and would know where and when the US Coast Guard cutters would be on drug interdiction patrols so they could avoid these areas. The guy said that even though the owners may report the theft to their insurance companies and the local cops he knew that generally missing boats don't receive any attention until long after their gone. Because of the heavy US surveillance Emilio said they would always avoid going near Cuba and as much as possible stay away from the Yucatan channel. Knowing this Emilio said they would never go west or the shorter route across the Caribbean but go east and well offshore into the Atlantic before heading south. When they were south of Grenada they would turn to a south westerly course and hug the Venezuelan and Colombian coastline to avoid detection." "Why didn't you and your girlfriend take the offer?" "Didi my girlfriend didn't like either one of them and thought they were slimy characters. They flashed a lot of money around and obviously were not worried about their next meal or drink. They bought us dinner and paid for four or five bottles of wine. Didi declined their offer outright, I told them I'd think about it and maybe see them in Saint Martin."

"Then what happened did you see them again?" "I flew back to Saint Martin and about a week later I hear someone rattling the anchor that's tied to my stern rail, it's Emilio shouting, Herve, Herve, we've arrived." "So your Christian name is Herve." "Yeah, okay, anyway Emilio and his partner Francisco come aboard my boat. After sitting down in the cockpit Emilio got right to the point and wanted to know if I had thought about his offer? He said the boat that he was going to take is at anchor in the lagoon, there's no one on board so he wants to be able to leave as soon as possible and it was important that he organize a crew right away. He said that normally he and his mate Francisco could handle things by themselves but because of the size of the boat they'd need to go at least 100 miles due east into the Atlantic before turning to a southerly course, so he wanted four people on board to cover the watches. Emilio knew the bridge on the Dutch side opened once in the morning and then around 4:00 in the afternoon; he wanted to leave when the bridge opened in the afternoon so he could be well offshore before anyone realized the boat's gone and maybe even be in Colombia before anyone's the wiser." "Is the boat still in Colombia?" "Yeah, I guess I shouldn't have said that." "Never mind go on." "Emilio said the American guy always contacts him through a friend who owns Le Bar in Gustavia on St. Barth's. He told him that he wanted the Irwin in St. Martin to give to a heavy weight in the Colombian government. He said the boat in St. Martin was the type of yacht this guy wanted. He told me the boat flew a Dutch flag, was owned by a German and knew that no one would be on board as the owner would be away for the holidays. Emilio said that all the boats they picked up were always taken to a small marina along

Colombia's Caribbean coast where they change the name, remove the hull identification numbers, and then repaint the trim and the boot stripe a different color. In effect the boats simply disappeared. Emilio told me that one time he was really curious who this guy really was so he called the American Embassy in Bogotá but he wasn't there. The telephone operator only said that he was an attaché in the commercial section. " "Herve, did Emilio tell you the name of the American in Bogotá? " "No, he never told me the guy's name."

"That's quite a story but now that I know the background and pretty much where the boat is why do I need you?" "You need me because I have the contact information on how to reach Emilio in Cartagena. I also know that he was obviously able to get two guys as crew who may still be on the boat. One call from me to Emilio at the Cartagena Yacht Club would see the boat disappear again and then you'd never find it. Even if you did find the boat with the hull numbers gone you couldn't make a positive ID. With no hull identification and the involvement of the American guy that got the boat stolen in the first place the Colombian authorities would laugh if you tried to recover it and don't forget the boat is registered in Holland not the US."

Pondering a response, "Okay, I agree the information may be helpful but underwriters would never agree to pay you the 10% reward because you had knowledge of the crime before it was committed. Of course you could also be charged with aiding and abetting which is a criminal act for not reporting what you knew to the French Gendarmerie or the Dutch police." The silence was deafening. "You can't do that." "You really don't think so? I wouldn't push your luck. You my friend Herve, owner of the yacht EVASION docked at the Marina Royale in Marigot have been a party to grand theft; you could end up losing your boat in addition to spending a few years in the slammer as a guest of the French Republic." I thought that Herve had hung up the phone but during the silence he must have quickly realized he was in deep trouble and would be better advised to keep talking and even more important to keep listening. Hoping to put the fear of God in him, while at the same time keeping the information line open, "Look Herve you made a big mistake in not reporting what was coming down to the authorities which would have prevented the theft in the first place. Now you are trying to illegally profit from what should have been said before it ever happened, naughty, naughty Herve. But having said that maybe I can help you out. The 10% is out of the question. In every case any reward that's paid is based only on the recovered value of the yacht and only after its safe return to the rightful owner. Any damage, theft of the gear or personal effects that was on the boat is deducted to come up with a recovered value on which the 10% is based.

But under the law as you aided and abetted in the commission of a crime you're a co-conspirator and clearly not entitled to any reward. What I would be willing to do is suggest to underwriters that if your information is reliable and we recover the yacht the underwriters would pay you a flat sum of $2,000.00." Obviously annoyed Herve shot back, "That's crazy, I give you the information that leads to the recovery of a yacht worth $250,000.00 and you give me a pittance of $2,000.00." "That's the deal. Take it or leave it. You can think about it for 24 hours and let me know. If I don't hear back from you by this time tomorrow I'll start moving." I hung up the phone and poured myself a glass of a very nice Cabernet Sauvignon. Ten minutes later the phone rang, "This is Herve, I accept your offer." "Okay. Herve call me tomorrow about noon." The next day at 5:30am Atlantic Standard Time I called the underwriter in Holland to give him the news and seek his approval of the $2,000.00 payment to Herve – if we got the boat back. Promptly at 12:00pm Herve called.

"Herve, I've spoken with the underwriter who isn't particularly happy with paying someone who was involved and was in a position to prevent the theft, but because he wants the boat back has agreed to pay you $2,000.00, but there are conditions. You must agree to fully cooperate and if we get the boat back and can prosecute the thieves you must agree to testify at their trial. Also I'd like you to come to Cartagena with me and identify Emilio?" "That's crazy these are bad people if Emilio sees me in Cartagena and finds I'm involved in any way with your efforts to recover the Irwin he'd kill me. You tricked me into giving you all the information and now you want me to risk my life for a measly $2,000.00. I don't think so." "Herve, I didn't trick you into anything you're the one who voluntarily told me everything that I needed to know. I can understand why you don't want to go to Colombia and may be able to avoid you having to do this if you will send me a full description of Emilio and his partner Francisco.

Write down everything you know about them. I want to know if they smoke and if so what brand of cigarettes, are they right or left handed, any distinguishing marks, tattoos or scars, the color and length of their hair, the color of their eyes, and the type of clothes they were wearing, include everything you and Didi observed. It wouldn't be in Colombia and because of jurisdictional issues I'm not sure where or how Emilio, Francisco or anyone else who may be involved could be brought to justice, but if we go to trial your testimony cannot be waived, and you must agree to cooperate fully with the Dutch and French authorities and that's it." "Okay, I don't like it but I'll agree. Didi's a pretty good artist so I'll get her to do some sketches of both of them and fax everything to you at the number on the Stolen Boat sheet." "How about the crew Emilio hired do you know who they are and what they look like?" "No, I never saw who he finally got, but it's got to be someone local; I'll ask around and try to find out." "Ok, in the meantime get me the sketches and everything you have on Emilio and Francisco and do it now. Time is of the essence because if they start altering the boats appearance and removing the hull numbers it will make my job even harder. Remember no boat – no $2,000.00." I didn't tell Herve that even if the hull identification numbers were removed I still might be able to identify the boat by using the serial numbers from the engine, transmission or the electronics; that is if I could get on board. Herve and his artistic girlfriend Didi didn't waste any time. As soon as the details and the sketches arrived I was on a COPA flight to Cartagena through Panama.

With the exception of being a quagmire of crime, corruption, and narcotics trafficking amongst other negative attributes, Cartagena is a beautiful walled colonial city reminiscent of old Spain. In an effort to blend-in I avoided the glitzy tourist hotels and stayed at a small inn used by businessmen located in what was described as a 'safe section' of the city. After checking in I took a taxi to the Cartagena Yacht Club to have a look around to see if I could spot Emilio, Francisco or maybe even the Irwin 52. After a Coke at the bar (the kind you drink not put up your nose) I hailed a taxi to drive me along the coast road just outside of the city where Herve said I might find the stolen Irwin. After searching for an hour or so I eventually did find an Irwin 52' tied up to a small dock along a breakwater to the west of Cartagena. From a safe distance and using binoculars I saw that the hatches were closed which in the sub-tropical heat normally means that no one is on board. I could see that the vessel's sheer stripes along her topsides were a brownish tan color and there was no name or hailing port on her stern. The stolen Irwin that I was looking for had blue sheer stripes, her name was *Elle* and her hailing port of *Curacao* had been painted on the transom. Even though there were some notable differences the yacht in Cartagena appeared to be the Irwin that had been stolen from Sint Maarten because of the personal items that were unique to the stolen boat. I wasn't sure how to pull it off, but I'd need to get a rubbing of her hull number on the transom, assuming it was still there. I felt even more confident that this was the *Elle* when I saw the custom stainless steel dive platform that had been designed and installed by the owner and a small royal blue and yellow telltale with the letter *E* in the middle that had been sewn by the owner's wife and tied to the upper mizzen port backstay. If I was right the *E* was for *Elle*. Returning to the Cartagena Yacht Club I found a seat at the end of the bar that was rapidly filling with the yachtie crowd preparing to avail themselves of the Happy Hour.

"G'day mate welcome to the Cartagena Yacht Club. My name's Pete I've got my boat here, you on a boat?" "No, just a landlubber doing the tourist bit." "Well Yank let me buy you a real beer, Katie love, give us two of those cold Fosters." "Katie's my lady and works at the bar during the week to earn a few pesos so we can eat. I'm a generous bloke so I let her have the weekends off so she can keep the boat clean." Pete even though a bit chauvinistic was an outgoing and friendly fellow who, in apparently craving for a bit of male companionship was anxious to tell me his story which I feel confident had been told many times before. "Ten years ago I did the single-handed bit and sailed from Sydney to the Marquesas then did a quick stop at Santa Maria in the Galapagos before ending up in Panama. I stayed in Balboa for a couple of days but got fed up with the rocking and rolling from the wake of the crew launches going back and forth to the ships anchored offshore. After getting through the Canal I stayed two weeks at the Panama Yacht Club in Colon then set a course for Bonaire where I planned to start a diving business. Two days out of Colon and a few miles southwest of the Colombian coast I got caught in a westerly and the bloody mast came down. I was able to jury rig a small sail and make it to Cartagena and I've been here ever since.

Had a few local ladies to keep me company then I met Katie a couple of years ago. She was down on her luck after having a fight with her bloke who kicked her off his boat. She had no money to get back to London so I gave her a job doing some varnish work on my boat and well, the rest is history."

"That's an interesting story. How big was your boat?" "32 foot from stem to stern, a great sea boat. I ended up selling her to a Brit who replaced the mast and rigging and sailed away. I never heard from him again. You know there are a lot of stories like mine around here. See the couple at the table under the Heineken sign? One night they say they hit a floating container offshore, patched the hole and made it to Cartagena. They had no insurance so they got the boat hauled at the Manzanillo Marina and have been here over a year trying to fix her up with money they make doing minor repairs and other odd jobs. The blond guy at the end of the bar is a Swede who's been around for about six months; he got hooked on the cheap drugs and doesn't seem to have any intention on leaving. See the two burly long haired guys sitting over there in the corner wearing the St. Maarten[34] T-Shirts? They're French, arrived a couple weeks back; from their obnoxious attitude they're both clearly pissed-off at the world. During the day they sit in the bar sipping on a few beers then at night find a boat with nobody on board and sleep in the cockpit. I don't know what their story is but it's not exactly Alice in Wonderland." Thinking to myself; hmm, French, St. Maarten T-shirts, two weeks and even though the faxed drawings weren't the best nor was Didi the artist that Herve had made her out to be there was a slight resemblance. I wondered if one of them could be Emilio and the other Francisco.

"Well mate enjoy your visit I've got to go on a walk-about to do some shopping. And by the way the restaurant here has got the best seafood in Cartagena and it's cheap." After Pete had left I took my Fosters and walked over to the two Frenchman. "Excuse me but I see you're wearing T-shirts from St. Maarten, do you live on St. Maarten?" With a heavy and distinctly French accent and clearly not interested in small talk the larger of the two mumbled, "We lived at Oyster Pond for awhile." Feeling lucky and hoping for a response I answered, "Near Captain Oliver's?" The mention of Captain Oliver's, a marina on the French side of the island located at Oyster Pond

---

34 The Dutch side of the island is called Sint Maarten while the French side is named Saint Martin

sparked an immediate interest. "You know Captain Oliver's?" "Oh sure I used to live on the Dutch side a few years back and sailed a small catamaran out of Captain Oliver's Marina, I'll never forget that terrible entrance on the windward side. Can I buy you a beer?" "Sure, sit down." Waving at the British barmaid, "Katie may we have three beers please." Becoming more relaxed in finding that I knew the island they seem pleased to have someone to talk to especially a fellow sailor. Wiping some beer that had dribbled from the side of his mouth with the back of his hand the larger of the two asked, "When were you last on the island?" "Oh, I haven't been back for a couple of years. How long have you been in Cartagena?" "Only a couple of weeks we delivered a boat." "So what are you doing now just playing the tourist bit?" "No, we want to get out of here but haven't been paid for the delivery or been given our return air tickets."

Hmm, return air tickets? Wondering where they were returning too I asked, "Where's home?" Taking a large swig of beer the one who I believed was Francisco said, "St. Barth's." "Well I guess while your waiting you can sit back relax and enjoy the scenery." "We have no intention of relaxing. After we got here that son-of-a-bitch we did the job for left and told us he was going to Bogotá to get our money, that was almost two weeks ago and we've not seen him since. If he's not back by the weekend we plan to take the matter into our own hands." "Is his boat still here?" "Yeah, it's tied up just out of town but the bastard wouldn't let us stay on the boat while he wasn't here. We're down to our last few dollars and have been forced to sleep in boats where the owners are gone because we can't afford a hotel." Asking Katie for another round and attempting to show a genuine concern, "You know if you don't get paid and the boats still here you could file a lien against the boat and a seaman's claim with the authorities for your wages, it's done all the time." "Well it's not quite that simple because the guy who hired us doesn't own the boat. I can't get into this because it's just too complicated." Bingo! These were the thieves that had stolen the Irwin from Saint Martin now enraged because their attaché paymaster hadn't come across with the money they had been promised.

Before I got up to leave I had to restrain myself because I really wanted to say, 'Sorry guys I guess there's just no honor amongst thieves.' The two thugs were not exactly pleased in being made to wait, especially because they were running out of money and had no place to stay. To keep them happy I wondered why they hadn't been allowed to at least sleep on the Irwin while they waited for their money. This seemed like a really stupid move on the part of their American paymaster. I then wondered how much they had been promised for stealing the Irwin. Under these unusual circumstances I pondered whether I should get creative and maybe attempt a potentially dangerous scheme to double cross Emilio's paymaster.

That night in my room I weighed the options. Emilio and Francisco were broke, no place to sleep, stuck in Cartagena with no way to get back to St. Barth's. It would be risky but suppose I were to tell Emilio who I was and that I was in Colombia to recover the Irwin. I'd level with him and take the chance that they weren't getting more from the American, which I didn't believe would be the case and offer them $5,000 each for the safe return of the Irwin to Saint Martin. While they might get upset and rearrange my physical features or even worse disfigure me permanently they would have little to gain. On the other hand Emilio and Francisco weren't stupid and being thoroughly pissed-off might see my proposal as a means to get even with the other American while at the same time cutting their losses and possibly even making a handsome profit. If they did agree to take the Irwin back to St. Martin I'd have to figure out before they'd arrive how to get the Irwin's owners to withdraw the theft report with the French Gendarmes in Marigot so they wouldn't be arrested upon their return. But before I figured this out I'd need to convince the two that my proposal offered a quick way to get them out of their current predicament. If they agreed to the deal it would be under the condition that they would permanently get out of the boat stealing business.

To guarantee their holding to their part of bargain I'd insist on them providing me with copies of the photo pages of the passports ostensibly to use with the Gendarmes to use for clearing the Irwin and its crew back into St. Martin. Because of the time differences and being a weekend I wouldn't have time to contact the underwriter to get his approval, but considering a hull value of $250,000.00 felt reasonably confident that he wouldn't object to the double-cross to get the boat back for $10,000. I also thought about what other options Emilio and Francisco really had. Even if they had been promised more money to steal the Irwin they had actually received nothing and in fact were out of pocket because Emilio had paid the delivery crew he had hired out of his own money. I reasoned it was worth a try.

The next day it was a warm and clear Saturday morning. After breakfast I went to the Market in the town's square and bought some T-shirts for Jason and a leather pouch for myself. I then stopped at a small cantina to have a coffee and some Arepas, the tasty South American biscuit that's made from flour, fried in lard and contains probably 10,000 calories. It's been said that even one Arepa has enough cholesterol to bring down a sumo wrestler. After leaving the cantina and before a return visit to the Yacht Club to present Emilio with my proposal I decided to take another look at the Irwin. As the cab rounded the corner passing a small cluster of shacks that bordered the water I could see clouds of smoke rising in the windless sky near where the boat had been moored.

The area from where I had looked at the Irwin previously was now jammed with people. I told the cab driver to wait as I quickly hoofed it around a fire truck and through the crowd who were watching a boat that was burning about 300' from the shore. The boat had been cast off from the dock and was now ablaze in the center of the channel. Once the highly flammable resin had ignited the Irwin became totally engulfed in flames and burned almost to the water line. The main mast had fallen forward and appeared like a battering ram lying over what was left of the bow. The mizzen mast lay sideways partially in the water with the lower half caught in the charred remains of the boat. As I approached a dismayed looking man holding some fishing tackle turned towards me saying, "You know if the boat had been left alongside the bulkhead the fire service might have been able to put the fire out. Who ever threw off her lines probably didn't realize that the current would move the boat downwind to the center of the channel where the water hoses wouldn't reach." "Yeah, the guy who cast her off probably wasn't a sailor and didn't realize what he was doing." In the distance over a small fence in an empty lot further down the channel I saw the two Frenchmen standing with their arms crossed and for the first time both had a smile on their faces.

The following morning I was on the COPA flight to Panama on my way back to Puerto Rico. After breaking the news to the underwriter in Holland I called the Marina Royale in St. Martin and left a message

for the master of the *EVASION* to call me. A short time later Herve
called, "Ed, how did everything go did you find the boat?" "Well I
found the boat but things did not go too well." "What happened?
Did you find the crew? Did you find Emilio? Did he find out who you
were?" "Calm down Herve. I never met up with the crew but I did
find Emilio and Francisco, they never knew who I was or why I was
in Cartagena. They thought I was just a tourist. Over a beer Emilio
told me that after they had arrived in Cartagena he had paid off the
delivery crew and bought them return tickets to Sint Maarten out
of his own money because he expected to be paid by the American
who had left for Bogotá. Emilio and Francisco waited patiently for
two weeks then last Saturday, because they hadn't been paid they
torched the Irwin." "What! They burnt the boat!" "Sorry Herve,
there's nothing left." "Are you still going to pay me for helping you?"
"Pay you for what the remains of a burnt boat in Cartagena? Next
time before you get involved in the nasty business of stealing boats
call me first. Good-bye Herve."

After completing my report on the Irwin I then decided to see
what I might be able to do for my new friend Jose on Margarita Island
and called Jean-Claude a French narcotics agent assigned to the Joint
Task Force working out of the US Coast Guard base in San Juan.
"Bonjour my friend any good tips on the new vintages coming in to
Guadeloupe?" "Ed, it's been a while how have you been my friend,
still working in Venezuela?" "Yeah the beat goes on, everything is
fine and we're seeing good results from the training. Jean-Claude I
know your line is secure but I'm not as confident that mine is. There
are some interesting things happening that I'd like to tell you about,
but not over the phone. Are you planning to be on the Base sometime
soon?" "In fact I'll be out on Saturday to do a bit of shopping at the
Navy Exchange." Because of my concern with security in using the
telephone or being seen in public with government agents I never
discussed sensitive information on the telephone or met with any
of my contacts in law enforcement except when we could do so in
the safety of the Roosevelt Roads Naval Station. The Base offered
maximum security and could only be accessed by those persons
with government identification and who had been given security
clearances by the Navy or the Department of Defense. The Base
provided me with a secure feeling that whom ever I met with and

what we discussed would not be overheard or observed by the public as a whole. Outside meetings in restaurants or other public places and being seen with persons who might be identified as federal agents was always avoided as it might prove harmful to my health.

After making his way across the Food Court to the booths situated against the inner wall a smiling Jean-Claude sat down, "Hi Ed, sorry I'm a bit late but the traffic getting out of San Juan was murder. What is it you'd like to discuss?" "Jean-Claude, through my contacts within the Venezuelan Coastguard I've met someone who has some important information that he'd like to share but wants to receive some compensation in return." "Compensation, exactly what kind of compensation is he talking about?" "He knows that the US Customs Service will pay 10% of the street value of seized narcotics to informants who can supply the necessary intelligence that leads to a successful bust. In addition to a monetary payment he also wants to obtain the agreement of Customs that if everything works out as he says he wants resident alien status for him and his family in the United States. The reason I called you first is because some of his information also involves shipments of narcotics through Guadeloupe and Fort de France that end up in France."

Now listening intently the Frenchman took out a small black note book and began writing. "Tell me more." "For the moment let's call him Charlie. He was introduced to me by a friend who is also in the Venezuelan Coastguard. My friend is reliable and even more important he's trusted by Charlie. Charlie works for the DISIP, the Venezuelan Security Service, but on the side he provides cover for a Lebanese drug lord who has a thriving business sending narcotics to the United States and Europe. It was during my last visit to Venezuela that I was first introduced to Charlie. After he gave me a run-down on what he had to exchange for his *compensation* we drove around and he showed me where everything is coming down. He knows a lot and I think he's for real." "This sounds more than interesting but why did you call me shouldn't you have called Customs or the DEA first?" "Jean-Claude, they definitely would have an interest in what's being offered but as you know there's always a scramble and the inter-agency rivalry to contend with. Customs, DEA, and the Coast Guard are always fighting to insure their agency gets the credit and the publicity surrounding a high profile seizure to make sure when budget time comes around their agency gets the funding. Because of the shipments that are going to the French Departments in the Antilles and mainland France I though you'd be better for the first contact and if you were interested you could sort of be the lead in bringing the others into the act. I trust you; I don't really trust the others."

"Thanks Ed, you're a real friend. You're right if Customs or DEA come across something they first fight amongst themselves and then generally throw me a bone at the last minute or cut me out completely. Also you'll be interested to know that the Gendarmerie also has a program that will pay informants a reward for actionable information. The payment is not a percentage but a lump sum. I also have a friend in the DEA who I owe a favor to and I'm sure he'd be interested." I then provided Jean-Claude with an outline of the information that I had and we agreed to keep in touch.

Monday morning Jean-Claude called, "I've spoken with the pharmacist and both your prescriptions will be ready on Tuesday morning at 10:30 at the pharmacy on the Base. For identification you must bring your papers with you to collect the medications. Please contact me if this is not convenient. Good-bye." To insure that telephone calls made over an unsecured line if monitored would have little significance the message contained simple codes. The pharmacist was the Drug Enforcement Agency. The pharmacy was the aspirin and pill section immediately behind the cash registers and check-out area of the Exchange. The two prescriptions indicated two DEA agents. A single prescription would have meant for me to look for one DEA agent. The papers for identification would be a copy of the LLOYD'S LIST newspaper that I would carry in my right hand. While anyone else might be carrying a local paper or one of the other stateside newspapers no one on the Navy Base would have a copy of the Lloyd's List. Being a subscriber I received this London based shipping newspaper every week. I arrived at the exchange at 10:00 and moved through the tobacco section briefly looking at the pipe tobacco and cigars before meandering over to where the aspirin was located.

"Are you Ed Geary?" "Yes." "I'm Larry Compton and this is Bob Weaver – DEA." Moving into the seating section of the Food Court, Compton and I sat down while Weaver remained standing. "How do you take your coffee?" "A little cream and one Equal, thanks." While waiting for Agent Weaver, Compton got right to the point. "Our boss has spoken with Jean-Claude and we understand you might have some information that may be of interest to the Agency." Without revealing his name or location in Venezuela I gave the two DEA agents an outline of the information that could be made available and what the informant wanted in return." After taking a sip of his coffee Compton who appeared to be the senior of the two began, "Ed, the information sounds very intriguing. I feel confident it will be of great interest, but you must understand I'm not authorized to agree to anything at this point. You'll have to give us the full details so we can submit it through channels to see if the demands of the informant can be met. I think the biggest hurdle will be the resident alien status for the informant and his family, this might pose a problem. Also if there were a number of successful seizures the informant would have to appear in court and testify."

With annoying arrogance Compton recited the words as if he was reading from the 'Wannabe DEA Agent Lesson Plan 101' that may have been part of his recent curriculum at the Federal Law Enforcement Training Center in Georgia. This pompous and supercilious novice acted as if he was doing me a favor, not the other way around. I was angry but restrained myself while getting right to the heart of the matter, "First, let me make it abundantly clear, unless all the conditions are met which includes the payments for the information and Green Cards for the informant and his family there won't be any seizures. If he were to be put in the witness protection program I'm sure he'd be willing to appear in court but there's a bit of a problem as he wants to live in Florida. It would need to be cleared beforehand whether or not his relocation to Florida would be acceptable to the US Marshalls Service who administers the program. On the other hand being Hispanic he and his family would go unnoticed and better assimilate in Florida instead of someplace like Iowa. But if you weren't willing to get him a new identity I can't believe that you would even ask that he agree to testify in court because it would never happen, you might as well ask him to commit suicide; you guys have been watching too many 'B' movies. Thanks gentlemen, this has been a total waste of my time." I got up and left. From a pay phone outside the Exchange I called Jean-Claude. "What a couple of clowns. These guys haven't got a clue as to what's going on in the real world. Jean-Claude maybe you should speak to someone at Customs to see if they might be interested because as usual the DEA is hopelessly lost in never-never land."

Two days later I received another coded call from Jean-Claude to confirm a meeting with US Customs; except this time it was the shipping company that had my order which was to be collected in the uniforms department of the Exchange. I met with a senior Customs agent (who was subsequently promoted to an important job in Washington) and laid out the whole program. Two weeks later we met again on the Base during which time the Customs agent confirmed that everything was a go. On my next visit to Margarita Island I met Javier and Jose; over dinner I gave Jose the details of my meeting with US Customs who said they would be in touch with him. Considering the danger of exposure I suggested that unless there was a problem Jose and I should not meet again. Jean-Claude and I met on the Base for lunch a few weeks later when I learned that Charlie had proven to be a valuable and reliable resource. Jose and I never spoke again but just before the holidays in 1994 I received a Christmas card with no return address and a postmark from Sarasota, Florida. Inside the card below the Merry Christmas greeting was a handwritten note, 'Mi amigo gracious por su ayuda'[35] it was signed *Pedro y Familia* and written below in parenthesis (Charlie). Folded neatly inside the envelope was a newspaper clipping from the Miami Herald newspaper. The story headline read; TIP LEADS TO CUSTOMS SEIZURE OF COCAINE WITH A STREET VALUE OF $30M.

"Jason, I'm going back to Venezuela on Wednesday, do you want to come along? The commandant has invited me to a naval graduation ceremony at the Circulo Militar in Caracas, no training, no work only a bit of play, it should be fun." "No, thanks Dad I've got a Spanish test coming up on Wednesday and I can't miss it, but if you will please bring me back a couple of the GUARDACOSTAS T-shirts." As always Goschenko was waiting for me at Maiquetia when I arrived. "Ed, I really appreciate your coming down for this graduation ceremony everyone is looking forward to your attending. I'm not supposed to tell you but the Picua group is going to present you with an engraved wall plaque to show their appreciation for the training. I'm sorry that

---

35 My friend, many thanks for your help

I won't be able to see you tonight because my wife has something planned for me to do, but I'll pick you up in the morning at 8:00. After what happened last month at the Eurobuilding I think you're wise staying at the Tamanaco Hotel." Goschenko dropped me off and after checking in I decided to take a swim in the hotel's expansive pool.

After a great dinner I decided to take a walk over to Las Mercedes shopping mall and browse the expansive number of shops. After picking up my pipe and tobacco from the room I went through the lobby and walked down the hotel's entrance road. Not far from the Eurobuilding hotel the Tamanaco hotel's entrance road also leads to the main boulevard of Las Mercedes which is situated below an overhead freeway. The entrance road is bordered on both sides by flowers, well manicured gardens, and lawns and is no more that a few hundred yards in length. When I was only a short distance from the intersection with Las Mercedes Boulevard a single shot rang out ricocheting off the concrete walkway in front of me. I thought to myself, oh shit not again. However, this time I was not completely alone as a taxi was just entering the hotel's entrance road from Las Mercedes.

For cover I quickly ran to the side of the cab and while simultaneously pulling open the rear door jumped in. "Please take me to the Tamanaco Hotel." "But mister you're at the Tamanaco Hotel." "Okay, take me to the reception." I gave the cabbie $10.00 for the one minute ride which clearly made his day. Once inside the safety of the hotel I asked to speak with the manager that was on duty. A Mr. Contreras soon emerged advising that he was the assistant manager and could he be of assistance. "Mr. Contreras, I was just walking down the hotel's entrance road leading to Las Mercedes when someone fired a shot at me. I didn't see the person but at the angle that the bullet hit the pavement the shot was fired from the hillside parking area to my left going towards Las Mercedes." Pulling a hand-held radio from his pocket Contreras summoned the head of the hotel's security office. A moment later the security chief appeared. "Take one of your men and immediately search the grounds along the entrance road. Someone has just fired a gun at this gentleman and who ever did this may still be on the property." With that the security chief while speaking on his radio, quickly disappeared out the front door of the hotel. Contreras turned to me, "Are you a guest in the hotel?" "Yes, the name is G-E-

A-R-Y and I'm in room 517." "I'm truly sorry about this and on behalf of the management do apologize for this terrible experience. As you know Caracas is a terribly violent city and many people have guns."

I thought to myself, Holy Christ here we go again another sermon about the crime, killings and whatever. "Mr. Contreras, I know that Caracas is violent which is why I don't wander around the city alone and stay in a hotel that I believe would and should have proper security. I strongly object to being shot at while I'm on the property of an upscale hotel that should have security personnel looking after guests who walk around the grounds." "Yes, but...." "Please Mr. Contreras let's not waste anymore time, while your security people look around could you please call the police, I want to file a report." "Yes, of course." Two police officers showed up about a half hour later and after first speaking with the hotels' security chief I told the police officers about the previous incident at the Eurobuilding Hotel. They took little interest in the Eurobuilding shooting saying that sometimes these things just happen. The complacent remarks by the police did nothing to raise my comfort level.

Once they had taken my statement and passport number they suggested that I report the matter to the American Embassy just in case something might happen to me. Considering my problems with Joseph Velling and the CIA mission at the Embassy who may have actually been responsible for the shootings the suggestion to report the matter to the embassy wasn't very helpful in putting my mind at ease. I returned to my room and decided to take a bath which I though might be relaxing, but not before closing the drapes and propping a chair under the door handle. Half in jest I thought that maybe if the assassin couldn't shoot me they might try an Alfred Hitchcock *Psycho* approach and cut me up in the shower or if that failed try to drown me in the bathtub. After settling into bed I turned on the television to see what was happening in the rest of the world when the phone rang. "Don't be stupid consider the offer that's on the table it's still not too late. Maybe the next time we won't miss." With that the line went dead as the unidentified caller hung up the phone. Now isn't that a sweet touch, I refuse to act as a spy for the CIA and now they are either trying to kill me or scare me to death. In either case they did get my attention and clearly I'd need to be extremely careful. No more walks alone and no more leaving the hotel based on anonymous phone messages.

After the Tamanaco incident I began staying at the Caracas Hilton, located in center of the city, which has a small garden area adjacent to the hotel's pool but no exposed entrance roads. While admittedly I didn't get shot at my stays at the Caracas Hilton brought on new challenges. The first fun and games came about when late one evening there was a knock on the door which upon opening I found a gorgeous olive skinned beauty in shorts and a halter top holding a gym bag. Before I could say a word she had pushed open the door and entered the room. Without hesitating she reached for my private parts saying, "I'm here to make you happy." Quickly regaining my senses, "Thanks, but I'm already happy so please leave." "I can..." "No you can't, out." Grabbing the lady-of-the-night by the arm I forced her and her gym bag through the open door slamming it shut in the process. This scenario at the Caracas Hilton happened on two subsequent occasions. The only difference on the other occasions was late at night when pretty ladies knocked on my door, I didn't open it. I reported the incursions to the hotel management who apologized and said they would deal with the problem – yeah right.

"Thanks for the T-shirts Dad they're really great, how was the trip?" "It was okay, the graduation ceremony was very nice and the group gave me a plaque in appreciation of the training, looks nice doesn't it?" "Another plaque; you know if you keep receiving all this stuff from the Venezuelan's we're going to need to get a bigger condo with more wall space. Oh before I forget, I came back to our place before going to school this morning to get some books and while I was here some guy called from Germany to talk to you about some stolen boats. I told him you were in Venezuela but would be coming back today; he said he'd call you back."

As the sun began disappearing on the horizon and the hands of the clock moved closer to 6:15 it was fast approaching the time when I was to assume my role as chief cook, "What do you want for dinner? I could grill some Dorado or Snapper or would you prefer pasta?" "Hey Dad you make the best spaghetti sauce in the world, let's have the pasta." After dinner and when the dishes were done we played chess with the usual results of Jason knocking off my royalty before my pawns could barely come into play. The rest of the week was fairly quiet which allowed me to complete a number of casualty reports for underwriters, get the Porsche serviced, and attend a meeting of the Parent Teachers Association at Jason's school. I was worried about the fallout from refusing to spy for the CIA but as I was committed I intended to remain focused on the training program in Venezuela.

SEVEN

Having been discharged by Washington (terminated sounds much too final) I had no further contact with the US Coast Guard attaché in Caracas or with Coast Guard headquarters in Washington. Under the auspices of the Venezuelan Navy the training of the Coastguard continued uninterrupted. In early January 1994 I was contacted by Eri Lopez-Spies a German now Venezuelan member of the Tiburon Auxiliary Group on Margarita Island. "Hello my friend how's everything; did you and Jason enjoy your Christmas?" "Yes thanks, Christmas was great and Santa Claus was very good to Jason how about you and Beatrice?" "We had some great weather so we took the boat out and did a bit of sailing. Spent a few days in Cumana and Puerto La Cruz and had a good relaxing time. Ed, the reason I'm calling is that we've got 15 new members who need to receive basic training, would it be possible for you to do some training sometime in January?" "No problem. I have to be in Caracas on the 12ᵗʰ and the week before I've got a ship inspection to do in Mexico. Once I arrange the flights I'll send you a fax with the details. Can I ask a favor? Once you have the dates I'd appreciate if you would book me a room at the Margarita Hilton at the military rate."

Arriving in Margarita in the middle part of January I was met at the airport by Eri, Javier, and Pablo de Castaneda the newly appointed commander of the group along with two of the new members. "If it's ok we'll stop by the hotel to check you in and then go out to the Coastguard Command Center so you can meet the lieutenant who has recently been promoted and is now the commanding officer in charge of the regulars." The Coastguard's base of operations or command center was actually a 40' shipping container that had been converted to an office and refurbished by auxiliary volunteers. A door had been installed on one side with a number of windows fitted around the container's perimeter. Javier had designed the interior and provided some desks, chairs, and tables from his interior design studio. Jorge Santana who owned a shop that sold and repaired marine electronics wired the command center and installed a VHF-FM radio and antenna. Once the alterations had been completed an auxiliary member who was a painting contractor had his crew apply a fresh coat of the blue and gray coastguard colors.

"Lieutenant Gomez, I would like to introduce Captain Ed Geary. Captain Geary is the officer responsible for the training of the auxiliary groups throughout the country." "Captain, it's a pleasure to have the opportunity to meet you in person, I've heard many good things about you from my colleagues." Lieutenant Gomez, a graduate of the Naval Academy was an excellent example of the new breed of well trained and enthusiastic naval officers that was emerging under the command and leadership of Briceño Garcia. Standing and moving towards a large chart mounted on the wall Gomez said, "Captain, if possible I'd like to begin the on-the-water training here in the area near Pampatar and would appreciate if three of my sailors can be included. When would it be possible for us to begin?" "How about 0800 tomorrow morning, I have some personal matters that I'd like to do this afternoon." Gomez smiled, shook my hand and ended the conversation with, "0800 will be fine." After leaving the command center I pulled Javier aside and quietly said, "Javier, I want to rent a car and take a drive out to Juangriego just to have a look around to see what's going on in the Arab community. So as not to attract any attention I don't want to be with you or go in your Bronco. I won't be long, so when I get back let's plan to meet at the Blue Topaz in about two hours." Javier, understanding my interest in Juangriego and the Arabs smiled, "That's fine I'll see you later."

After picking up a rental car I drove to the other side of the island and Juangriego. In driving by their T-shirt shop there was no sign of Hassan or Abbas amongst a half dozen Arabs congregating around the shops entrance. A few minutes later in passing the warehouse of VENEZ Import-Export I observed Hassan standing next to the open drivers' door of his Mercedes yelling instructions to someone inside the warehouse. Abbas was placing a large box with the letters KOTEX printed on the sides into the trunk of the Car. Joking with myself as I drove away I laughed thinking could Hassan and Abbas also be in the business of smuggling women's sanitary napkins? Later while driving down the main street of Porlamar, which because of its upscale shops has been nicknamed the Rodeo Drive of Margarita by the well traveled Venezuelan elite, I noticed a glassware shop that had large signs announcing its annual clearance sale.

Having the need for a set of champagne flutes and as the shop was only a block away from the Blue Topaz I pulled into an open parking space deciding to take a look at what they had to offer. Rather than carrying it into the shop I put my briefcase in the trunk and locked the car. I was pleased with myself when I was able to purchase a set of duty free Waterford Crystal glassware at half price. Returning to the car I unlocked the trunk to put the glassware inside when my heart started pounding – my briefcase was gone. I quickly looked around but other than what appeared to be normal people going about their business there was no one that looked suspicious or who was carrying a tan Samsonite briefcase. Just at that moment I turned to see Javier walking along the boulevard from the direction of the Blue Topaz which was only a short distance away. "Hi Ed, how was your visit to Juangriego?" "Javier, someone has broken into the rental car and now my briefcase is gone. Can we quickly drive around the area in case the thief might still be around? Fortunately I had my wallet, passport, and air tickets in a fanny pack around my waist, but the briefcase contained documents, some sensitive reports and letters to Briceño Garcia, my camera, agenda, and a number of training files." "My car is just around the corner, let's go." After driving around the area for about twenty minutes we found nothing and proceeded to the police station to file a report.

"No, there was no sign of forcible entry. There were no windows broken and the trunk hadn't been pried open." As I relayed the circumstances of the theft the desk sergeant penned in the details of his report repeatedly questioning me on how the briefcase could have been stolen without something being broken or any signs of the trunk being forced. "Sergeant, when I left the car all four doors and the trunk were locked. I was in the shop for no more than twenty minutes and the car was parked on the main street. I can't tell you who or why but my briefcase is gone and I'd really like to get it back." Once he had completed the report he called another officer and had him put out a radio alert to the patrol cars in the area to keep an eye out for the briefcase or any of the known thieves they had a file on. "Captain, I'm sorry this happened but theft is a growing problem on Margarita. You lost your briefcase but many times these thieves take the whole car, you should consider yourself lucky." "Thanks sergeant, that's very comforting, my briefcase and all its contents are stolen in broad daylight on the town's main street and you tell me I'm lucky." "I'm sorry you feel that way Captain. If we find your briefcase I'll contact you at the Hilton." "Javier, I'm ready for a drink." With that we drove back to the Blue Topaz where we promptly ordered two Polar beers. Javier putting his hand on my shoulder, "Ed, I really feel bad this has happened to you. But I don't think it was simply a petty theft, it's just too smooth. The kids that break into cars look on the seats inside, if they see something they smash a window, grab whatever it is and run. With no broken windows and no marks to indicate the trunk had been forced opened; I think whoever took your briefcase had a *jimmy tool* or a key to the car. And my money would be on a key so as not to attract any attention on the main street." "But how would they get a key?" Javier smiled, "If someone was watching you and wanted what you had in your briefcase $10.00 would buy a duplicate key from a friend inside the car rental agency. The thieves would follow you in hopes that you'd leave the car with the briefcase and anything else of value in the car. You accommodated them and now they have your briefcase."

The list of those who may have any interest in the contents of my briefcase was very short; the list could be limited to the US Coast Guard, the CIA and its agent Joseph J. Velling. Having started very early in the morning to travel from San Juan to Maiquetia then on to Margarita on top of having my briefcase stolen I decided it best to decline Javier's offer of joining him for dinner. Dropping me at the front of the Hilton and before leaving Javier was his ever gracious self, "Ed, I'm really sorry about today but have a nice dinner, a bottle of wine and get a good night's sleep. I'll pick you up at 0800 in the morning." When I got to my room I was mentally exhausted, I took a bath put on a robe and fell asleep while watching the Evening News. The theft of my briefcase bothered me but what was more troubling was the thought of being followed. Waking a short time later I concluded that dressing and having to go down to the restaurant was just too much. I decided to order dinner from room service.

"This is Captain Geary in room 314. I'd like to order a tossed green salad with oil and vinegar, the grilled New York sirloin medium please, and a baked potato. Please also let me have a bottle of mineral water and a small bottle of the Cabernet Sauvignon, no. 22 on the wine list. Oh and please add a little extra butter for the potato." "Thank you sir, your order will be delivered to your room in about 30 minutes." Having dozed off I was awoken a short time later by the knock on the door. In opening the door a uniformed waiter tray in hand entered the room, "Please set the tray on the table near the window." After I signed the bill the waiter left. The wine was excellent but after eating the salad, half of the steak and only a few bites of the baked potato I began experiencing severe stomach pains. I sat down on the bed and don't remember anything until I heard the loud ringing of the telephone. I felt terrible. In rolling over in bed I saw that it was light outside and the clock read 8:15. "Ed this is Javier, are you alright? I've been downstairs with Moncho and Gozo since 7:30 we were concerned when you didn't come down, is everything okay?" "Javier, I don't know what the problem is but I feel awful." "Stay put we'll be right up."

Moncho was Francisco Mendez who as well as being an auxiliarist from Grupo Tiburon was also a medical doctor who regularly attended guests at the Hilton and the other upscale hotels in Margarita. Benny Nieves known by his nickname Gozo, a local fisherman had been a member of the Margarita auxiliary unit for the last two years. A few minutes later the door swung open and Javier entered the room followed by Moncho and Gozo. "After what happened yesterday I don't think it's a good idea to leave your door unlocked," said Javier clearly upset. After looking at me in a bathrobe in the prone position on the bed Moncho turning to Javier said, "Javier, I'm going downstairs to get my bag out of the car." Gozo remained standing while Javier sat on the edge of the bed, "Ed, you look terrible." "Thanks, at least now I know that I look as bad as I feel." Returning a short time later Moncho inserted a thermometer under my tongue, while pulling out his stethoscope and placing the cold instrument on my chest, He said, "Take a deep breath. What did you have for dinner last night?" "I had a salad, a piece of steak, some baked potato, and a little wine. Room service brought the meal to my room about 8:30 last night." Moncho looked around the room and said, "Where's the tray?" Raising my arm to point to the table near the window, "It's on the table...... it's gone!" "I asked the waiter to put it on the table near the window and I left it there after finishing the meal." "If that's all you had to eat maybe there was something in the food that made you sick."

Moncho picking up the room's telephone, "This is Dr. Francisco Mendez, please connect me with Paco." Paco, a friend of Dr. Mendez, I soon learned was the Hilton's manager of food and beverage. "Paco, this is Moncho I'm in room 314 with Captain Geary a guest, can you please come to the room right away." Moments later a worried food and beverage manager knocked and entered through the partially open door. "Moncho, is there a problem?" "Paco, last night about 8:30 Captain Geary had dinner delivered to his room and after he had eaten the meal became very ill. What I want to know is who prepared the meal and the name of the waiter who brought the meal to the room. I also have a problem with finding that without Captain Geary's knowledge someone entered the room during the night and removed the tray with the remaining food. The person who removed the tray then left without fully closing and locking the door." The now trembling food and beverage manager wiping his brow apologetically offered, "I'm truly sorry for this, I don't know what happened but assure you I will find out. We have had no reports of guests becoming ill after eating and no one should have entered the room without first seeking the guest's approval. This is highly irregular." "Paco, please get on to this right away I need some answers immediately." With that the food and beverage manager quickly left the room. Closing his bag Moncho looked at me, "Ed, it's possible the salad ingredients weren't cleaned correctly or maybe the meat wasn't properly cooked. I'd suggest you drink a lot of liquids and get some rest. If you need to contact me call the front desk to let them know and I'll come right over."

"Javier, I really do feel dreadful and need to recover before starting the training. Can we reschedule for tomorrow?" "Sure Ed, no problem. Is there anything we can do for you now?" "No, I'll be alright I just need to sleep for a while. Maybe we can meet for dinner later?" Javier turning to leave, "Sure, I'll give you a call at seven." Punctual as ever which is unusual for a Latino, Javier was on the phone exactly at seven, "Hey amigo how do you feel, ready for some dinner?" "A little better but still a bit weak in the knees, I'll be down in 5 minutes."

When I entered the restaurant I found Javier sitting at a corner table with a waitress waiting to take his order. Ordering a churrasco, well done and baked potato he turned to me, "How about you my friend, the churrasco steak is excellent here?" "You know Javier after having had meat last night, I think I'll pass." I opted instead for a bowl of consommé and a large bottle of water *con gas* hoping it might help reduce my still rumbling stomach.

"Moncho, Moncho, over here." Javier now standing was beckoning to Dr. Mendez who had just entered the restaurant. "Good evening, how's the patient doing, feeling a bit better?" "Hi doctor, glad to see you, thanks for taking a look at me this morning. I do feel a lot better but my stomach is still messed up and I have a bad case of diarrhea. For dinner I'm having a little soup and mineral water." "That's a good idea, drinking a lot of liquids will help your recovery. What ever you had must have been quite bad. I've spoken again with Paco, the cook that prepared your meal and the waiter who brought it to the room. I also took two steaks that were in the same package as the one you had last night and had a chemist at the hospital check the steaks for contamination. After the tests he reported the meat was Okay. No one else reported being ill after dinner last night and the only medical calls I had yesterday from the Hilton involved a guest that had fallen at the pool and another who had left her prescription medicine in Caracas." "Moncho, have you any idea who took the tray out of my room?" "Oh yes, I did follow up with this. I checked with room service and house-keeping. The house-keeping supervisor said that a chambermaid was doing the evening turn-down and putting chocolates on the pillows on the 3rd floor which is the concierge level and when she came to your room she said that the door wasn't closed. She said except for the light from the hallway upon entering the room it was completely dark. She saw the tray and decided to remove it, but at first hadn't noticed you in the bed. Because she had entered the room without knocking and hadn't seen you until she was leaving with the tray she was frightened that she might lose her job so she left without fully closing the door which may have woken you up. It clearly wasn't the right thing to do and she has been reprimanded, but it sounds plausible." Taking a sip of the carbonated water, "Moncho, I appreciate what you've done but right now nothing seems plausible. I hope it's just a case of some bad food but because of what happened to me in Caracas I hope it wasn't a case of someone trying to poison me. Maybe it sounds plausible, but what happened seems implausible; I am given tainted food, someone enters my room when the door is locked, then a chambermaid says she removes the tray with the remaining food and then leaves my door open, it just doesn't sound like a coincidence.

Considering what happened last night I think it's important that you know what's been happening to me in the last number of weeks. What occurred last night might just be another episode in a scheme by the CIA to either scare the hell out of me or maybe kill me." I then told Moncho and Javier of the shootings in Caracas and the attempt to run the lieutenant's car off the road while driving to Valencia.

"In November last year I was approached by a CIA agent from the US Embassy in Caracas who wanted me to become a spy and engage in espionage against the Venezuelan military. Because of our close relationship the CIA was particularly interested in Briceño Garcia. When I refused the US Coast Guard discharged me and as of December 31st stopped supporting the Venezuelan training program. As part of the intimidation and a vicious campaign against me I think the CIA is clearly trying to send me a message." Turning a bit pale Javier asked, "Does headquarters and Briceño know about this?" "Yes, even though the US Coast Guard has dropped me Briceño has asked that I continue the program under his command. You may think what happened last night sounds plausible, but I don't think so." Putting his hand on my shoulder, Moncho first glancing around the room then looked at me, "This is incredible, the United States is supposed to be our friend, you are our friend who has worked hard for the Navy and the Coastguard and now they try to maybe kill you because you won't become a spy, so much for good neighbors. What are you going to do?" "There's no question that I'll have to be very careful. I've written to a number of people in Washington and told them of what the CIA is up to in hopes that the termination of the Venezuelan Initiative can be reversed but in the meantime with Briceño's blessing I plan to continue the training." Between January 1994 and early February 1995 the training did continue but at a reduced level.

"Hey dad it's really great to have you back, how was Margarita did you see Jenetta?" "Yeah, it was an interesting trip and a lot happened. I didn't see Jenetta or Hector but did have a meeting with Briceño who sends you his regards. I told him about what the CIA asked me to do and when I refused that the US Coast Guard discharged me. He was surprised and disappointed to learn of what had happened but told me not to worry. Briceño wants me to continue the program and reminded me that I'm still a Captain in his command."

I had told Jason about the CIA's plan to destabilize the government in Caracas, but so as not to unnecessarily worry him, hadn't said anything about the recent attempts on my life. "Dad, something strange happened yesterday. After school I came back to Villa Marina to pick up some books I needed for my homework assignment and saw this guy walking down the second floor steps in front of our door. It looked like he may have come from our apartment. When we passed each other I was looking at him but he looked away and wouldn't make eye contact. About an hour later just before Lucy picked me up I was looking out the front window and saw a gray four-door sedan with two guys inside parked across the street under the big Banyan tree along the marina's fence. It was strange because the guy in the driver's seat was the same person I had seen on the steps, another guy was sitting in the back seat. When Lucy came to pick me up I went downstairs and the car was gone. " Just to be sure it wasn't my friend Joe Velling I asked Jason, "What did the guy look like that you saw coming down the steps?" "He was short; I guess about 5'2" and heavy set. He had short black hair like a GI crew cut, short sleeve shirt, and a tie. I didn't speak to him and I'm not sure if he was a Puerto Rican but he was definitively a Latino."

The man Jason saw being short, having dark hair and somewhat overweight was not the non-descript pale face Velling. A few days later the duo in the gray sedan appeared again parked under the Banyan tree which is directly across the street from our apartment. For a number of weeks the men and surveillance cars changed, but all continued to park under the Banyan tree so as to have an unobstructed view of our condominium.

In view of what I though would be only a temporary set back in the training, in the early part of 1994 I turned my thoughts to another Venezuelan assignment that I had been working on but wasn't pressing for my attention. The case involved a $250,000.00 yacht that had been stolen previously in Sint Maarten. A short time after the yacht had disappeared she was sighted on the Dutch island of

Curacao then later turned up in Venezuela. In monitoring the vessel's whereabouts after she left Curacao she made a number of port calls to different marinas along Venezuela's Caribbean coast. I followed the yachts movements but each time I was ready to move in and recover her I'd find that she'd left, sometimes only hours before. The cat and mouse chase went on for a number of weeks. I was soon to learn that I was not the only person with an interest in the yacht. In Venezuela when a vessel moves from port to port she is obliged to clear-in and clear-out. From the clearance papers obtained from the port authorities we learned that the people on board included a number of Europeans. In checking the names through INTERPOL we found that all were fugitives and at least one was identified as a member of a Russian crime group. Nicknaming the file The French Connection II it was an interesting case that would soon come to involve a lot of legwork, investigative research and a bit of luck. The case had all the ingredients of a good mystery novel. It also at least temporarily, took my mind off of what was happening with the CIA.

Soon after pin-pointing the location of the stolen yacht at the Macuto Sheraton marina in Venezuela and learning that she had paid for a months dockage, I placed her under 24 hour surveillance with the assistance of fellow officers of the Venezuelan Coastguard. I later had a bit of a laugh when I found that my Coastguard surveillance team was being watched by French narcotics agents operating out of the French embassy in Caracas. I learned of the French surveillance after receiving a call from a friend, Jacques Deauville, who was police commissioner and head of the French narcotics task force in Venezuela. The information from the gendarmerie indicated that the people on board were using the vessel for what they believed would be a secure location and control point in a clever distribution plan involving a large consignment of Colombian cocaine that was to be delivered by ship to Europe through West Africa. After some small talk Jacques got right to the point of his call, "Ed, my men have the yacht under surveillance and reported to me that you have people watching the yacht as well. I learned of your involvement in the case after it had been stolen in Sint Maarten. Knowing how you work I assume you're just waiting for the right opportunity to pounce and recover her for the insurance company. I would like to meet with you as soon as possible but ask that you please do not do anything until we can discuss the situation. When will you next be in Caracas and be able to meet with me at the French embassy? If you'll let me know when and what flight you will arrive on I'll send a car and driver to meet you at Maiquetia."

The next day I booked the flight and called Caracas, "Hi Jacques, I'll be arriving tomorrow on the afternoon American Airlines flight." "That's fine I'll send a car and driver to meet you." The short flight of just over an hour was made even better when American Airlines upgraded me to first class. Jacques' driver was there to meet me and 45 minutes later I was having coffee at the Embassy with the charismatic French cop. "Ed, I do appreciate your being able to come so quickly. Let me give you a bit of the background and tell you why this case is so very important to the French government. My people in the Gendarmerie in Saint Martin confirmed that the yacht was stolen and that you were involved in its recovery. Because of its value I also know you want it back. As the owner and his wife had returned to the States and weren't expected back until the fall the targets didn't expect the theft to be reported quite so soon. Our targets had the yacht stolen by two petty thieves that were known to hang around the Marina Royale in Marigot; after they took the boat they delivered her to Cartagena. The focus of our investigation is on a multi-national group of French, Italian, German, and Russians who are involved with one of the major European crime syndicates; they're using the yacht for what they believe is a safe refuge while finalizing a plan to orchestrate the movement of a large consignment of cocaine from Cartagena, Columbia. They aren't aware that we have had them under surveillance for a number of weeks monitoring all their telephone and high frequency radio calls. Our surveillance started even before they left Cartagena. From the radio intercepts we know that a Honduran flagged freighter is to rendezvous with a Russian cargo ship that is presently at anchor in Pampatar on Isla Margarita. The problem we have is that at the moment we haven't been able to determine exactly when the rendezvous is scheduled to take place. INTERPOL has sent us the reports on the Russian, German, and Italian nationals on the yacht who have warrants outstanding for drug trafficking. In the case of the Frenchmen onboard we have warrants outstanding in France not only for trafficking, but also for murder. At the moment we are just waiting for the information as to when the transfer is to take place between the ships. We are also waiting for the Warrant from Paris for a French woman who we learned joined the others when the yacht arrived at the Macuto Sheraton.

My government has spent a great deal of money on the case which will be lost if you were to shall I say, 'prematurely' recover the yacht. Needless to say those on board are not a nice bunch." "Jacques, I really want to help but I simply can't take the risk of losing this high value yacht, the insurers want it back undamaged and as soon as possible. But to help you out maybe we can make a deal. Let's say that if I were to agree to pull back my surveillance team and delay seizing the boat would you be willing to continue the 24/7 surveillance but with a little something extra? This is what I have in mind. As part of your surveillance I would ask that you covertly place a satellite tracking device somewhere on the hull which is to be constantly monitored. You confirm to me every 24 hours that the vessel hasn't moved, but if for any reason the vessel does move from the Macuto Sheraton you would agree to immediately call me so I could have the naval authorities detain the vessel. I simply can't take the chance that she would leave the jurisdiction of Venezuelan waters; particularly if she would sail eastward to the Atlantic." Rising from his chair Jacques extended his hand, "You've got a deal."

Everything went as planned until a week later when I received a call from Jacques saying the yacht had unexpectedly left the Macuto Sheraton and was sailing east on a course towards Isla Margarita. The following day I was on a plane to Venezuela. In a penthouse overlooking the harbor in Pampatar the French had set up a command post with long range listening devices allowing us to overhear every conversation inside the yacht down to the flushing of the toilet in the aft cabin. When the occupants sat in the cockpit they were repeatedly photographed through high definition telephoto lenses with such clarity that you could see the individual tattoos on the left arm of the Russian. To record and decipher the conversations Jacques had agents on duty who in addition to French were fluent in English, Russian, Italian, and German.

The moment Jacques received confirmation that the arrangements had been finalized for the transfer of the cocaine between the ships, now anchored offshore he was ready to pounce on his prey. Removing his eyes from the telescope Jacques looked at me saying, "Ed, what do you think of our penthouse pretty nice huh?" Then quickly rotating the telescope to me, "Here, watch closely they've started to move. The navy boats have closed the loop around the yacht and our people are now on board. They're in the process of moving the bad characters up to the bow. Having them in custody has really made my day. Ed, I really appreciate your working with us, this wouldn't have happened had you not been willing to help." "No problem Jacques. Hey, we've got a common interest in getting the bad guys, I just hope when the underwriters find out that they loaned their $250,000 yacht to the Gendarmerie for a drug bust they're not too upset. At least there aren't any bullet holes to fill." Jacques now speaking into his hand held VHF radio, "Omega Seven, Omega Seven this Alpha One please report." "Alpha One this is Omega Seven. Targets in custody, Victor November (Venezuelan Navy) has boarded both Sputnik (Russian ship) and Roatàn (Honduras ship) – full compliment (the officers and crews of both ships) in custody. Toulon was quiet. (No shots were fired) The powder is safe (Cocaine seized). The radio message from French narcotics agent Omega Seven confirmed that simultaneously with the boarding of the yacht heavily armed officers and sailors of the Venezuelan Navy had boarded the Russian and Honduran ships that were anchored offshore before the first kilo of cocaine had been transferred. I later asked Jacques why they used the name *Toulon* to indicate that no shots had been fired. "Because my American friend, Toulon with exception of a few drunken sailors from time to time is generally a quite place because it's where ships of the French Navy are based." The entire operation took less than an hour without the use of firearms and with no one being injured in the boarding's. We celebrated that night like only the French know how. The following month I received a letter of commendation on the letterhead of the

AMBASSADE DE FRANCE AU VENEZUELA
SERVICE COOPERATION TECHNIQUE
INTERNATIONALE DE POLICE

thanking me for the joint cooperative efforts that lead to the seizure of a shipload of narcotics and the arrest of the traffickers.

After returning from Venezuela the fax on the top of the important stuff on my desk immediately caught my attention. It was from Geert Halvorsteen an underwriter with one of the large insurance groups in Holland. "Ed, Nelly told me that you would be returning tomorrow;

I would appreciate if you could call me on my private number ASAP in the morning. I have a problem in Suriname, our former beloved colony."

"Good morning Geert, what's up?" "Ed, thanks for calling. Would you be able to take a couple of days off from your Venezuelan training to help me with a little problem I have? How good are your contacts in Suriname and how soon could you get to Paramaribo?" "I've got some reliable contacts in the marine community and my attorney, Myles Tralins is the lawyer for the Surinamese government in the United States. Why, what's the problem?" "Three days ago one of our German assureds had one of his bulkers[36] arrested in Paramaribo for allegedly carrying drugs. Under a charter agreement the ship had sailed in-ballast[37] from Barranquilla, Colombia to load aggregate in Suriname that was to be delivered to George Town in the Cayman Islands. After being loaded in Suriname the ship was boarded by the local police who arrested the master for drug smuggling. The first officer was left in charge and told that the ship couldn't leave. After a thorough search by the local police and the US Coast Guard which included the unloading of the cargo the authorities who couldn't find any drugs now plan to start cutting up the ship to find where they think the drugs might be hidden. The Ukrainian master swears there are no drugs on his ship; after he was arrested they put him in a god-awful jail. The first officer is trying to stop the authorities from cutting up the ship and a lawyer we retained through a reference from the local Ship's Agent hasn't done a thing. Can you help us?" "How soon can you fax me the paperwork?" "There's really not much more than what I've just told you. The lawyer that's supposed to be working on our behalf hasn't sent us anything, but I'll send over everything I've got the moment I put the phone down." I thought to myself, hmm, German ship coming from Colombia, transiting the coast of Venezuela and supposedly taking aggregates to the Cayman Islands; I wonder if this was one of the ships on the CIA's protected list. Could it be that the CIA hadn't paid or not paid enough and their Surinamese *collaborators* had tipped-off the authorities in Paramaribo? If this was the case maybe the CIA's cohorts were sending a subtle message – don't mess with us. On the other hand I wondered if the German

---

36 A ship employed exclusively in carriage of bulk cargoes
37 Empty

ship might somehow be involved with the Arabs in Juangriego on Margarita. Interesting…

One of the problems with Suriname and they have many, is that Suriname Airways has only one plane since the other one crashed, which limits their service to the country to only one flight a week from Miami; the one weekly flight, if it actually flies is generally full. My only option appeared to be a bit of networking and creative thinking with my dear friend who also happened to be my lawyer Myles Tralins in Miami. "Good morning Myles, I need a little help. Dutch insurers' have a problem with a ship that's been arrested in Paramaribo and they have asked me to try and sort out the mess. I called Suriname Airways and it seems that all their flights for the next two weeks are fully booked. They also told me I must have a current Visa." Taking me off his speaker phone, "Ed, I have Suriname's ambassador staying with Janet and I this weekend and later this morning I'll be speaking with him to find out what time he'll be arriving in Miami on the flight from Washington. Let me have the name of the ship and I'll have the ambassador look into the matter and find out what the status is. Call me back after lunch."

Having told Myles the substance of my conversation with Geert and the particulars about the ship and the master who had been jailed I was hoping that he might be able to provide the influence and the help needed. About 2:30 I called Myles's office, "Hi Myles, any luck?" In his usual matter-of-fact manner he responded, "Ed, it seems that the local police in Paramaribo received an anonymous tip that your ship was transporting a substantial consignment of narcotics so the acting chief of police had the vessel arrested. The local police searched the vessel but found nothing so they called the American Embassy and asked if the US Coast Guard could send down a team from Miami to do a search with their drug-sniffing dogs. The Coast Guard flew in a team on a Hercules 130 but after a full day and a thorough search of the ship they reported that she was clean and there were no drugs on board. Still not being satisfied the acting chief of police seemingly convinced that there were drugs on board decided that he should start cutting open all her compartments to find where the narcotics were hidden. The local paper and TV station picked up the story so if no drugs are found this acting chief is going to look pretty bad." "But Myles, please explain to me if the local cops and the Coast Guard didn't find any drugs why are they still holding the master in a god-awful jail cell and still have the vessel under arrest?" "Politics, pure politics; I've spoken with the ambassador and his suggestion is that we both fly to Suriname because the only way the situation is going to be resolved is through personal contact. When the ambassador leaves Miami he's flying back to Paramaribo and said he'd be happy to intervene if we are there too." Now encouraged by the prospects I asked, "Are you telling me that you'd be willing to come along?" "I've got some depositions scheduled but I can get one of my associates to cover for me. In any case even though I represent the government I've never actually visited the country. It should be fun." Clearly pleased I said, "That's great I really do appreciate let's say your 'intervention'. So the underwriters will know what's planned, first thing in the morning, I'll send a fax letting them know the game plan and that you've graciously offered to assist – for your normal fees of course; this way when you send your bill there won't any surprises.

The problem is how do we get there? I've checked with Suriname Airways and all their flights are full for the next two weeks and this situation can't wait that long, I..." Myles cut me off, "Let me try something. I'll have my travel agent look into it and see if she might have better luck if the airline knows that it's official business and who I am." About an hour later Myles' travel agent Roberta from the Travel Shoppe phoned me. "Mr. Geary, Mr. Tralins called me about booking a flight for both of you to travel to Suriname, but I'm sorry to say that there simply is nothing available from Miami which is the only place they fly from in the United States. I know this may sound a bit silly but KLM the Dutch airline has a code share arrangement with Suriname Airways and under the code share they have a daily flight direct from Amsterdam's Schiphol airport. I could get you both out of Miami in the afternoon to connect with the KLM flight to Suriname the following day or there is another alternative, but it's a bit expensive.

Caldwell Air Charters would be willing to fly you from Trinidad's Piarco airport to Suriname and back for a flat $4,000.00. They told me they have a twin engine aircraft that's available along with a pilot and co-pilot. Mr. Caldwell said the total cost of the charter would be $4,000.00 and he quoted it wet. [38] I could book Mr. Tralins on the

---

38 Includes fuel

American Airlines flight from Miami to Trinidad that arrives late afternoon at Piarco. The American flight from San Juan leaves at 5:20pm with an estimated time of arrival a bit after 8:00pm. You and Mr. Tralins would have to overnight in Trinidad then leave the next morning for Suriname. Caldwell said the flying time is about three hours." "Excuse me Roberta but will Caldwell accept a personal check to pay for the charter?" "No checks, but Mr. Caldwell said that you could pay the $4,000.00 in cash or with an American Express card. Before calling you I spoke with Mr. Tralins and he said this would be fine with him but as you were paying the bill I should first clear everything with you." "Roberta, that sounds great. Please call Caldwell and definitely confirm the plane is still available. I don't want us to end up in Trinidad and find the plane has been booked on another charter. It's important that the plane remain overnight in Suriname so we can return the next day, if not we'd be stuck trying to get back. Hopefully Caldwell won't charge more for the overnight, but tell him I'll pick up the bill for the pilots' hotel and meals. Tell Caldwell I'll pay for the charter with my American Express Platinum card. Once you've confirmed the charter with Caldwell then go ahead and book Myles to Trinidad. I'll book my flight direct with American Airlines. Please get us two rooms at the Trinidad Hilton and four rooms at a good hotel in Paramaribo for the next day. When this is done I'd be grateful if you'd send me a fax confirming the arrangements. Oh by the way, please ask Caldwell if there are any other charges under his *wet* charter just to be sure that he's included the cost of airport landing and parking fees in the $4,000. I need to have all the details so I can let the underwriters know what the total costs will be."

A short time later Myles called, "Ed, I understand from Roberta that everything is set for our visit. After I spoke with her I called the ambassador in Washington to let him know of our plans and to be sure everything was all right with him. He then asked if we had Visas to enter Suriname; I don't and I assume you don't either so here's the deal. My plane gets in earlier but I'll wait at the airport for you to arrive; the Suriname ambassador to Trinidad will have his driver meet us at Piarco to take us to the Hilton. When he picks us up at the airport we'll give him our passports which he will take to the Suriname embassy to be stamped with our visas. When the driver collects us in the morning to take us back to the airport he'll return our passports which will have the necessary visas. The visas cost $50.00 US dollars each; he suggested we tip the ambassador's driver $20.00 or $30.00 for his efforts." With a sigh of relief I answered, "Sounds good to me, I'll see you at the airport in Trinidad."

Outside the arrivals hall at Piarco Myles was waiting with the embassy driver. "Ed, this is Gregario from the Suriname Embassy." Shaking his hand I acknowledged the introduction, "Hi Gregario, nice to meet you. I really do appreciate your assisting us with the visas." "No problem, I'm pleased to help. I'll drive you to the hotel and then pick you up in the morning at 8:00am." With that we were off to the Hilton. After checking in and leaving our bags in the rooms we met in the restaurant. Myles being the connoisseur he was selected a great bottle of Lafitte Rothschild that we shared over dinner while talking about our children. Myles was a doting father who spoke proudly about his two sons and Sarah his lovely daughter who he thought was growing up too quickly. I kept pace with Myles in affirming the happiness and pleasure derived from raising a son who was rapidly becoming a young man who had always made his father very proud too.

In the morning Gregario was waiting while we checked out, he then drove us to the charter company base at Piarco airport. The six-passenger aircraft was comfortable and spacious considering there were only two of us. We both read while occasionally gazing out the window as we flew over eastern Venezuela, Guyana, and along the coast of Suriname. When we landed at Paramaribo's airport we found it was deserted. With the limited number of tourists' who visit Suriname, immigration and customs authorities don't hang around the airport and in any case it's only about an hour's drive from the city. The lone policeman on duty at the airport called the authorities in Paramaribo who sent an immigration officer to the airport to stamp our passports.

After a bone-jerking ride in a vintage Chevy sedan we arrived in Paramaribo and checked into the dilapidated down town hotel that Roberta had recommended. After dropping our bags in the room I took a cab to the German ship to meet with the first officer while Myles met with the ambassador who had arrived earlier. Walking down the quay where the ship was moored I could see that the ship's cargo had been unloaded and was piled high alongside the dock. Three armed police officers were standing near the ship's cargo hatches which were open. After making my way up the ship's gangway which was guarded by another two uniformed police officers I was greeted by a gentleman who introduced himself as the first officer. "Captain Geary, I am very happy to see you and pleased that you were able to come so quickly. The ship has been thoroughly searched by the local police and a US Coast Guard inspection team from Miami. They didn't find any drugs because we don't have any drugs on board. Even though they found no drugs, the ship is still being detained and the police refuse to release the master from jail. The lawyer that was hired through the local Ship's Agent is still on board. I think you should meet him."

In entering the ship's lounge the lawyer was easily identifiable sweating profusely wedged between a bench seat and a table fixed to the deck in the center of the room. The chief engineer and other ship's officers were in bright blue overalls with baseball caps. The lawyer was wearing a wrinkled white shirt with a poorly knotted tie that by its red and other multicolored stains indicated a recent meal of spaghetti, red or white wine or both. His Ben Franklin type glasses kept sliding down his large hair filled nose as a result of the perspiration migrating from a bald head that was partially obscured by the little remaining hair having being swept from left to right over the top of his slightly pointed head. The first officer made the introduction, "Captain Geary, this is Mr. Stoltenberg who was appointed by the Ship's Agent in Paramaribo." Approaching the lawyer I said, "Mr. Stoltenberg it is a pleasure to meet you and I do appreciate your intervention, but don't quite understand why the ship remains in detention."

Struggling to move his excessive body mass that was crammed between the seat and a table bolted to the deck Stoltenberg rose to his full 5' height exposing a body reminiscent of an out-of-shape sumo wrestler. Looking up at me while extending his hand, "Captain, I don't quite understand why you are here. I have told the owner and his insurers that everything is under control and that I've taken care of everything. There simply is no need for you to get involved."

Not wishing to aggravate an already difficult situation I decided to be a bit diplomatic. "Mr. Stoltenberg, my task is to attempt to resolve what has become a confusing and expensive situation that appears to be going nowhere. The owner and his insurers are concerned that even after the cargo was removed and when no drugs or even traces of narcotics were found by the local police or the US Coast Guard why on God's earth is there any justification to start cutting up the ship's various compartments?" Pushing back on his glasses and raising his head to look down his porous, greasy nose he said, "Here in Suriname we have a big problem with drugs. The ship is being detained because a reliable police informant has said there are drugs somewhere on the ship and the authorities are determined to find them."

Sitting down at the table I looked directly at the lawyer, "Please help me understand Mr. Stoltenberg if the numerous inspections of the ship and her cargo haven't found any drugs who is detaining the ship and why?" With a sarcastic smirk while slowly moving his hand over his remaining hair that had fallen over his narrowed eyes the lawyer responded, "The US Embassy." I turned to the first officer and placing my hand on his shoulder, "Let me see what I can do. I'll visit the Embassy and be back later today. Thanks Mr. Stoltenberg, I'll be in touch."

With that information in hand I had the waiting taxi drive me to the US Embassy located in central Paramaribo. "I'd like to speak with the Ambassador please. My name is Ed Geary and I'm here with regard to the German ship you have detained." The guard looking at my identification, "I'm sorry sir the Ambassador isn't here, maybe the chargé d'affaires might be able to help you." "Thanks that would be appreciated." Less than two minutes later from behind a door that appeared capable of withstanding a full frontal assault from a Sherman tank a demure chargé d'affaires entered the reception area. "Mr. Geary, I'm Caroline Morgan what is it that you need help with?" "Madam, I understand that you are holding a German ship and I don't understand why." "Mr. Geary, please come with me I think you should speak with Anthony Garza our legal affairs officer."

Down a short hallway the first door to the left lead to a room with a desk and a small sign marked LEGAT. Ms. Morgan made the introduction, "Mr. Garza, this is Ed Geary he's here in reference to the German ship that the Coast Guard team did a drug search on." "Son-of-a-gun Ed Geary don't you remember me? Tony Garza I was the FBI liaison officer at Roosevelt Roads from 88' to 90' I took over

for the ole' 10/7[39] Pete Wilson after he got posted back to the States."
"Tony, of course I remember, you used to hang out at the marina.
We first met when Jim was the marina manager and he threw the
Christmas party at the Rosy Roads Yacht Club; how long have you
been in Suriname?" "Well it's been about a year now. When I left
Rosy I did some advanced training at the Federal Law Enforcement
Training Center in Georgia then was offered this assignment. What's
up with you do you still have that go-fast, what was its name, oh yeah
Ms. PIGI?" "Yep, I've still got the boat but don't have much time to use
her. I've been on a training mission for the Coast Guard in Venezuela
while trying to keep up with my normal marine stuff which is why
I'm in Suriname. What's the deal with the German ship, why are you
still holding her?" "Who told you we were holding her? The Coasties
put the dogs on board and after they made a thorough search and
found nothing they finished up their inspection and said the boat was
clean and could go. Who said we're holding the boat?" "Some sleazy
lawyer who works for the Ship's Agent told me the ship couldn't leave
because the US authorities wanted her to remain in port." "That's
bullshit. The reason the boat's still here is because the little jerk who's
the acting chief of police wants the job as Commissioner of Police. The
last Commissioner got fired and the job's open. He's made a big deal
about this huge drug bust that he was in charge of, but they never
found any drugs. At big bucks for the US taxpayer we flew in a Coast
Guard team on a 130 from Miami who searched the boat and found
nothing. There are no drugs on that boat.

I think he believes that if he has a big drug bust that gets splashed
all over this backwater of a country the good publicity would get him
promoted. He's the one holding the boat, not us." Shaking my head,
"What a bastard, how about a little help?" Standing and walking
around his desk Tony said, "What exactly do you need?" "I want to
get the ship out of here ASAP and stop this clown from claiming that
it's the US embassy that's holding her. Could we ask Ms. Morgan to
call the Attorney General of Suriname and tell him that the German
ship named the *DAGMAR* was searched by the Coast Guard, there
were no drugs found on board, and her cargo of aggregates is clean
too. The ship is therefore no longer of any interest to the United

---

39 A term frequently used by law enforcement officers in radio transmissions to indicate "I'm out of
    service"

States Government and the US embassy has no further reason to detain her.

At the same time she should formally request that the Attorney General immediately release the ship's master from jail and remove the police officers who are presently on board. I'd appreciate if she would also tell the AG that her verbal requests will be confirmed in writing and personally delivered to his office by messenger. With the ambassador away Ms. Morgan as the Chargé d'affaires should sign the letter. Please make a copy of the letter for me. Picking up his phone Tony said, "Hi Caroline, it's Tony could you pop down to my office for a minute there's a matter that needs your attention." After explaining what was needed Ms. Morgan returned to her office to call the Attorney General and prepare the requested letter for delivery. Twenty minutes later Ms. Morgan returned to Tony's office, "Mr. Geary here's your copy of the letter, I've spoken with the Attorney General who said he would call the jail to have the ship's captain released from custody and first thing tomorrow morning he will prepare an order for the release of the vessel, anything else?" "Thanks, but I think if I asked for anything more I'd be pushing my luck. I really appreciate your help and am very grateful that you were able to resolve the problem so quickly. If I thought she might read it I'd be happy to send a letter to your boss Madeline Albright telling our noble Secretary of State of the fast and efficient service provided by the US embassy in Suriname. Seriously though, I really do appreciate the help and the speedy response. Tony, I hope it won't be as long before we meet up again. Next time I'm in the "O" club at Rosy I'll have one for you or better yet why don't you organize a visit to Puerto Rico and I'll take you to dinner." Shaking hands as I got up to leave Tony smiled, "Don't be surprised if I show up sooner that you think, we've got the Navy flying back and forth from Rosy about twice a month bringing in the embassy supplies. I might just catch a ride and surprise you. Are you still in Villa Marina?" "Yep, same place same phone number, give me a call."

When I returned to the hotel Myles was waiting. I showed him the letter and told him what had transpired at the Embassy. In turn he told me that the ambassador had suggested that we meet tonight for dinner at his private club. The ambassador's club was an interesting experience; before dinner while having a drink at the bar a rather inebriated gentleman put his arm over my shoulders and while virtually using me to hold himself upright in slurred words said he would like to personally welcome me to 'his' country. Over dinner I asked the ambassador who the gentleman was who had extended the kind but rather alcohol induced welcome to Suriname. The ambassador casually said, "Oh, that was the president of Suriname." Not knowing of my visit to the US embassy or the release of the vessel by the Attorney General, the ambassador assured Myles that he had taken care of everything and in a few days the ship should be able to leave. We probably should have told the ambassador that the attorney general had already agreed to release the ship and the master, but clearly knew the honorable ambassador hadn't spoken with anyone or done anything to help us.

Myles and I decided to let him find out for himself. The next morning at 0900 hours on the way back to our chartered plane we stopped by the ship, as well as having his ship freed the Ukrainian master was overjoyed that he had been released from jail. About 0830 hours the bailiffs from the attorney generals office had delivered the release papers that permitted the ship to sail on the tide. I told the master to immediately cast off his lines, leave and don't look back. I later found that the sleazy lawyer who had been appointed by the Ship's Agent sent an un-itemized bill to the Dutch underwriters for $60,000.00 for his efforts which in real terms could not have amounted to more than a few hours. The cargo of aggregates that had been off-loaded from the ship ostensibly for the search of drugs was later found to have been *disposed* of by the surveyor appointed by the Ship's Agent who was supposed to be acting in the best interests of the ship. While I didn't have any further interest I learned a month or so later that the cargo of aggregates found its way to a local construction company whose owner was a member of the lawyer's family. The following month the Surinamese ambassador to the United States sent a bill to Myles in the amount of $14,000.00 for professional services in securing the release of the vessel. To save Myles from any embarrassment considering that his client was the government of Suriname I called the ambassador to tell him that I knew and he knew that he had done nothing to secure the release of the German ship and recommended for his own edification that he obtain a copy of the letter that the American Embassy had sent to the Attorney General.

With ambassadorial courtesy I suggested that His Excellency was little more than a common crook albeit with diplomatic immunity and that I would neither approve nor recommend that his personal bill be paid. Before terminating the conversation I diplomatically suggested that his Excellency should *go forth and multiply.* The investigation and ultimate resolution revealed that the Central Intelligence Agency wasn't involved with the episode in Suriname, probably because the Agency may not have had a Station in Paramaribo.

EIGHT

Along with his two sons from a previous marriage who he idolized, Myles' wife Janet was an intelligent, sophisticated, beautiful, and charismatic lady blessed with grace and charm. Myles adored Janet and Sarah, their young daughter who had become the light of his life. Having lived in Caracas for a number of years Janet became fluent in Spanish and developed a warm feeling for the people and culture of Venezuela. Knowing of my efforts in training the Venezuelan Coastguard and frequent visits Janet and I often spoke of this fascinating country. Myles too knew Venezuela well as he dealt with and was involved in the legal matters of PDVSA, Venezuela's national oil company.

"Hey Myles, what's up? How are Janet and Sarah?" "Hi Ed, they're fine both looking forward to our holiday in Aspen. How's Jason?" "Oh, he's fine. You know in talking with him about the CIA and the Coast Guard clowns that kept him out of the Coast Guard Academy I'm not really sure if he truly wanted to attend the Academy in the first place. In any case he's been accepted into Washington College in Chestertown, Maryland and is looking forward to leaving Puerto Rico for a while. Instead of not having to pay any tuition at the Coast Guard Academy it'll cost us a few shekels for Washington College but if he's happy that's the most important thing. Sometime down the road he can frame the letters from Briceño Garcia and Martin Fossa recommending him for acceptance to the Academy, they'll make great conversation pieces for the wall of his study. Hey, how many guys get personal letters from the commanding admiral of the Venezuelan Navy and the Commandant of the Coastguard recommending them for acceptance to the US Coast Guard Academy?"

"Ed, does the CIA still have you under surveillance in Puerto Rico and in Venezuela?" "Yeah, I'm still in the cross-hairs and they continue to watch everything we do while the beat goes on. During one of my visits to Caracas Jason came home from school and found a guy coming down the steps of our building and later saw him watching our condo from a car parked across the street in front of the marina. I checked the apartment when I returned from Caracas and couldn't find anything out of place but just to be sure had a friend sweep the place for bugs. It was fortunate we did the sweep because we found that the telephone and the fax lines had listening devices in the mouthpieces. I've asked my friend to come back every few days to do follow-up sweeps just in case they get back in." "Ed, please be careful and watch your back. Considering how many times they tried to do you in and now with bugs on your phone lines it's pretty clear you're dealing with some very nasty and dangerous people. Even cats only have nine lives and your numbers are dropping fast. By the way did you get any response to your February 25th fax to that guy Louis Leon at the Senate Intelligence Committee? Could be he's discussing it with the chief counsel Michael Sheehy on how to deal with the hot potato you've dropped in their lap. Have you heard anything back from them?" "No, they're all stonewalling me." "What about the letter you wrote to Clinton? Are you still planning to write to Kramek the Coast Guard Commandant and Woolsey at the CIA?"

Myles turned off his speaker phone as I continued, "I can understand that Clinton is much too busy with his personal problems with wet cigars and White House interns but I'm surprised that I haven't even had an acknowledgement from one of his minions. I'm waiting to see if I get anything back from the West Wing before writing Kramek and Woolsey. As Velling and Ecker have confirmed that both Kramek and Woolsey are nothing more than political hacks in collusion, I'm pretty sure they'll follow the same path and continue stonewalling me. I'm also convinced that everyone inside the Beltway who's involved in the case is hoping I'll just give up and go away. I've clearly been deemed a threat to national security because if they don't put a lid on the exposure and the Conspiracy gets out a number of heads could roll." "Ed, I'm really sorry that after all you've done to help the US Coast Guard the government would be so vindictive. In any case if they don't respond or make any effort to resolve the matter we'll sue the bastards. I recall you told me that you had met Kime, but never met either Kramek or Woolsey. Woolsey's nothing more than one of Washington's political delinquents and Kramek's probably from the same evil mold. Unfortunately, the government has too many of the Kramek and Woolsey types who only advance through the system by devious deception that requires walking over a number of warm bodies along the way. I know we've discussed this before but please keep all your notes and records in a safe place just in case we are forced into litigation."

In an effort to assure Myles the records were secure, "Everything's safe and secure. The training manuals, miscellaneous correspondence, and the big red book with the photographs probably wouldn't be of too much interest but in any case I've secured them in a file cabinet that's got a welded steel bar through the handles with two locks on top. I'm sure if push comes to shove they'd get in but at least it'll take them a bit of time. I unfortunately had a lot of stuff in my briefcase that was stolen which is now probably in my CIA file in Washington. I had a number of reports and confidential letters in my briefcase, the other correspondence to the Minister of Defense, Chief of Naval Operations, Briceño, Naval headquarters, training, and my travel schedules are secured inside the empty cavity of an old HP printer that's under a bunch of junk in a bedroom closet. If anyone rummages through the files I have on Venezuela they'll find only inconsequential correspondence. I've also installed motion detectors in my office and in the dining and living rooms." "Ed, it sounds like you've got everything covered but just in case we need a back-up why not make a copy of the sensitive stuff you've got and send it to me for safe keeping?" "Myles, that's a good idea I'll do it right away and send a copy of the file to you by Federal Express to insure it gets there."

"Ed, if you've got a moment I need your help with a personal matter." "Sure Myles, what's up?" "What's your opinion about Hylas Yachts?" In knowing that Myles had a Hans Christian 41' sloop named the Symphony which he cherished, kept in pristine condition, and used frequently in the Caribbean and in the Mediterranean, I was curious, "Hylas makes a nice boat Myles, but what's wrong with the Symphony? She's a perfect boat and in wonderful condition." "Well Sarah's growing up and I think we're going to need a bigger boat with more room that we could live on part time in the Mediterranean. What Janet and I are thinking about doing is selling the house at Coco Plum and getting a nice townhouse close by so we could spend part of our time in Florida and maybe the summers in Greece or Spain. I'm looking at a larger Hylas or maybe a Moody 54'. What do you think?" "What a great idea! Both the Hylas and the Moody are good boats and would be ideal for a live-aboard situation. Buying a new boat would allow you to select the cabin lay-out that suits you best. I'd also recommend that you make sure that whichever one you buy meets the United Kingdom Maritime and Coastguard's Code of Practice requirements. Like the Symphony you could register and flag the new boat in the USA, maybe Delaware, but if you eventually sold the boat in the Mediterranean most likely because of the size it would be re-flagged in the UK and used as a charter yacht for carrying passengers. Any UK flagged commercial vessel carrying passengers would have to be inspected to be sure it meets the requirements of the Code. Also it's important to keep in mind that if your new boat met the Code requirements and you ever wanted to sell her the value could be increased by maybe 10% or more." "Ed, whatever boat I buy new or second-hand you'd do the survey to make sure it was properly constructed, seaworthy, and met this Code you're referring to. I've requested some brochures on these and some other yachts and once I have the details from the builders we can talk more. In the meantime the underwriters have asked for an updated survey as I am in process of renewing the insurance on the Symphony. There's no rush but I need to get the survey to the underwriters in Hamburg in the next 60 days. When are you next planning to be in Miami?" "Myles, I have a survey coming up on a 58'Hatteras in two weeks and could add a couple days on to my return to look at the Symphony." "That would be fine you could stay with us while you're here." "As soon as the date is confirmed for the Hatteras I'll let you know." "Thanks Ed. Keep me posted on developments and in the meantime keep your head down and only sit with your back against the wall." With that Myles hung up the phone.

Between October 1991 and January 1994 the Venezuelan Mission had proven itself to be the best of times and the worst of times. On November 15th 1993, ten days after refusing to become a spy for the Central Intelligence Agency Captain Alvin Sarra USCG Chief Director of the Auxiliary informed me that "the Venezuelan mission didn't fit the USCG profile and that the mission is to be discontinued with effect from November 26, 1993". "Good morning Myles, I just faxed you a copy of the letter I received from Al Sarra the Chief Director of the Auxiliary telling me that the Coast Guard is dumping me and the Venezuelan Mission with effect from the 26th of this month. Now isn't that sweet a few days after I tell Velling to take a walk and I won't spy for them the Coast Guard cancels the Mission." After a short pause Myles asks, "Who is Sarra's boss? I'd suggest you move up the chain of command because maybe the higher-ups don't know what's really going on." On November 30, 1993 I wrote a letter to Rear Admiral William J. Ecker USCG, Chief, Office of Navigation Safety and Waterway Services, Al Sarra's boss at headquarters. I had first met Ecker the previous November during the NACON '92 in San Francisco. A first impression of Ecker was that he wasn't a great leader nor did he possess the management skills required for those in command, but he had been successful in conning his way to the top. While not being a great leader he clearly enjoyed the cocktail circuit and was quite happy when socializing with a drink in his hand. As he was one step above Sarra I sent a letter to Ecker not knowing at the time that he was involved and was fully aware of the CIA's conspiracy against the Venezuelan's. In my written appeal I detailed the CIA's proposal offering me an *opportunity* to be paid from an illegal fund that would be deposited in an unlawful numbered offshore bank account and that the CIA would have me promoted to commodore if I'd spy for them within the Venezuelan Military. In a carefully worded letter dated 13 December 1993 Ecker responded," …The Commandant joins me in thanking you for the interest and enthusiasm you have brought to this initiative, for the time and personal funds you have willingly expended, and for the success of your efforts." Ecker's letter like any well scripted soap opera always includes a word from the sponsor, in this case the CIA. *"The proper channel for your efforts is with and through the attaché in Caracas. It is important that your efforts coincide with the direction and focus established by the ambassador and must also have his staff's prior approval."* Oh my, what a nice touch. My only request to this star adorned desk jockey in Washington was for his help and protection from the CIA. In his response he doesn't offer help or protection but tells me that I need to join in with the CIA's spy games and everything will be just fine. Ecker's letter did however confirm that he, the US Coast Guard, and the Central Intelligence Agency were collectively involved in the conspiracy to destabilize the elected government of Venezuela.

"Myles, as you can see by the letter I faxed to you this morning Ecker has not only confirmed that he knows exactly what's going on with the CIA but he's also told me that if the program is to go forward I'll have to work at the pleasure of the ambassador and his attaché our dear Mr. Velling. I was hoping that if the Flags at headquarters knew what was going on I'd get some help. Boy, I was dead wrong, it's obvious that they're all deeply involved up to their sanctimonious necks and are now trying to cover their asses."

"Ed, I think it's patently clear that the enemy has been identified. How do you want to handle the situation? Shall we file a suit against the government?" "Not yet. I still have faith that if I can get to the right person that's high enough in the government the issues can be resolved. I'm going to contact a friend who's a producer with 60 Minutes who's done a number of stories on the CIA to see if there may be others in the business sector that may have experienced a similar problem. If I can locate someone else who might have had a similar problem maybe I can find an inside track to the right people in Washington who can help me. In the meantime I think that my friends in the Venezuelan military are clearly in danger and I need to warn them of what the CIA's got up its dirty sleeves. I've got a meeting scheduled at naval headquarters in Caracas in early January and will be with the Minister of Defense and the Commanding Admiral of the Navy. I also have a meeting scheduled with the Commandant of the Coastguard. I'm going to prepare a letter of what the CIA's trying to do so when we meet I can give it to them personally." Myles was momentarily silent, "Ed, do you think that's a wise move. Could they maybe think you might be working with or imbedded with the CIA and..." Abruptly cutting him off, "Myles, these individuals both professionally and personally are my friends. I trust and believe that they know me well enough to know that I wouldn't betray or spy on them for any reason or for any amount of money. I also believe that by exposing the conspiracy and making a full disclosure of the CIA's activities and their attempt to recruit me as a spy it will show that I have nothing to hide and have no hesitation in laying everything out on the table. If there's any question about my honesty or integrity it can be brought out in the open and addressed in a face-to-face meeting. If they trust what I will tell them and believe that it's true

I think they'll allow the program to continue while at the same time take the necessary steps to protect themselves and their families." Never forgetting that he was a lawyer Myles asks, "Please fax me a draft copy of the letter so I can look it over from a legal perspective." "Sure, no problem. I'll be in touch."

With the exception of being followed and from time to time having the condominium debugged every few days Christmas was a happy time. Together Jason and I decorated a 6' tree which stood in the living room adorned with multi-colored lights, bright ornaments, and lengths of silver strand. Our house-bound cats, two sisters named Port and Starboard viewed the ornaments as dangerous creatures from outer space and frequently attacked them, often bringing the tree crashing to the floor. I had decided many years ago that because of the nature of my practice as a marine surveyor I didn't need an outside office or the required commute to work each day. My secretary Nelly Ortiz was quite happy working in our rather nice condominium even though I had to give up smoking my pipe during normal working hours to insure a peaceful co-existence with a non-smoker. Nelly's husband Manny, the manager of a Bible Study camp also didn't smoke or drink. In admiration and respect for their religious convictions shelving my pipe during the day was a small price to pay. Our three bedroom condominium was situated in a gated community directly across the street from the Villa Marina Yacht Harbor and was located in a garden setting with swimming pools and tennis courts. I had converted one bedroom into an office with the normal necessities of typewriters, general office equipment, fax machines, and a VHF-FM radio. I was able to safeguard my general files in locked cabinets with sensitive material secreted inside a gutted HP printer which proved particularly comforting after I learned that I was a person-of-interest to the CIA. The condo had four occupants, Jason and I and Port and Starboard, our feline companions.

"Dad, finished with that thing for Venezuela yet? We promised Poncho and Lucy we'd be at their place by 4 o'clock and it's now 3:15 and that's American not Puerto Rican time!" "Jason, 'that thing' is a very important letter to the Admirals and I want to get it done before we go, give me 15 minutes. I'll finish the draft and then in the morning you can proof it for me for errors." In addition to his schooling in Puerto Rico Jason had also attended schools in Saint Thomas, US

Virgin Islands and Dutch Sint Maarten in the Netherlands Antilles. Jason was born in California and in addition to English, he spoke a little French, was conversant in Dutch, and fluent in written and spoken Spanish. While Nelly handled most of my correspondence in Spanish Jason had become a great proof-reader on the weekends.

In spite of the actions of the CIA and the US Coast Guard to terminate me and end the Venezuelan Program I reasoned that if the Minister of Defense and vice admiral Briceño Garcia approved, after December 31, 1993 I would continue the program as a Captain in their Navy. Having been summarily discharged I had no other option but to disassociate myself from the US Coast Guard and their CIA co-conspirators. On December 18th 1993 I completed a three page letter to the Minister of Defense and the Commander of Naval Personnel and faxed it to Myles. A short time later the phone rang, "Mr. Geary, Mr. Tralins is on the phone and would like to speak with you." "Hi Ed, I got the letter and it looks fine. You seem to have covered everything and I'm glad you didn't mention Velling by name. Publicly identifying a CIA officer could get you in a lot of trouble. I also think you were wise not to mention the oil issue or go into the details about Chàvez because right now other than the CIA and the US Coast Guard no one really knows who his supporters might be. At this point the main focus should be on espionage, you, the Coast Guard, and the CIA, not the side issues." "Myles, I'm glad you approve of the letter but wish I could have made it a bit shorter. It's just that I'll have the opportunity to have the attention of these heavyweights together at one time and think it's a good point in time to tell them what's really going on behind the scenes. Because Briceño is a personal friend I think I'm also going to prepare a separate letter for him along the same lines but with a few more specifics." The letter was captioned "Sensitive Information – Prepared; 18 December 1993 Delivered: 12 January 1994 and was written both in Spanish and English. The letter was addressed to Vice Admiral Radames Munoz Leon, the Minister of Defense of the Republic of Venezuela with a copy for Vice Admiral Briceño Garcia. On January 12th 1994 at naval headquarters I personally handed the letter to them during our meeting. I prefaced the letter by telling them, "Gentlemen, I am sorry to have to advise you that the US Coast Guard has terminated the Venezuelan Initiative with effect from December 31, 1993."

After reading the letter the Minister of Defense rose and looking at me said, "Captain, if this letter would have come from anyone else I would find its contents difficult to accept, but knowing you as well as I do personally I can fully understand your concern. Under item 7) of the letter you have made reference to a Second Secretary of the U.S. Embassy in Caracas who identified himself as an agent of the CIA. Can you tell me the name of the Second Secretary?" "Admiral, unfortunately under the laws of the United States if I reveal the name of a CIA operative I could go to jail." "But Captain you're in Venezuela not in the US." "Yes, I realize that but next week I'll return to Puerto Rico which is under the jurisdiction of the United States." "Alright Captain I understand your reluctance, but tell me is the US ambassador Martin Skol aware of what his staff are up to?" "I know the ambassador is aware of the Venezuelan training mission and my work with the Armada, but at this time I can't say for sure what he may or may not know about the CIA's activities." Considering the direct instructions given to me in Rear Admiral Ecker's letter it was pretty clear that the ambassador was fully aware of what the CIA and the US Coast Guard were up to but decided it best to avoid exposing the ambassador, at least for the moment. "Captain, you've willingly committed yourself and worked diligently to expand and train our Coastguards and demonstrated a professionalism that we all have admired and appreciated. The Ministry of Defense awarded you the *Honor Merito* and not long ago the Ministry of Foreign Affairs presented you with a Foreign Service commendation at the cocktail party hosted by our Consul General in San Juan. For your country to treat you in this way is reprehensible and inexcusable. However, I believe you have followed the right course in bringing this matter to our attention. Because the actions of the US government clearly involve a number of our government ministries I feel obligated to first discuss the matter with the Minister of Foreign Affairs." Admiral Munoz Leon took his hat from the desk and visibly distressed turned towards the door; I rose, we exchanged salutes and he left. Briceño Garcia leaned back in his chair and now staring at the ceiling, "The knowledge that our supposedly friendly American neighbors want you to spy on us is very alarming. It also must be terribly disappointing for you to learn that when you refuse to become involved in their scheme they want to calmly dispose of you. This is ridiculous. Your work has been exemplary and to the great benefit of our Navy and Coastguard. I have repeatedly written letters of praise for your work in Venezuela to the Coast Guard attaché and personally spoke with the Commandant in Washington. This is absurd."

"Admiral, I'm truly sorry. But because I refused to become a spy the Mission was terminated and the Coast Guard and the CIA now wish to punish me. I should add that amongst the other officers of general rank the CIA have expressed a particular interest in you personally. Admiral, I was astonished and disappointed when I received word from Washington that the Coast Guard would no longer sponsor the Mission, but that's not all. I am to be demoted and discharged from the Coast Guard" The Admiral rose from his desk and rubbing his forehead, "Demoted and discharged? Have you done something that I'm not aware of to warrant such actions? And wait a moment, what sponsorship are they talking about? Captain Goschenko and the Navy provided for your transportation and except for the few times that you were offered accommodation and meals at our military installations at Mamo and Puerto Cabello am I not correct that you paid your own hotel expenses? Unless the US Coast Guard reimbursed you for your air tickets between San Juan and Maiquetia I know that you personally paid all these costs as well." "That's correct, I paid for the air travel and my hotel costs and did not receive any payment of any kind from the Coast Guard or the US government for my time or for any of my expenses." "This is crazy that they should now refer to *their* sponsorship, they have sponsored nothing. What are your plans, is it your intention to stop the training?" "No, with your permission and authorization I would be willing to continue the Mission but not as a Captain with the US Coast Guard Auxiliary but as a Captain in the Armada." "I'm pleased to hear this. Consider it done. You have my full authority to continue as an officer in the Armada and we will forget about these people in Washington. I am also very disturbed to learn that McKenzie and the American embassy have not limited their activities to diplomatic interests and fully accept your account of the matter. I'm not certain how we'll deal with the spying issue but as Admiral Munoz Leon stated we have departments in the government that can take the appropriate action. I'd like to know the name of this Second Secretary the one who's behind all this?"

"Admiral, unfortunately I can't reveal the name of this individual because under American law I could be prosecuted and probably jailed for what they call *outing* an agent of the Central Intelligence Agency." The Admiral didn't press the issue further. I was pleased and happy to learn that the Mission would be able to continue with the Admiral's approval. "Thank you sir, I do appreciate your support and will continue the mission on behalf of the Armada not the US Coast Guard." "Then it's settled. Carry on Captain." I stood, saluted, and left.

Considering that Briceño Garcia and his family were a target of the CIA and as such exposed to danger, during my next visit to Caracas I met with the Admiral and gave him a typewritten letter that contained more specific details of the CIA's request for personal information concerning his private affairs, family and children, and the other general officers of the armed forces, the plan to destabilize the elected government, and the particular information the US government wanted me to obtain about Venezuela's military establishment. The letter did not name the CIA operative Joseph J. Velling. After reading the four page letter the astonished admiral then asked, "Captain, you're a very brave man. In spite of being offered money and promotion to commodore you were not willing to betray the trust and friendship of your many colleagues in Venezuela, I commend you. Unless you have reconsidered your position and believe it best to discontinue the training I would as I told you in our last meeting, like you to continue with the program as an officer under my direct command. You must however be extremely careful as your movements will no doubt continue to be closely monitored by the CIA. In view of the potential danger do you wish for me to assign a navy officer to act as your aide and meet you upon arrival at Maiquetia with orders to accompany you at all times while you're in the country?" "Thank you sir, but I really don't believe that will be necessary." Having fully informed the admiral of the conspiracy and relieving myself of this terrible burden I extended my hand, "Admiral, I thank you for your confidence. I do appreciate your support and will indeed continue the program. I assure you that I have disassociated myself from the US Coast Guard, the CIA, and any other agency of the United States government that may attempt to compromise my integrity or that of the Armed Forces of Venezuela."

In February 1994 I returned to Venezuela for advanced training of the Caracas Picua auxiliary group that was scheduled to take place at the Carenero Yacht Club near Higurote in the state of Miranda. "Geary, Geary, over here," shouting and waving from the hoard of people outside the arrivals area at Maiquetia airport was Goschenko in his Class A uniform. "Ed, why aren't you wearing your uniform? I did tell you that I planned to drive directly to Carenero this afternoon so we wouldn't have to deal with the morning traffic. I've booked us in a hotel near the port. Why didn't you wear your uniform?" "Nicholas, it's a long story I'll tell you while we drive." Over the next 3 hours I told Nicholas about the CIA and my meetings in January with the Minister of Defense and with Briceño. During the journey Goschenko said nothing but frequently pounded the steering wheel in expression of his emotions. After we had checked in to the hotel and found a local restaurant for dinner, "That's terrible. I had thought that the shootings at the Tamanaco and the Eurobuilding were just random acts of violence that's so normal in Caracas and the food episode at the Hilton in Margarita was just bad luck. But maybe they weren't." "Nicholas, I don't know if the CIA was really trying to kill me or just scare me. The US Coast Guard and the CIA were infuriated when I turned down their offer to spy for them. They are irritated too because I exposed the conspiracy in writing letters and can't be convinced to drop the matter. It could be they just want to scare me into submission hoping that if they harass me enough I'll quietly disappear into obscurity. When I was at the Comandancia last month Briceño asked me to continue the training as a Captain in the Armada and in so many words said screw the US Coast Guard. I put my US Coast Guard Auxiliary uniform in moth balls and after January 12th will only use my Venezuelan uniform, but to avoid attracting too much attention I won't wear it to travel in. That's why I didn't wear it today." The next afternoon on the drive back to Caracas Goschenko expressed his concern over the CIA's interest in the military but was pleased that Briceño had agreed to continue the training programs. "Ed, tonight I've got you booked in the Hilton and tomorrow will collect you at 0800. It shouldn't take us more than a couple of hours to reach Valencia where we'll meet with Pepe, the commander of the Rescate group. Pepe wants to organize the training for next month as he's recruited about 10 new members. Let's stop for some coffee and Arepas."

About an hour out from Higurote on the road back to Caracas Goschenko turned off the main highway and proceeded south down a narrow road. "Nicholas, where are we going?" "I want to show you my farm." "You have a farm?" "Yes, it's not very large but it has a small house and a few fruit trees. When I want to get away from Caracas I sometimes come out here with my son." A couple of miles from the main highway we turned again to a small lane where off to the right was a small farm house surrounded by trees and a waist high wood fence. "Well here it is, this is my farm. Maybe someday when I retire I'll come out here to live, it's very peaceful and away from the congestion and crime in Caracas." "This is nice Nicholas. Can we go inside?" "No, I didn't think of showing you my finca pequeño[40] until we were on our way back to the city and I don't have the key with me, there's really not much to see anyway. It needs a lot of work and I'd rather wait until I get it fixed up before I show it to you."

It was now getting close to 5:00pm and we were still some distance from Caracas traveling at about 40 miles per hour on a winding two lane road which at the time was the main highway back to the metropolitan area. "Nicholas, have you noticed that Ford truck behind us? It's been following us ever since we turned back on the main highway. There's been a number of places with open road where they could have passed us but they've remained about three car lengths behind us for the last 45 minutes or so." "No, I haven't been paying attention. The road can be very dangerous with a number of large trucks moving very slowly, sometimes you don't see them until you come around a curve and there they are." About ten minutes later we approached an open area where off to the left you could see the new freeway that was under construction.

Other than the truck behind us there were no other vehicles in sight. Just at that moment the Ford truck sped up to pass us and when the truck's back bumper was just to the left and almost touching the front of Goschenko's Mitsubishi the driver swerved crashing into the front bumper of the Trooper." Struggling with the steering wheel to keep control Goschenko yelled, "Coño! What is that son-of-a-bitch doing?" Fortunately Goschenko maintained control and the road's shoulder was reasonably level so we came to a stop without rolling over. Taking a holster from the driver door's side pocket Goschenko

---

40 Little country house

pulled out his gun and jumped from the car just as the truck disappeared around a bend in the road. "What a crazy fool. He could have killed us. I guess we should consider ourselves lucky but look at the damage to my car." "Nicholas, do you think we should report what happened to the police?" "No, I didn't see the license plate number and all I can say is that it was a dark Ford truck of which there are thousands in Venezuela. We'd spend hours with the police for nothing because they wouldn't do anything anyway. In any case we probably won't see any police cars before we get to the outskirts of the city."

The Caracas Hilton is a great hotel located in central Caracas directly across a main boulevard from the Belle Arts Center and near all the major plazas. Goschenko had booked me a nice room on the concierge level and what was even better was that he got me the room at the discounted military rate. After taking a shower I ventured down to the lobby and the numerous restaurants located within an indoor garden setting. Choosing an Italian eatery I decided on the buffet table figuring that if someone wanted to try and poison me again they might have a bit of a problem with 50 or so other diners picking at the same anti-pasta. Over a great Caesar salad I pondered the events of the afternoon. It's no secret that when I'm in Venezuela and traveling with Goschenko our movements are known to a number of people in advance. Could the incident with the Ford truck simply be a case of being in the wrong place at the wrong time, or could the same people who tried to run us off the road when the lieutenant and I were driving to Valencia be involved?

I somewhat answered my own questions a few weeks later when Goschenko and I were scheduled to visit Carenero but at the last minute I had to cancel because of a bad cold. "Nicholas, this is Ed. My cold has really gotten worse. I've got a fever, I can't stop coughing and I really feel terrible. I think I should stay in tonight. If you don't mind swing by the hotel so I can give you the training aids and the new inspection decals to take with you to the class tomorrow. Please tell the auxiliary members that I'm sorry I couldn't make it but I will make it up to them on my next visit. I'm going back to Puerto Rico on an early flight tomorrow to try and recover. I'll give you a call later in the week." Goschenko came by the hotel and after a coffee left Caracas late in the afternoon for the drive to Carenero.

After a light dinner washed down with bit of Merlot I felt a little better and returned to my room. While brushing my teeth there was a knock on the door. Leaning out of the bathroom, "Hang on a minute I'll be right there." Looking through the peep hole I could see the visitor was a female and wondered who it was. In turning the handle the female who I quickly found wasn't a lady, pushed the door open and barged into the room. "Who the hell are you? Setting a fairly large gym bag on the floor and reaching for my well, private parts she said, "I'm here to make you happy." "Thanks, but I'm already happy now get the hell out of here. Who sent you?" "A friend and you don't have to pay…." With one hand I picked up the gym bag and through the open door tossed the bag while forcing the female into the hallway. "Fuck off coño!" After slamming the door shut she continued to bang on the door while I called the front desk and asked them to send someone from security to my room. By the time a security officer arrived the lady of the night had disappeared.

After breakfast the next morning I stopped by the reception desk and spoke with a Mr. Perez, the front desk manager. "Mr. Perez, I'm sorry to say but I think you have a serious problem with hotel security. Last night around 10:00pm a prostitute knocked on my door and before I realized who she was she had forced her way into my room. Not good Mr. Perez when hookers are allowed to cruise the hallways of the Hilton late at night looking for customers." Peering over the top of his gold rimmed glasses and looking somewhat indifferent, "What is your room number sir?" "Concierge level room 717." Focusing on the front desk computer screen, "Oh yes, Captain Geary. Captain, I do apologize for the inconvenience. Only those persons who are registered in the hotel are allowed on the guest floors. We do not permit unaccompanied visitors to enter the lifts. I will make a report of this and again I apologize. We have had a problem with some of the hotel's porters who when they see a single male occupant register seem to feel that the gentleman may enjoy female companionship and allow these ladies access to the guest rooms. I'll see that security is made aware of the problem." "Security should already be aware of the problem because last night I called them while the woman was still beating on my door."

When I called Coastguard Headquarters to schedule a training visit I was told that Captain Nicholas Goschenko had been in a terrible automobile accident. The Coastguardsman said Goschenko was in stable condition in a Caracas hospital's intensive care unit. The duty officer continued, 'Captain Goschenko was first taken to a military hospital and then was moved to a private hospital where he is now recovering from major injuries that he sustained in a serious automobile accident on the road to Carenero. Captain Goschenko is expected to live but may suffer from impaired hearing and the partial loss of vision in his left eye. His Mitsubishi Trooper was a total wreck. The hit and run accident involved two vehicles." "Can you tell me what the other vehicle was?" "Just a moment let me look at the accident report." After a short pause, "Witnesses reported to the police that the other vehicle was a dark colored Ford truck. The truck fled the scene before police and the emergency services arrived." "Thank you lieutenant, I'm sorry to hear of the accident but do appreciate the information. Please send a message to Captain Goschenko that I am sorry to hear of the accident and hope he has a full and speedy recovery." I thought to myself hmm, a dark colored Ford truck, I wondered if this was this just another coincidence?

NINE

"Mr. Geary, Mr. Tralins would like to speak with you." "Hi Ed, sorry I missed your call but I was in a deposition. What's up?" "Remember my being used for target practice, the poisoned food in Margarita, and the incident when a car used as a battering ram tried to run a Navy lieutenant and I off the road as we were driving to Valencia in the lieutenant's car?" "Yes, I remember." "Well recently I was with Goschenko driving back from Carenero when a Ford truck tried to run us off the road. I didn't think much about it at the time but I just spoke with Coastguard headquarters in La Guaira and learned that Goschenko is in a hospital in Caracas as a result of a hit and run accident. What's a bit bizarre is that on the day of the accident I should have been with Goschenko but returned to Puerto Rico because of a cold. The accident that almost killed him involved a Ford truck and I'm wondering if it may have been the same Ford truck that tried to run us off the road earlier in the month. His Mitsubishi Trooper is a total wreck and Goschenko is in bad shape. He may have hearing loss and lose the sight in his left eye. It could be a coincidence but......" "Ed, coincidence or not you've got to be careful. I think that the CIA wants you out of the picture." "You know I think your right. Oh and there's been another interesting development.

A couple of days ago I got a call from Lowell Bergman you know the producer with 60 Minutes. I sometimes see or speak with him when he passes through San Juan on his way to the British Virgin's. When he's not traveling Lowell generally splits his time between New York and California. This time he called me from his home in Berkeley. He was curious about the problems in Venezuela and said he may be interested in doing something for 60 Minutes. Lowell said he thought it would make an interesting story and might even help me in my battle with the Coast Guard. Lowell thinks I've got a lot of great stuff in my file but we could really nail the bastards if I could get Velling on tape." "Ed, what does he mean exactly?" "Lowell says I should try and arrange another meeting with Velling while wearing a wire. I'd record the conversation and if 60 Minutes actually ran the story the tape would be irrefutable corroboration of the claims made in the pleadings; the frosting on the cake so to speak. It also might be a good time to spill all the beans about how the US wants to gain control of Venezuela's oil. What do you think?" Pondering the idea and turning his speaker phone off Myles said, "Do you think you could get Velling to meet you considering the letters you've written and the number of people who know about what he's been up to? Where would you want to meet him?"

"I honestly don't know whether or not he'd risk being seen with me. But maybe to give him a level of comfort I could try and set up the meeting at the Officers Club at Rosy Roads, which is where we met before in October and November. I don't think it would be wise for me to meet him in a hotel or some other public place, or if he suggested the meeting take place in Caracas. I also couldn't go to the embassy because I'd be searched by security. They'd find the wire and recorder and well, that would be the end of any meeting." "Ed, your friend is right. If you could record him repeating the offer it would be undeniable evidence. How will you do it?" "I'll just call him at the embassy in Caracas and try and set it up when he's back in Puerto Rico." 'Okay give it a shot. I'll put together a list of key words that I want you to memorize for the meeting and interject into the conversation. Right off the top of my head the words that come to mind are spy, NOC, CIA, Chàvez, oil, and US Coast Guard, these are important. You also want him to talk about the CIA getting the US Coast Guard to promote you to Commodore, how they will pay you, how they'll open an offshore bank account for you and also try to get him to tell you as much as possible about the relationship with Chàvez without making him nervous." "Let's see what I can do. I'll keep you posted." After a half dozen telephone calls to the embassy and only receiving a recording I decided to send Velling a fax on my private letterhead. On February 15th 1994 I sent the following fax to the United States Embassy in Caracas.

To Fax Number: (58) (2)285-4226

Attention: Joseph J. Velling, Esq.

From: Capt. E.S. Geary
Date: February 15, 1994
Subject: Subject matter of our Oct/Nov 1993 meetings

<u>Message:</u> Dear Mr. Velling: I would like to reconsider your proposals concerning your agencies interest in the Venezuelan Naval Establishment. I have attempted to contact the Embassy on 284-8031, 285-2222 and 285-3111 for the last week, but all I get is a recording. Please call me and we might be able to meet at the Officers Club as we did before.
Regards, Ed

I sent a copy of the fax to Lowell Bergman and to Myles Tralins. I did not receive a call or a response to the fax from Velling or anyone else at the US Embassy in Caracas. Considering that Admiral Ecker had terminated the Department and my position as its chief on December 31, 1993, I found it odd that Admiral Welling would write me letter dated February 24th 1994 addressed to Captain E.S. Geary, USCG (A), Department Chief Pan American Auxiliary Liaison (DC-PAAL). On the same day I received the letter from Admiral Welling I replied on my official USCG Auxiliary letterhead deciding it was a good time (assuming he didn't know about it already) to let Welling know about the CIA's clandestine efforts to spy on the Venezuelan Navy. My letter to Welling included reference to my January 12th meeting with Vice Admiral Radames Munoz Leon, Minister of Defense and Rear Admiral Briceño Garcia who said he would report the matter to Vice Admiral Julian Mauco-Quitana and the Chief of Naval Operations. My letters to Admiral Welling clearly hit a sensitive nerve in Washington. In a letter dated March 29th 1994 Captain Alvin Sarra, Chief Director of the Auxiliary who had conveniently overlooked Admiral Welling's congratulatory letter to me dated February 24th 1994 apparently a bit miffed and no doubt suffering from an advanced form of senility disorder before being put out to pasture tells me, ...*While you as a private citizen are free to correspond with whomever you wish, in your USCG Auxiliary dealings you are expected to use the Chain of command....... You are reminded that it is inappropriate for you to continue using that letterhead, the business card and, when representing the USCG Auxiliary, the title of "Captain". This type* *of misrepresentation is punishable under chapter 14 of the United States Code section 892 by a fine of not more than $500. You are hereby directed to stop.*

As evidenced by Admiral Welling's official and congratulatory letter of February 24th 1994 addressing me as Captain and Department Chief Pan American Auxiliary Liaison I clearly hadn't engaged in any misrepresentation. I wasn't punished under Chapter 14 of the United States Code section 892 and it didn't stop my efforts to expose the Venezuelan Conspiracy. The training of the Venezuelan Coastguard Auxiliary continued through the spring and early summer months of 1994 with monthly visits to Margarita Island where Coastguard units Tiburon, Sierra, and Delfin assembled for weeklong exercises. As a precautionary measure whenever I left the Hilton it was always in the company of four or five other officers and I never again ordered from room service.

In early February after sending a collection of documents and making numerous calls to Louis Deleon of the House Permanent Select Committee on Intelligence and Michael W. Sheehy the chief Counsel I followed up with a fax on February 25th 1994 that included another six pages that detailed and documented the conspiracy being undertaken by the CIA and the Coast Guard. When I called three weeks later I was told that the matter was under investigation and Deleon asked if I would be willing to testify before a Senate Committee. I readily agreed to appear before the Committee. In mid May 1994 I telephoned and spoke with Mr. Sheehy who said that they had confirmed and received an admission from the CIA that they had indeed attempted to persuade me to 'snitch' (their word not mine) and provide intelligence on the Commands of the Venezuelan military establishment. Sheehy further confirmed that the USCG had agreed to allow the Venezuelan program to continue on the condition that I work through Joseph J. Velling, the CIA agent who was still shrouded under the guise of a commercial attaché at the US Embassy in Caracas. Sheehy said that Rear Admiral Ecker's letter of December 18th 1993 further confirmed the findings of the investigation carried out by Senate Committee; if I refused to work for the CIA the US Coast Guard would terminate me and the program and this is exactly what happened.

I then received a letter dated June 13th 1994 from Mr. Sheehy that skillfully contradicted what he had told me previously. In spite of the fact that the Senate Committee investigation had proven the culpability of both agencies Sheehy had arbitrarily decided to absolve the CIA and the US Coast Guard from any wrongdoing. The letter incredulously avoided any reference whatsoever to the spying activities against the naval establishment of the Republic of Venezuela which he had previously confirmed.

Using ambiguous, illusory terminology sculptured and offered in such a way to shield the Coast Guard from public condemnation Sheehy's letter stated, ..."*I was advised (by the USCG) that your position was disestablished by order of the head of the Coast Guard Auxiliary based on a judgment that the program had grown beyond the scope of what the Coast Guard felt it should be involved in.*"

While this statement is true it relates only part of the story. The Sheehy letter deliberately omitted all the findings of the Committee's investigation that he had originally read to me over the telephone,

"....following an investigation by this Committee we have confirmed that Joseph J. Velling in his capacity as an agent of the Central Intelligence Agency assigned to the United States Embassy in Caracas made contact with and requested that Captain Edwin S. Geary of the US Coast Guard Auxiliary engage in espionage against the military establishment of the Republic of Venezuela. He [Geary] was further requested in writing by Rear Admiral William Ecker, USCG to liaise, coordinate, and continue his activities in Venezuela identified as the Venezuelan Initiative under the direction of the CIA Mission and the Embassy of the United States in Caracas. Captain Geary declined and refused to engage in the Coast Guard and the CIA's espionage activities. Having originated the Venezuelan Initiative and appointing Captain Geary as its chief the Coast Guard determined it did not possess the required expertise in the area of espionage and insisted that his efforts be transferred to the control and direction of the CIA because....**

the program had grown beyond the scope of what the Coast Guard felt it should be involved in."

The CIA and the US Coast Guard had been caught and exposed in a conspiracy against the Venezuelan Coastguard and Navy and were now using the Senate Committee in an effort to silence me by means of intimidation. Not being satisfied or willing to accept another government agency attempting to quash the matter, which now included the US House of Representatives Permanent Select Committee on Intelligence, after receiving the letter I called Mr. Sheehy and surprisingly he answered the telephone. Mr. Sheehy, obviously uncomfortable in having mistakenly picked up the phone and taken the call was still very cordial. "Mr. Sheehy, I have received your letter dated June 13th 1994 but was surprised and disappointed to find you have not included your findings that confirmed the CIA's attempt to recruit me nor the Coast Guard's involvement that you personally relayed to me in our previous telephone conversation. You confirmed that the Committee's findings were further corroborated in Admiral Ecker's letter that for the program to continue I'd have to work at the pleasure and under the direction of the CIA attaché Velling and the ambassador in Caracas." "Yes, I do recall our conversation. The CIA and the Coast Guard have confirmed what you have told us. The CIA acknowledged they had attempted to recruit you but deny they had any involvement with the Coast Guard's decision to stop the mission. As you have pointed out Rear Admiral Ecker documented the Coast Guard's position quite clearly, work for the CIA through their attaché under the direction of the ambassador and the mission could continue. It was your decision not to work for the CIA and the Coast Guard closed the mission. Captain, you will appreciate that we must be extremely careful not to agitate an already delicate and difficult situation. I'm sure you will also understand that I cannot provide you with a letter that makes any reference to the CIA's overseas operations. I'm sorry Mr. Geary, Good bye." So much for integrity and truthful public servants…

"Myles, I just hung up the phone with Michael Sheehy of the Senate Intelligence Committee. I received a letter from him this morning that's nothing more than another Washington white-wash. As you know when I first spoke with him he acknowledged everything that I had told him about the CIA and the Coast Guard and said he would put it in writing and he just acknowledged it again five minutes ago in a phone call. Sheehy had originally told me that he would write me a letter confirming what he had first told me over the phone but he didn't. I guess the CIA or the Coast Guard or both got to him because his letter is just a bunch of general crap and doesn't contain any of the specifics he related to me in this and the earlier phone calls. I also found that the staff lawyer that asked if I would be willing to testify before a Senate Committee is gone. When I asked to speak with him I was told that he has been reassigned and the request for me to testify has been shelved." "Ed, what do you expect from the Washington crowd. I'm sure when it got out that the lawyer Deleon had asked you to appear before the Senate Committee they dumped him. They're all there to cover for one another and none of them want to rock the boat. The CIA's under real scrutiny because of the mess of the Aldrich Ames fiasco and if something like this came out Senator Patrick Moynihan would have more ammunition to close them down. I think you're turning over a lot of rocks and in doing so you're exposing a lot of the Washington worms hiding beneath them." "Myles, while I appreciate what you're saying I just can't let the matter die or be buried without a fight." On August 11th 1994 I wrote a two page letter addressed jointly to James Woolsey, Director of the Central Intelligence Agency and Vice Admiral Robert E. Kramek, Commandant of the US Coast Guard; the letter contained a personal appeal for their intervention and assistance. In response James V. Hirsch the Acting Executive Director of the CIA sent me a two paragraph letter dated 27 September 1994 that denied any involvement simply declaring, hey it's not us. The Commandant responded through Thomas J. Burnaw, Director of the Auxiliary for the Seventh US Coast Guard District in Miami who sent me an obnoxious letter telling me that with immediate effect I had been kicked out of the Coast Guard Auxiliary. Burnaw said that as the decision was rendered by the illustrious Commandant, "that the action is considered final and not subject to further review or appeal." When they're cornered the pen pushers have such a wonderful way with words.

After more than a year of futile attempts to resolve the issues surrounding the CIA and US Coast Guard's failed efforts to recruit me as a spy Myles and I agreed that the only option I was left with was to file a lawsuit in the United States District Court in Miami naming the Commander, Seventh United States Coast Guard District as the defendant. In addition to a wrongful termination from the US Coast Guard Auxiliary the US Coast Guard had demoted me, purged my service and personnel files, and withheld decorations and medals that were awarded for my exemplary service. While the lawsuit could have named the Commandant of the Coast Guard and the Director of the CIA it would have meant defending the action in Washington D.C. with much greater inherent costs. The civil action case number 95-0323 CIV-Nesbitt named Joseph J. Velling as the CIA operative and the principals within the US Coast Guard who had violated my rights of review as cited under 5USC Section 706(2)(A). The lawsuit did not ask for monetary damages but only that I am returned to duty at the rank of Captain, my service and personnel records were to be restored, and I was to receive the decorations and medals that had been rescinded by Captain Gregory Magee when he was Commander of the USCG Greater Antilles Section.

In early March 1995 a number of leading English and Spanish language Florida newspapers picked up the story with reporters calling me in Puerto Rico for interviews. An extremely supportive print media released a number of stories detailing the scandalous and unlawful activities of the US Coast Guard and the Central Intelligence Agency and their efforts to destabilize the elected government of Venezuela.

On March 9th 1995 I received a telephone call from Julio Aliaga, a Cable News Network correspondent with CNN America in Miami requesting an on-camera interview. The following day on March 10th 1995 I received a faxed letter from Mr. Aliaga that Ms. Susan Candiotti of CNN Miami would be conducting the interview on March 17th at my home in Fajardo, Puerto Rico. Mr. Aliaga advised that Ms. Candiotti would be accompanied by the cameraman, Ben Gonzalez and Darrall Johnson the sound technician. As soon as I received the fax from CNN I called Myles. "May I speak with Mr. Tralins please?" Myles secretary responded, "Just a moment." "Hi Ed, what's up?" "Myles, I've received what I think is good news. CNN picked up the story of the Venezuelan Conspiracy from the Miami papers and the District Court filings and have asked that I do an on-camera interview for CNN International. Susan Candiotti and the CNN crew will be coming to Fajardo on the 17th and will be at my place at 8pm." "Hold on a minute, have you agreed to this?" "Myles, as you know I've been speaking on and off with Lowell Bergman from 60 Minutes but I'm not sure if he's really interested or what he's waiting for. I know he was disappointed when I couldn't get Velling on tape but if CBS isn't interested in the story I don't think I should pass up the opportunity with CNN. I had asked Lowell to let me know if Don Hewitt or Mike

Wallace is interested in doing the story right away or if it may be something they are considering for further down the road.

In any case I think that if CNN runs the story it would be aired a number of times over a number of days and would get virtually worldwide exposure. If 60 Minutes does the story it would have limited exposure in the US and be seen only once on a Sunday night." "Ed, as your lawyer my advice is to hold off on this type of publicity. You're not asking for any monetary damages only some items that while important to you are inconsequential to the Coast Guard. I believe that if we don't rub their noses in the dirt publicly I can get Arnold Aikens the US Attorney to agree to what's been demanded in the lawsuit without incurring further costs." "Okay Myles, if you don't think it's a good idea I'll tell CNN that you want me to hold off on the interview."

On March 11th 1995 I faxed the following to CNN in Miami,

Dear Mr. Aliaga: It was nice speaking with you last week and I thank you for your faxed letter of 10 March 1995. While I was pleased to learn of CNN's interest in the conspiracy against the Venezuelan Naval Establishment and the Admirals who are in command on reflection and following discussions with my counsel, Mr. Tralins feels that it may be improper for me to carry out the interview scheduled for next Friday. In view of the possibility that the agencies activities that have been revealed to date may go much deeper, on advice of Mr. Tralins I must, at least for the time being decline the opportunity to conduct the interview with CNN on Friday, March 17th. I sincerely hope you appreciate and understand my reluctance to go on camera at this time, but feel the matter best be addressed through due process which to date I have been denied.

The faxed letter was signed Capt. E.S. Geary

In view of the extensive newspaper publicity that the Venezuelan Conspiracy had received and in anticipation of the story being covered by the electronic media such as 60 Minutes or CNN, on March 30th 1995 I wrote a letter to Vice Admiral Jesus Enrique Briceño Garcia who now was the Commanding Admiral of the Venezuelan Navy to keep him apprised on what was happening. In the letter I enclosed a synopsis of the background and a copy of the lawsuit. On April 18th 1995 I received a faxed copy of a letter that Myles had received from a Richard Kendle II and his acknowledgement. In his letter dated 13 March 1995 Mr. Kendle said he had read the Miami

Daily Business Review article COAST GUARD AIDE SAYS THE CIA SANK HIM and felt there were some similarities to what had occurred to him through actions of the Coast Guard in Miami. Mr. Kendle had been an Environmental Protection Specialist with the Coast Guard in Miami and early in 1994 had written a letter to the Secretary of Transportation Federico Pena and the State of Florida as he was concerned about the Coast Guard's contamination of the waterways with abandoned mercury batteries. Mr. Kendle, who holds an engineering degree, a law degree, and is an MBA and who had received numerous awards and promotions, wrote to the Secretary of Transportation because he was concerned about the effect of mercury poisoning on the public. In writing to Myles Tralins he closed by saying, "If my situation can be of any help to Mr. Geary, please feel free to call me. The newspaper article brought back the pain and anguish that the Coast Guard inflicted on me and I don't think that Mr. Geary and others should suffer from a 'dictatorial situation' at the Coast Guard District Headquarters in Miami." At the time neither I nor Mr. Kendle would realize how helpful his interest and experiences with the Coast Guard would be.

It was June 20th 1995 at about 10:30PM when the phone rang in our condominium at Villa Marina. "Hey dad, can you grab the phone I just want to finish folding the laundry. If it's Carlos Gonzalez I'll call him back in 15 minutes." Carlos one of Jason's close friends was also in his 1995 graduating class at Fajardo Academy but it wasn't Carlos who was calling. Hearing coins being dropped into a pay phone I answered, "Hello" "Captain Geary?" "Yes, who is this?" "There's no need for you to know my name. I have something to tell you that I'm sure will be of interest. Have you had your phones swept, are they clean?" "How do you know about my phones…." "Don't ask just tell me." "They were swept this afternoon and yes they're clean." "I want you to listen very closely because what I have to tell you could be very important in your case against Admiral Leahy and the Coast Guard." "How do you know about my case against Leahy?" "Let's just say I read it in the papers. If it were to be revealed what I am about to tell you could get me in a lot of trouble so listen carefully because I'm only going to say it once and it's my nickel. The information is for you and your lawyer no one else. If it's made public or repeated in anyway someone might figure out where it came from. So don't repeat it, agreed?" "Okay mums the word, but who are you?" "Forget who I am. I know about your case and believe that I might be able to help you. You're taking on some of the most powerful people in the US government and unless you're careful they'll bury you." "Bury me? What do you mean by that?" "After being shot at, run off the road, and being given a bit of poison in your baked potato at the Hilton you shouldn't have to ask. If you had eaten all of the potato that night we wouldn't be talking right now. The poison that was used induces heart failure and death appears to be from natural causes. Depending on the lab where the tests are done the compound could have been identified had the food been analyzed. Didn't you ever wonder why they removed the tray from your room that night?" "Who are *they?*" "You're obviously a smart guy and should be able to figure that out without too much effort." Now I was even more curious. The lady caller was articulate, and guessing from her voice would say that she was probably in her mid 30's. By her matter-of-fact demeanor, choice of words and explanation of 'bury me' she clearly had intimate knowledge of what was really going on. I wondered, was she on the Admirals deck at Coast Guard headquarters, in the legal affairs office in the 7th Coast Guard District in Miami, the Directors office at Langley or maybe in the US Attorneys office? "Has your lawyer told you about the 'Whistleblower' provisions? This might be an easier path for you to follow because the case would be treated differently in view of the protection and rights afforded to Whistleblowers. It may be worth considering because right now the US Government intends to make your life miserable and expensive. All your interrogatories are going to be returned unanswered under the guise of national security. The government knows what you're claiming is true and that you've got a good case but because of national security issues they can keep a lid on things for a long time and legally stone-wall you. I hope you'll consider pursuing or at least look at the possibilities that would be available as a Whistleblower."

"Didn't you ever wonder what happened to Velling?" Having often thought about his disappearance, "Yes, I was......" "Never mind just listen. At the time you weren't aware of it and it wasn't a coincidence that Velling left the CIA in September 1994. Within ten days of your letter being delivered to Director Woolsey Velling was quickly removed from the CIA mission in Caracas and told to immediately submit his resignation. Velling wasn't too bright and was little more than a pawn. The US Coast Guard played a significant role in his termination. The Coast Guard had full knowledge of what was going on, but thought you would accept the deal the CIA offered you especially after Admiral Ecker gave it his blessing. When Ecker approved and told you to work through the Embassy and attaché Velling you blew his mind when you refused. The CIA and Coast Guard were outraged by your letters to the Senate and House Oversight Committees exposing the affair. You really stirred things up when you got Sheehy to admit the collusion between the CIA and the Coast Guard, when they learned of what he had told you they immediately put a muzzle on him before he could do any permanent damage. Once they found out about the letters you were writing there was a major disagreement between the Admirals and the CIA on how you should be dealt with. Because you were technically and legally part of the Coast Guard, the Commandant had the final say and he was hoping you would lose interest and drop the matter. When you didn't lose interest and persevered, against the wishes of his underlings the Commandant delayed your disenrollment until the CIA got Velling out of the picture. Velling was gone in September you were gone in October." "I really appreciate your help and the *inside information*. You must be very close to the source." "A lot closer than you can imagine. Wait a minute I need to feed this thing."

After hearing a number of coins had dropped in the phone I continued, "But why are you doing this especially considering the risk your taking?" "I graduated from school believing in the rule of law. The United States is a country that is based on the premise of law. When the rule of law of our great nation is violated I get upset. From what I've seen you did a great job doing what you did in Venezuela but when you decided not to compromise your honesty and integrity you upset a lot of people especially when you wrote Clinton and the others. No one in Washington likes their dirty laundry hung out on the street where everyone can see it. Trust me I've got first hand knowledge of what's going on. The CIA and the Coast Guard have done everything possible to hide what was going on and hoped you'd give up and the matter would simply go away. They purged your service and personnel records and embarked on a vicious program of character assassination. I've seen letters to people at headquarters who you clearly thought were your friends but they weren't. I recall one letter dated 1 February 1993 that you sent to a Lieutenant Lynne Drusemark-Mountcastle at the USCG in Miami complimenting her on a Fishing Vessel Inspection program that was presented during the Venezuelan's visit to Base San Juan. The same day Mountcastle sent a memorandum addressed to 'M'at headquarters that stabbed you in the back. The file also contains a copy of a Routing and Transmittal Slip dated 3 February 1993 from a Chief Warrant Officer named Wayne Hennessey that included copies of some newspaper articles that you had sent to him in New York. On the routing slip he sent forward he wrote below the remark – *Oh no, I'm on his list! Nice LTR HD.* Hennessey also had drawn a caricature of you showing a pipe smoking sailor with captain's shoulder boards and *VZ* written on the cap. From the other letters and memos that are in the file that you sent to Hennessey you obviously think he's your friend. Could be that his insensitive remarks are nothing more than what is to be expected of a struggling warrant officer who feels that by belittling your efforts he'll stay in the good graces of his superiors. There were others that you though were your friends too but all of them engaged in a bit of hypocrisy at your expense. For their own benefit they all stabbed you in the back to maintain a favorable position with their superiors. Hold on I've made a list, there are others but remember these names, Magee, McKenzie, Sarra, Ecker, Roseberry, Lanz, and this Mountcastle that I've already mentioned. If you're in contact with any of these people be careful and don't confide in them because just like the 'Miranda Decision – anything you say can and will be used against you.' They're all competing for recognition and promotion and using you as a stepping stone, but when it's over they'll quickly be forgotten. You may think that they are your friends but they're not; they're in a position to hurt you even more than your enemies. While it may not be evident in the court proceedings everyone that's involved is nervous because they know that if they don't stop you Velling's will not be the only head rolling from the guillotine. Everybody involved is taking damage control very seriously. The cover-up and circle-the-wagons effort by both agencies was necessary to conceal a poorly planned CIA operation that backfired because you blew the whistle. Oh, and by the way I'm curious why you didn't ask for monetary damages in the lawsuit?" "I wasn't interested in profiting from the situation; I just wanted to have my records restored." "Okay, I was just curious. Usually when people sue the government they always like to add a million or two for their pain and suffering. Considering what you've gone through and what you're going through now if anybody is deserving of damages for pain and suffering you'd be on the top of the list. You'll be interested to know that for the security clearance you needed to work for the CIA Velling had pulled all your personal background information. When you backed out they feverously checked and rechecked your background in an effort to find something you'd be ashamed of. Unfortunately, they couldn't find any skeletons in the closet that could be used against you or to force you to drop the matter. You were followed everywhere to keep tabs on your drinking habits and to see if you were womanizing. You were shadowed by the CIA but disappointed them when they found that you normally drank a Coke when everyone around you was sucking on a Heineken. The Agency also discovered you weren't a womanizer because you were either home alone, doing what you do on boats or had your son in tow when you went out. One CIA report to the directorate first suggested you might be a closet gay and then later had to admit that they couldn't find any evidence to support this. Even though they said you didn't attend church regularly the reports described you as a choir boy in diapers whose single parent activities were limited to working, eating and when you slept it was always alone. That's why they reverted to the prostitutes in Caracas. The CIA figured that maybe when you were away from home and didn't have your son to care for you might be more inclined towards a roll in the sheets with a hooker. But boy-o-boy you really upset their plan when you threw the hooker out of your room at the Hilton. The gym bag that the 'lady' carried into your room had been fitted with a hidden camera and a recording device. When you threw her and the bag out you may have thought you only had hurt her feelings, but the way her gym bag hit the floor destroyed a Sony video camera that cost the government over $1,000.00 to repair. But on the other hand had you succumbed and enjoyed the ladies free entertainment you'd have been nailed to the cross or maybe burnt at the stake."

"Hmm, I've never been labeled a choir boy before and assure you I don't wear diapers…." "Hey, Captain that's a CIA assessment not mine." "I'm going to fill in my attorney with what you've told me and appreciate your help. Can you call me again in a few days in case my lawyer may have some other specific questions?" "I don't know if I can do that but I've got to go now. Stay vigilant and keep your head down. Good bye and good luck." The line went dead. I continued to hold the phone in disbelief wondering if I had only imagined what had just just taken place.

Knowing that Myles seldom arrived at the office before 10 and not wanting to bother him at home, the next day I became a clock-watcher waiting in anxious anticipation to share the news of my late night call. At exactly 10:05, I called. "May I speak with Mr. Tralins please, Ed Geary calling" "Good morning Ed, what's up?" "Myles, late last night I received a rather strange call. At about 10:30 a woman called me from a pay phone. She told me a bunch of stuff about the case and then suggested I should look into what she called the Whistleblower provisions. She says that the government is going to ignore answering the interrogatories claiming they don't have to answer because of national security issues." "Ed, hold on a minute who was this person who called you and why is she speaking with you about the case. Is she a lawyer...?" " Let me back up a little bit. I don't who she is or where she's getting her information from but she knows a lot of details about the case. She also told me a bunch of stuff about the CIA and the Coast Guard that would only be available to someone on the inside. As an example she knew when and why Velling left the CIA and that I hadn't eaten all of my baked potato at the Hilton in Margarita. She even told me that had I finished the potato I probably would have died from the poison. I think she's got to be a lawyer or maybe Para-legal in the US government somewhere, she just knows too much."

"Ed, it sounds like the government may be trying to set you up for a fall. Did you tell her anything about the case or discuss anything...." "No, Myles she talked and I listened. Before she started talking she asked if my phones were clean and had been swept for bugs. She knew that my phones had been tapped by the CIA and before she said anything wanted assurances that the phone line was clean. What also was strange is that she was calling me from a pay phone and had to keep adding money. She told me that Velling had been forced to resign from the CIA in September and that the Commandant had waited until Velling was out of the picture before he discharged me in October. She also said that the CIA had tried to poison me at the Hilton in Margarita using a compound that would induce heart failure and was hard to trace. She didn't say what the poison was but told me it had been mixed inside the baked potato and had I eaten it all I would have died." "Ed, this is quite amazing but I don't know how we can use it. We discussed the shooting incidents and the bad food at the Hilton in Margarita but we've got nothing to tie in the CIA. Before the call last night you weren't sure whether they were trying to kill you or just scare you; the caller confirmed that they were indeed trying to kill you but we've still got no hard evidence. If we would have had been able to analyze the food we might have been able to confirm it was laced with poison, but we don't have the food. If she's not willing to come forward and testify all we've got is hearsay which isn't admissible in court. If I tell Aikens the US attorney that we have this information I'm sure he would be able to find out who the lady is and...." "No, Myles we can't do that I assured her that the information would remain confidential and only be privy to you. What do you think about her suggestion of the Whistleblower route?" "I agree your caller has provided some remarkable information but I'm a bit concerned about her suggesting another route if she truly believes the CIA and Coast Guard is worried about exposure. She's right though, there's no question the government intends to delay the proceedings as long as possible hiding under the crap of national security hoping to wear you down. But if as she says they are indeed worried about adverse publicity, exposure and where the case might lead maybe I can get Aikens to agree to a Stipulation for Compromise Settlement. You're not asking for any monetary damages so they may be inclined to settle the case and thus avoid the publicity." "Myles please hold off on contacting Aikens for the moment. The Coast Guard is fighting us on a number of points that I consider important like preventing me from retiring as a Captain. Let me first see what I can find out about this Whistleblower thing. Maybe it's a possibility."

In late July 1995 I wrote to the National Whistleblower Center, 415 Florida Avenue, NW, P.O. Box 26382, Washington, DC 20001-9996. Almost by return I received a letter from Ms. Linda Nunes-Schrag of the National Whistleblower Center with the names of lawyers identified under the National Whistleblower Attorney Referral Service (ARS). The letter also provided the names of reporters who are involved in whistleblower cases. I drafted and sent letters detailing the CIA's Venezuelan Conspiracy to Maggie McNeil of Reuters in Washington, Edward Lipton of National Public Radio in Chicago, Ron Yates of the Chicago Tribune, and Hal Lancaster of the Wall Street Journal. I was disappointed when the replies I received were lukewarm, the 'don't call me – I'll call you syndrome'. I quickly realized that maybe I should have contacted the New York Times or the Washington Post who have always proved to be much more aggressive when important issues need to be aggressively exposed.

I watched as the days and weeks passed while nothing happened. Myles kept pressing the US attorney who kept stone-walling or engaging in legal maneuvers while I was incurring more and more legal fees. My informant had warned of this and she was right on the mark. To help me out financially Myles graciously cut all his legal fees in half.

The following week as I lifted the telephone I could hear the sound of coins dropping into the box which told me that the caller was my friend somewhere in the shadows of government. "Captain Geary is the phone clean?" "Yes, both phones and the apartment were swept today and there are no bugs." "Good. Got a pen? Write this down. Tell your lawyer to look into the case of Richard Kendle, he currently lives in Washington DC. Between November 1989 and November 1994 Kendle worked for the Coast Guard in Miami as an Environmental Protection Specialist under a civil service GS-12 and was fired for reporting the Coast Guard's contamination of the waterways in Florida with abandoned mercury batteries. After making individual reports to the State of Florida and Federico Pena, the Secretary of Transportation the Coast Guard had intelligence officers search his desk and his briefcase for any information about the battery program accusing him of violating the chain of command. Kendle has an engineering degree, an MBA, and a law degree and after contacting the US Office of Special Counsel was told that his rights had been violated…." "Wait, wait, and hold on a minute. Kendle has already contacted my lawyer. In March when he read about my case in the Miami papers against the Coast Guard he sent a letter to my lawyer offering to help us. Myles, my lawyer has already spoken with him and is obtaining all the details relating to his case." "That's good I'm pleased to learn this. Kendle is one smart guy and the facts and circumstances of his case can definitely help you."

"Look you know my name but not knowing your name I'd like to be able to refer to you as something more than hey you. I don't wish to sound crude, but considering all the hush-hush information you're providing from a pay phone that may not necessarily be in an underground parking garage but probably is somewhere in the shadows there's a noticeable similarity with Watergate, any objection if I refer to you as Deep Throat?" "Yes, it is crude but I guess under the circumstances and if you follow the path of Woodward and Bernstein who never exposed their Deep Throat I'll go along with your thinking." Having agreed to a name for my caller, "Please tell me what's going on? The US attorney keeps talking about reaching a resolution but then dances around the issues and refuses to get down to specifics. Amongst the items I have insisted on is that they restore my records, award me the commendations that were given then taken away, and apply a retirement date of October 1995 which will give me the minimum 15 years for service retirement." "You'll remember I warned you that the government would drag things out hoping that by exposing you to more legal fees they'd just wear you down. It's all part of their plan to punish you for causing so many problems. Oh, and something else, the government knows that you've been talking with Lowell Bergman at 60 Minutes and with CNN about doing a story. The CIA hates Bergman but at the same time respects his thoroughness while fearing the stuff he digs up. They were particularly upset with 60 Minutes because of the story about the missing drugs involving the National Guard General at Maiquetia and the CIA. I don't know exactly but there were some other bits and pieces that Bergman dug up some time back that exposed the agency's dirty dealings in Central America. In one case 60 Minutes exposed the connection between an Nicaraguan army colonel who was the person in charge of a death squad that had been trained and was funded by the CIA. Washington isn't concerned with revelations printed in the grocery store tabloids but exposure and publicity by respected news organizations like CBS' 60 Minutes and CNN scare the hell out of them. Your lawyer should let you do the story either on 60 Minutes or CNN or both would be even better." "That's interesting. Myles was of the opinion that media exposure would act to delay any settlement, but from what you tell me it might have the opposite effect." "I think if you do the stories you and your lawyer may be pleasantly surprised. Got to go, watch your back."

Myles continued with his research on Kendle and two other cases where the Coast Guard and the State Department had violated the rights of whistle blowing officials while preparing for trial. I continued paying his reduced legal bills and having my phone and home regularly swept for bugs. After evaluating the prospects and exposure I decided that a CNN interview that would be aired repeatedly in the United States and overseas would provide greater coverage. There was no question that a piece on 60 Minutes would be good, however it would only be aired once on a Sunday night in the continental United States and then filed away into the archives. In the spring of 1996 I contacted Julio Aliaga the CNN correspondent who I had declined an interview with in 1995 and arranged for an on-camera interview. The interview was filmed in the law offices of Myles Tralins at One Biscayne Tower, 2 Biscayne Boulevard, Miami, Florida. After the clip was aired I began receiving a number of calls from concerned citizens who wished me well. Complimentary calls also came from government ministers, army and navy officers throughout Latin America who were impressed with my dedication, commitment, and loyalty in not releasing the confidential information demanded by the American Central Intelligence Agency and the United States Coast Guard. Less than 30 days after CNN International ran the story the assistant US attorney Arnold Aikens called my attorney and said they would agree to the settlement on the terms that had been on the table for the last year. At 9:00PM on Friday June 7th 1996 the day after the headline appeared in the Miami papers: MARITIME EXPERT SETTLES DISPUTE WITH U.S. OVER REFUSAL TO SPY I answered the phone to hear the clicking sound of coins being deposited in a pay telephone. The caller said, "This is Deep Throat. I thought I'd let know that you can now safely eat baked potatoes again." And then the line went dead.

EPILOGUE

In 2002 the Chàvez government began allowing Colombia's anti government Marxist guerillas and specifically the Revolutionary Armed Forces of Colombia, known by its Spanish acronym as FARC unimpeded movement across the open border between the two countries. The FARC who have been carrying on a successful campaign of terror funded primarily by the drug cartels for over 15 years continue to pass between Colombia and Venezuela without being challenged. Ironically there are an estimated 23,000 Venezuelan soldiers stationed on the expansive border with Colombia who from orders from Caracas pay little or no attention to the FARC rebels who regularly cross between the two countries. On August 19, 2003 US Defense Secretary of Defense Donald Rumsfeld met with Colombian President Alvaro Uribe in Bogotá ostensibly to offer support and assistance aimed at backing Colombia's war against drug traffickers and the cocaine cartels. The US media reported that Rumsfeld made the comment that the drug war, "may end up having a military solution as well as a political solution."

On August 21, 2003 President Uribe met with Chàvez in Paraguay during the inauguration ceremonies of the new Paraguayan president in an effort to have Chàvez broker a peace with the rebels. In late September 2003 an American OV-10 spy plane was reported to have been shot down over northeast Colombia killing the pilot. In view of Chàvez's professed anti-American agenda the plane is believed to have been deliberately attacked by Venezuelan authorities. The OV-10 Bronco, a multi-purpose light attack aircraft used by the US Marine Corps during the Vietnam War for reconnaissance and tactical support operations was operated by a secretive Reston, Virginia based U.S. defense contractor called DynCorp. DynCorp is reportedly financed by the CIA. A former cabinet minister's aide said that the border between Venezuela and Colombia was an open border and that border crossings were permitted, the aide also said that he doubted that Chàvez had ordered the downing of the US spy plane. The incursion into Venezuelan airspace of the OV-10 was followed by a flight of 15 US owned Black Hawk helicopters that violated Venezuelan airspace when they crossed from the northeast direction of Colombia reportedly in search of FARC hostages; these forays by the US military allow Chàvez to continue to claim that the CIA is still trying to kill him. News reports in September 2003 said that Chàvez had learned that the CIA was planning to shoot down his plane while traveling to speak at the United Nations in New York which was to be followed by a visit to Venezuela's CITGO oil company in Houston, Texas. Chàvez further revealed that his government is in possession of a video which his security forces secretly recorded of a CIA officer giving a class to Venezuelans on surveillance. Jokingly Chàvez said, "The technique could not have been very good, since we managed to film him." He argues that this is evidence that the CIA continues to be involved in clandestine activities in Venezuela. Having been briefed by agent Velling on the CIA's intentions on insuring the flow of oil to the United States I don't think there's any question that the Agency remains committed in its efforts for another regime change but this time the focus is on removing Hugo Chàvez from his position as the president of the Bolivarian Republic of Venezuela – one way or the other.

A STATE OF DENIAL

In view of Velling's ineptitude and blunders in Venezuela he was forced to resign from the Central Intelligence Agency in September 1994. According to the information received from *Deep Throat* after I had gone public there was an urgent need to get Velling out of the picture – quietly and quickly. The general consensus was it was better to have one head rolling from the media guillotine rather than the heads of a multitude of admirals and political cronies' in Washington who had conceived and been involved in the flawed attempts to infiltrate the Venezuelan military establishment. In becoming the sacrificial lamb Velling, the erstwhile James Bond wannabe found his career as a spymaster abruptly and unceremoniously terminated.

However, as Velling had been ejected from his government job under the guise of a *resignation* my attorney, Myles Tralins was confident that at some later date, those individuals who were spared exposure and beheading by his resignation would, in traditional Washington fashion find a suitable method and means to reward him. Velling complied with his DC cronies and disappeared silently into anonymity. Even though he had dropped off the radar screen, Myles intended to issue subpoenas to order Velling, Ecker, and a host of others to appear at trial, but was repeatedly stalled by issues and claims of national security.

After the meetings with Velling in November 1993 I never spoke or saw him again. It was not until early 1995 that I learned from Stan Yarbro of the Miami Daily Business Review that he had found Velling living in Seattle, Washington. Unless there might be two Joseph J. Velling's who live in Seattle, Washington Myles Tralins was right on the mark in his observations that the Velling of CIA infamy would be rewarded and *taken care of* for his sacrificial resignation in September 1994. Velling, the incompetent buffoon of Caracas notoriety who was rewarded and nicely *taken care of* is now: Captain Joseph J. Velling, JAGC, US Navy Reserve. He continues to be on the federal payroll by means of a gratuitous position with the United States Social Security Administration in Seattle, Washington.

A COUNTRY IN CHAOS

Venezuela is a beautiful country divided into 23 states favored with a year-round tropical climate and an abundance of natural resources including oil, natural gas, iron ore, gold, diamonds, bauxite, other minerals, and hydropower. Venezuela was one of the three countries that emerged from the collapse of La Gran Colombia in 1830, the other two being Colombia and Ecuador. Up until 1959 the country was ruled by generally benevolent military strongmen who encouraged social reforms while allowing the expansion of the oil industry. While the military obediently watched in the background the traditional elite maintained a dominate position in the corridors of government while manipulating and controlling the heartbeat of the country's economics. Not unlike most of Latin America the rich got richer while the poor struggled to exist. In 1993 the level of corruption in Venezuela reached a peak when the president, Carlos Andres Perez fled the country. He was later impeached after being charged with misusing $17 million from a security fund for personal election debts and a lavish inauguration. A subsequent investigation found that the $17 million in fact may have been closer to $40 million that was stolen. In January 1994 Venezuela's Banco Latino failed causing a run on the country's currency. A warrant was issued for the arrest of Banco Latino's chairman Gomez Lopez but unfortunately he had already left the country. Ricardo Cisneros another Board Member and reported crony of George Herbert Walker Bush quickly left Venezuela after he too was charged with being involved in the failure of Banco Latino. As a result of the looting and monetary shenanigans within the financial community almost the entire private banking system had to be nationalized at a cost of $8.5 billion. Financial controls were imposed on the weakened currency and the exchange rate was set at 170 Bolivar's to one US dollar. A year later the financial climate in Venezuela remained in chaos forcing the Bolivar to again be devalued this time by 41%, setting the new exchange rate at 290 Bolivar's to one US dollar. In part due to the declining economic state of the country in 1996 Venezuela reopened the oil sector to private foreign investments.

In spite of the attempts on my life in 1993 and 1994 I continued the Coastguard training and bore witness to the internal strife, crime, and corruption that was growing at an alarming rate throughout the country. Revolution was clearly in the air.

In October 2004 my first book 'Gotcha' was due to be published with a brief reference to the Venezuelan Conspiracy including the role played by the CIA in installing Hugo Chàvez as president. Prior to the publication of 'Gotcha' I decided that if I was to visit the country again it should be before revelations of the CIA/Chàvez *connection* became widely known. If the president's past connection with the CIA were to become public knowledge and publicized by his opposition Chàvez, in an effort to maintain his credibility would be forced to quickly deny & distance himself from any past connection with his proclaimed enemy, the United States of America. Once the *connection* was exposed I also wondered if I might be on an immigration watch list at the airport, refused entry and promptly put back on the next plane to Puerto Rico by the Border Control, Departamento de

Extranjeria (DX).

With this in mind I made the decision to visit Caracas before Christmas in 2004. In an effort to locate my friend Nicholas Goschenko after an exhaustive search on the Web I located a marine group named the Organización Nacional de Salvamento y Seguridad Maritima de los Espacios Acuáticos de Venezuela, A. C. or ONSA, a nautical organization based in Caracas. On the ONSA's webpage I was pleased to find that their National Coordinator was none other than Nicholas Goschenko. I sent him an email advising of my proposed visit to which he immediately responded in his normal warm and friendly manner.

Through an exchange of e-mails we arranged to meet at the Simon Bolivar/Maiquetia airport on December 21st 2004; Goschenko had also arranged for a hotel for the five days I would be in Caracas. Upon my arrival I was met by the same wonderful Goschenko I had worked with 10 years previously. He was accompanied by his new business partner a lovely lady named Maria Elena Gutierrez. On the drive into Caracas Goschenko began reciting the events that had taken place over the last few years. He said that the right-wing neo-liberal thieves who ran the national oil company first suggested and then forced him to immediately retire with a small pension. PDVSA's anti-Chàvez management wanted the pro-Chàvez Goschenko out of the company insisting that he quietly retire or he would be fired. In spite of many years of faithful service he was being victimized because of his support for Hugo Chàvez and the Bolivarian Revolutionary Movement.

Having few options left he decided to retire from PDVSA and move to Miami, Florida. According to Goschenko while he was living in Miami he received a call from Chàvez' organizers in Caracas asking him to return to Venezuela to become involved and work in the 1998 presidential election campaign of Hugo Chàvez. Because of the untenable situation he had been placed in by the corrupt management at PDVSA for his support of Chàvez he decided to return to do whatever he could to help in his election campaign. After losing his job at PDVSA he was financially devastated and couldn't afford to keep his car or his farm in the country. He said that after almost 20 years with the national oil company he was now obliged to live on a small PDVSA pension and the money he made as a partner with Elena in their editorial publishing business providing magazines to the passengers of Venezuela's bus companies. Goschenko said his wife Daniela was still bravely fighting the cancer that had unremittingly continued to threaten her life as it had for so many years. Goschenko was thankful that by accepting retirement PDVSA hadn't canceled his medical coverage that paid for Daniela's chemotherapy treatments. Even though I hadn't seen Nicholas for many years I was saddened and distressed to hear of his present predicament. On the other hand considering the unwavering support he had given to the Chàvez campaign I was surprised to find that he had so little to show for his efforts and was still struggling financially five years after the revolutionary forces had taken control of the government. I asked if it had been wise to be so vocal in his support for Chàvez to the extent of sacrificing his job and everything else he had worked for over the years. With a stern look he said that Hugo Chàvez and the Bolivarian Revolutionary Movement was changing the country for the better and wasn't stealing the way all the other politicians had done in the past. He said that because of the respect, friendship, and admiration that Chàvez had for Fidel Castro the United States had labeled him a communist. Goschenko was adamant saying, "Chàvez isn't a communist he's a modern socialist and humanist who is working for the good of all Venezuelans, not just the rich. If he (Goschenko) had to make sacrifices for the good of the revolution he was more than happy to do so."

Goschenko knew of the shootings in Caracas and the poison incident in Margarita. Shortly after the attempt to run Goschenko's car off the road while we were traveling from Carenero I had made him aware of the CIA's efforts to recruit me as a spy against the Venezuelan military. I also told him the background of what I knew about the CIA's plans and because of oil why they wanted Chàvez in the Miraflores palace. Being a computer expert Goschenko was on the Internet daily monitoring current events in Venezuela where he had seen 'Gotcha' and the CIA – Chàvez *connection*. When I told Goschenko that I was writing another book with the entire background of the Venezuelan Conspiracy he asked for an autographed copy when it was published. Goschenko said that he and many other Chàvez supporters had known since 1992 that after the impeachment of Carlos Andres Perez the CIA was focused on weakening the government of

Venezuela and was prepared to go to any lengths to gain control of the country's oil.

Goschenko had also astutely monitored the recent insurrections closely and said that only a short time after Chàvez had been elected the CIA and NED had attempted to remove him but had not succeeded. The business owners continued their efforts to oust Chàvez which lead to planning the rebellion that resulted in the April 2002 coup where the military installed Pedro Carmona Estanga in the Miraflores for a day. Goschenko said that the anti-Chàvez riots on April 11th where 19 people were killed had been organized by the CIA and was backed by military attachés at the US Embassy. He said that he was told that the riots had been paid for with funds from the American National Endowment for Democracy and that Venezuela's security police identified the US military attachés that were involved. Goschenko said that the security police had found that the attachés had actually been at the Fuerte Tiuna military headquarters with the anti-Chàvez coup leaders on April 11th."

Goschenko went on to explain the social programs that had been introduced by Chàvez and the good that was being done with the country's oil money was for the benefit of all Venezuelans not just the power brokers who ruled in the past. There was no question that Nicholas Goschenko was unwavering in his support of Hugo Chàvez and the Bolivarian Revolutionary Movement.

During my stay in Caracas with Goschenko as my guide we visited the Miraflores palace where ministers loyal to Chàvez hold court and rule the country under the socialist doctrines frequently mandated by the popularly elected president. In our visit to Naval and Coastguard Headquarters we found the right-wing commanders of the old guard who once ruled with absolute sovereignty had been replaced with admirals unconditionally loyal to Hugo Chàvez and the Revolution. Goschenko said that at the present time the majority of the population, 6 out of 10 supports Chàvez and the Bolivarian Revolutionary Movement, adding that the popular vote has been evidenced in three democratic elections monitored as free and fair by the Carter Center and the Organization of American States (OAS).

I was sad to find that many of my friends from years past, the engineers, doctors, small and large business owners, and the captains of industry whose companies had fueled the economy of this once model democracy had long since fled the country. Some relocated to Spain and Portugal, while others immigrated to the United States. The National Endowment for Democracy, USAID, and the CIA through military attachés continue to fund and support a number of right wing groups in an effort to remove Hugo Chàvez from power. Goschenko said that the US backed traitors that participated in the April 2002 coup are the same conspirators who organized the insurrection and the strike in the oil industry in late 2002 and early 2003 that cost the Venezuelan economy a few billion dollars.

The self serving policies, flaws and deterioration of American foreign policy is nothing new and goes back to the reign of George the 1st (H. W. Bush) and even before when he was the erstwhile director of the CIA. These same incoherent foreign policies that were *rubber stamped* by Bill Clinton worsened and have further deteriorated under George the 2nd. The cowboy diplomacy and foreign policies of the Bush dynasty (both Georges) are acknowledged to be seriously flawed, many times perplexing and incomprehensible in part because of the lack of truthfulness. This lack of truthfulness was further evidenced when only a short time after his move to the White House George W. began to hype his perception of the dangers with Saddam's possession of weapons of mass destruction, weapons of mass destruction that didn't exist.

During the same period in devious support of the Bush Administration George 'slam-dunk' Tenet and the less-than-illustrious CIA began peddling false intelligence surrounding Iraq. Tenet's bogus intelligence contributed to the less-than-informative daily news briefings by then US Defense Secretary Donald H. Rumsfeld, probably better known as the court jester, who falsely promoted America's successful invasion to eradicate the non-existent weapons of mass destruction from Iraq. Rumsfeld continued his gibbering claims of success and accomplishment against a background of demonstrated incompetence and repeated demands for his resignation from respected politicians and a multitude of generals, mounting US casualties, and a denied civil war in Iraq. After the gravely premature 'Mission Accomplished' declaration by the president, Rumsfeld at least temporarily crawled back under his rock sheepishly retreating to the safety of his bunker at the Pentagon. When pressed for answers from an inquiring press corps Rumsfeld simply responded by telling them to back-off. Mr. Rumsfeld continued his feverish grasp at publicity in his statement comparing Chàvez with Adolph Hitler and concern with the election of Evo Morales as the president of Bolivia.

Finally becoming aware of the deteriorating situation in Iraq the American people spoke loudly and clearly during the 2006 mid-term elections; with the Democrats taking control of both Congress and the Senate Bush was reduced to presidential lame-duck status. Deciding to cut his losses even before the final mid-term election results were in Bush went into damage control mode and jettisoned his unpopular Washington pal by quickly dumping Rummy. Bush junior replaced the infamous Secretary of Defense with Robert Gates another non-descript political hack and crony of his father.

Not to be outdone the less-than-illustrious Secretary of State Condoleezza Rice added some spice to the stew when she remarked at a Congressional hearing that "Chàvez is leading a Latin brand of populism that has taken countries down the drain." Amusingly Secretary Rice's statement was made the same month a US military attaché in Caracas was caught bribing Venezuelan armed forces officers for military secrets. Of course we should not forget the notorious George Tenet who upon his retirement from the CIA to write a book received the highest civilian award granted to American citizens. Much like the job awarded to the inept Joe Velling, Tenet was *taken care of* and given an award which if for no other reason is consistent with US government incompetence. Just prior to his retirement it was revealed that while under Tenet's dubious leadership the CIA provided bogus intelligence that caused then Secretary of State Colin Powell to give false testimony at the United Nations that lead our country into an avoidable war that has cost the lives of thousands of young soldiers while providing thousands of others with life altering injuries.

Havana, Cuba is a prime example of hard-line communism perpetuating itself at the cost of the population. A visit to the island finds that Cubans born after 1959 have been brainwashed to a point where Fidel and Raul Castro and the other radicals who are in charge are revered and virtually worshiped. Those born before Fidelito's revolution while not necessarily wanting another Batista still have fond memories of the freedoms experienced under the sometimes benevolent dictator. Clearly no one would wish to see the rebirth of

Batista type doctrines or worse yet see another hard line communist Cuba emerge in Latin America. This is especially true considering the virtual isolation of the island with its populace exposed to the miseries and hardships presently endured by most Cubans.

While the plight of the poor does require urgent attention many Venezuelans are far more educated, sophisticated, and worldly to accept the hardships and isolation experienced in Cuba; on the other hand if Nicholas Goschenko may be cited as an example, Chàvez by touting his humanistic and socialistic ideals may unknowingly be leading them all along a left-wing path fueled by oil wealth. The jury is still out, but there may be a slight chance that with the massive oil revenues at its disposal the Chàvez regime could ultimately be successful if they are diligent and aggressive in protecting the rights and the civil liberties of all its citizens, but so far the results haven't been encouraging. When Chàvez assumed the presidency in 1998 the price of oil was about $11.00 a barrel, in 2006 it hovered between $56.00 and $75.00. The Chàvez regime repeatedly touts that it is responsive to the populace and the country's needs as a whole claiming that the Bolivarian Republic of Venezuela will achieve the success it is seeking and become a model for the region. To gain the support of the masses the charismatic leader focused his efforts towards the 80% of the population which are poor and live in poverty. Chàvez may have given the poor self-esteem but nothing more because most of the population is still poor. Some economic analysts report that one-fourth of the country's 26 million are even worse off living in *extreme poverty*. In the last 8 years it appears that Chàvez and his Bolivarian ideals have brought the country closer to chaos than success. As an example since Chàvez took control of Venezuela in 1998 the crime rate has doubled. In 2003 alone there were over 11,900 homicides which is about 46.5 per 100,000 and corruption is at an all time high.

In the current political climate, the court of international opinion appears to have rendered a verdict that the self serving, flawed and dubious foreign policies of the past and present Washington administrations are accountable and solely responsible for the movement to the left and the popular election of socialist revolutionaries in Latin America. The corrupted policies of saber-rattling and forced regime change promulgated by the President and his self-serving politicos' in the administration to eliminate those who oppose them have resulted in the appalling back-lash against the United States. As Hugo Chàvez is still in power the final chapter of this spy story is yet to be written.

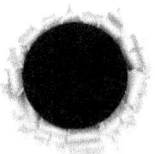

Tuesday, March 7th 1995 – Miami Daily Business Review[41]

Coast Guard aide says CIA sank him
Suit alleges agency got him dismissed for refusing to spy
by Stan Yarbro of the Review Staff

Captain Ed Geary, a US auxiliary Coast Guard officer pictured with his friend Admiral Jesus Enrique Briceño Garcia, commander of the Venezuelan Navy

......In the tropical heat of a hot October evening in 1993 while attending a Navy League meeting at the Roosevelt Roads Navy Base in Puerto Rico I, Captain Ed Geary, a US civilian maritime expert and auxiliary Coast Guard officer recalled seeing a man in his early 30's dressed in a long-sleeved shirt, Brooks Brother's suit and shiny loafers. The man was clearly a federal employee of some kind, but I didn't think much of it at the time. I now regularly think about that first meeting with the man who later identified himself as Joseph J. Velling. Geary has filed a federal suit in Miami, alleging that Velling as a CIA agent tried to recruit him to spy for the CIA in

---

41 As reprint permission of the text of the original article was denied this is an edited excerpt of my original interview with Stan Yarbro of the Miami Daily Business Review.

Venezuela. When he declined, Velling used the US Coast Guard to retaliate against him. His lawyer, Myles Tralins of Miami's Tralins and Associates, says that the Coast Guard violated its own rules by summarily dismissing his client." The lawsuit names the District Coast Guard commander based in Miami, Rear Adm. William Leahy, as a defendant. Coast Guard representatives in Miami, speaking for Leahy, and in Washington said they could not discuss the case citing the pending litigation…. The US Embassy in Caracas confirmed that Velling was assigned as a political officer there from July 1993 until September 1994. The State department's Foreign Service personnel office said that Velling resigned that month……

Later when the case was settled the matter received further media attention.

Thursday, June 6th 1995 – Miami Daily Business Review[42]

Maritime expert settles dispute with U.S. over refusal to spy
Consultant says CIA retaliated after rebuff
By Noreen Marcus of the Review Staff

……Marine expert Ed Geary's year old suit in Miami federal court was dismissed last month following a confidential settlement in April. The only part of the settlement that could be made public was Geary's status as US Coast Guard Auxiliary Retired, said Myles Tralins, his Miami attorney. The Coast Guard had earlier refused to discuss the lawsuit for Geary's refusing to spy on his friends, senior Venezuelan naval and coast guard officers and now the settlement guarantees it won't be discussed at all.

---

42 As reprint permission of the text of the original article was denied this is an edited excerpt of my original interview with Noreen Marcus of the Miami Daily Business Review.

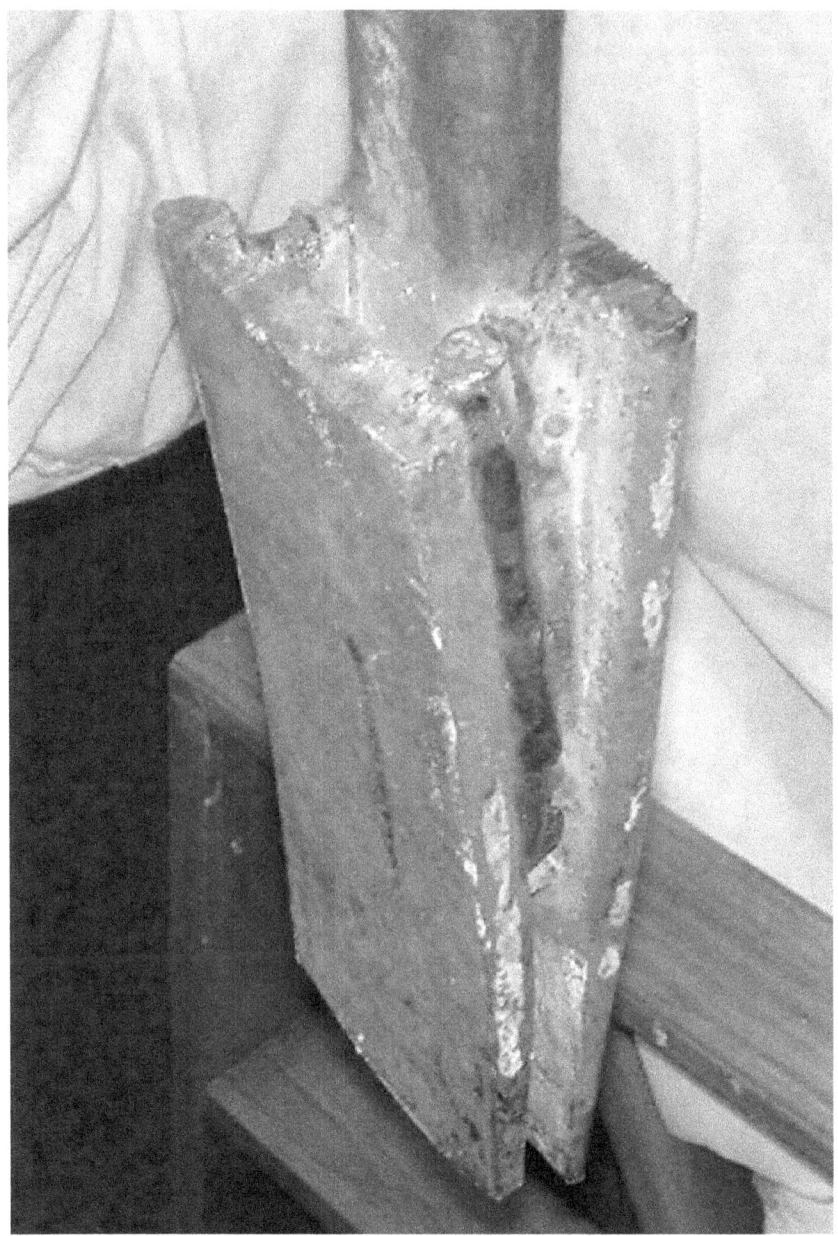

The tool used by drug traffickers to open containers without breaking the customs seal.

The author at the Officers Club at Venezuelan Coastguard Headquarters – La Guairá

Officers of the Venezuelan Coastguard Auxiliary

Training at the US Coast Guard Base in San Juan, Puerto Rico

Base San Juan – Headquarters of the
US Coast Guard Greater Antilles Section

From left to right: Captains'. Nicholas Goschenko, Carlos Presencia Jurado, Gregory Magee,
Carlos Luis de Casas Bauder & the author

Classroom training in Venezuela

Classroom training was carried out throughout Venezuela

On the water training exercises on Lake Maracaibo

UNITAS: US & Venezuelan Coast Guard joint training exercises
on Venezuela's Margarita Island

An unmarked Venezuelan Coastguard Auxiliary patrol vessel during an offshore boarding of a go-fast suspected of narcotics trafficking.

Graduation day: Venezuelan Coast Guard Group Picua at the Coast Guard School at La Guaira

The formal graduation ceremonies

The author with Admiral Briceño Garcia, Commanding Admiral of the Venezuela Navy

Rear Admiral Eliseo Martin Fossa Commandant of the Venezuelan Coastguard with the author and aide at the 1st Auxiliary Conference in Caracas

About the Author

Captain E.S. Geary has appeared as an expert in admiralty and maritime cases in Federal, State & local jurisdictions throughout the USA and Europe. He holds a US Coast Guard masters license for commercial vessels amongst other credentials and qualifications.

- Former US Coast Guard Department Chief – Pan American Auxiliary Liaison – Rank: Captain National Policy Advisor to the Commandant of the Venezuelan Coastguard – Rank: Captain

- Graduate: US Army Military Police Academy

- Maritime Fraud Investigator

- National Panelist in Admiralty – American Arbitration Association

- Member: American Society of Appraisers and ASA Senior Appraiser of Yachts & Ships

- Licensed & Registered Professional Engineer

- Fellow & Life Member: Institution of Diagnostic Engineers (UK) – Forensic Engineering

- Certificated ISO 9001:2000 & ISM Code QMS Internal Auditor – Maritime (International Register of Certificated Auditors – UK)

- Member: Yacht, Designers & Surveyors Association (UK)

- Nominated Nautical Surveyor approved to carry out work for the UK Maritime & Coastguard Agency

- Member: Society of Naval Architects and Marine Engineers (USA)

- Member: Royal Institution of Naval Architects (UK)

- Member: American Society of Naval Engineers

- By Appointment Maritime Valuation Expert and Consultant:
    US Department of Transportation – Maritime Administration (MarAd)
    US Department of the Treasury – Internal Revenue Service
    US General Services Administration

He is a member and past director of the International Association of Marine Investigators who in 1996 voted him the Marine Investigator of the Year.

"Success should be viewed as a journey, not a destination"